Father
& I

Father
& I

A Memoir

CARLO GÉBLER

LITTLE, BROWN AND COMPANY

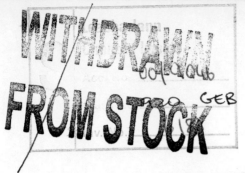

A *Little, Brown* Book

First published in Great Britain by
Little, Brown and Company in 2000

A CIP catalogue record for this book
is available from the British Library.

ISBN 0 316 85388 7

All photographs from Carlo Gébler's own collection,
apart from the photograph on page 78,
© Newnes and Pearsons, 1961

Typeset in Berkeley by M Rules
Printed and bound in Great Britain
by Clays Ltd, St Ives plc

Little, Brown and Company (UK)
Brettenham House
Lancaster Place
London WC2E 7EN

For my mother

Acknowledgements

I gratefully acknowledge the financial support of the Arts Council/An Chomhairle Ealaíon and the Arts Council of Northern Ireland.

Many people and institutions have supplied me with information or confirmed the facts; they include the Amalgamated Transport and General Workers' Union, John Carroll, Cedric R. S. Christie, Joe Devlin, Adrian Gébler, Clancy Gébler-Davies, Helen Lanigan-Wood, Desmond MacNamara, David Marcus, Edna O'Brien, Graham Rawle, Roc Sandford, Jeremy Sandford, Donald Swain and Peter Robinson.

Simon Callow, Greg Darby, Gina Marcou, Glenn Patterson and Mary Ann Wilson read the manuscript. Thank you.

Portions of this work (in a slightly different form) previously appeared in *Prospect*, *Fortnight*, the *Irish Times*, the *Black Mountain Review* and the *Mail on Sunday* magazine.

I have changed one or two names. All inventions and lapses of memory, all errors of fact and idiosyncrasies of chronology are, of course, my own.

'Life is lived forwards but understood backwards'
FRIEDRICH WILHELM NIETZSCHE

'Memory tells us not what we choose, but what it pleases'
MICHEL EYQUEM MONTAIGNE

Prologue

Bang in the middle of the twentieth century my father took a wife who produced a son whom he called Karl.

Then he lost that wife, took a new wife, acquired a new son and he called me – Karl. (Carlo, as I now am, only came years later.)

This is about my father, the life we had together, and the discoveries I made in later life about his life before I was born. Our relationship was a failure and yet the story has a happy ending, of sorts. My late discoveries humanised the old man.

This is a memoir; not a biography. I have tried to stick to what I remember. Close family members appear infrequently; odd though it seems, this reflects what I remember of them, which is very little.

You can't change the past but, with understanding, you can sometimes draw the poison out of it.

PART ONE

chapter one

Towards the end of his life, my father lived alone in Dalkey outside Dublin, in a house called Cnoc Aluin. The house, with its stone walls several feet thick, was once a keep or guard house, he said, first Danish, then English, and the walls of his basement were part of the original military building. Just right, I thought, an old paranoiac like you, you would end up in a fortress.

In Cnoc Aluin there were just a coal fire in the back sitting room and portable electric fires in the bedrooms.

These comprised of a copper reflector and a heating bar. This was actually a white clay sock with a corkscrew coil in the middle.

The bars were fragile. One little knock and they crumbled like chalk. I grew up with these fires in London; I knew all about them.

My father kept his spare heating bars in a basement room in Cnoc Aluin. He had hundreds; he bought them cheap when the English manufacturer went bankrupt.

One day, in 1990, the bar in the fire in his bedroom went.

He fetched a new one from his store. The next part of the sequence is a mystery. He had a stroke or a seizure or something, then fell and hit his cheek against the corner of the copper reflector.

At the time I lived, with my family, in the nursery at the top of a big house outside Enniskillen.

The telephone rang in the kitchen and I picked it up.

'This is Stan,' said a voice. The accent was received Irish over a Canadian core.

This was Stan Gébler-Davies, my cousin, son of my father's younger sister, Olive. I last heard Stan's voice in 1964; I was hiding under the table in the hall in the house where we then lived in south London and Stan was shouting in through the letterbox. My father had locked him out.

'I have bad news,' said Stan. Then he explained. My father was in hospital, he said. My father didn't know where he was. He didn't know who he was. He didn't know what day it was. He didn't know he'd written books or fathered children or married three times. The fall had accelerated his dementia. What might have occurred incrementally over years had been hurried through in a few seconds. Everything that had once been in his head was now erased.

I wasn't surprised. Through the 1980s I saw my father once every year or two, and each time we met I thought he was more forgetful, more confused and more frail than the time before. He had a wife in those days. Jane was much younger than he was and I always thought she would outlive him. But she hadn't; she pre-deceased him; she'd been dead now for a little over a year.

'I want to help him,' continued Stan, 'but I can't. The social worker insists it must be family.'

And, technically, I was family; I was his son; we had lived together, when I was a child. Then had come the separation, my mother from him, him from my mother. He had sought to turn me against her. I wouldn't. I couldn't. He was furious. How, he asked, could I betray my one true parent, him, the parent who would show me the straight way, the right way, and nail my colours to the mast of the corrupt parent, her?

Obviously, he said, because I was a mummy's boy; and obviously because I was weak, corrupt, venal, disloyal, and irredeemably bourgeois. My mother gave me money, sent me to public school and let me watch whatever I wanted on television. That's why I took her side, he said.

Our relationship, never good, got very much worse after this. Following the divorce, as the years rolled by, we saw less and less of each other and, when we did, he was frosty and suspicious, while I was frosty and polite.

When Stan rang, we were barely in contact, my father and I. And I had long since ceased to think of us as being members of the same special unit, the Géblers. However, the Irish state had other ideas.

'You're his next of kin,' said Stan, 'so it has to be *you* who sorts him out.'

Then Stan added, 'I know your brother's in London but with you being in the North, you're much closer,' as if the geographical argument settled it.

I said nothing. I had complicated feelings about Stan. A couple of years after my father locked him out of our house, Stan and my father had a rapprochement. After some prompting from my father (and with some help from him as well, I believe) Stan had written one or two nasty pieces about my mother that were printed in *Private Eye* in the early 1970s. My father and Stan remained friends, even after my father left London and went back to Dublin. Indeed, during these later years, my father indicated to me that Stan was more than just a friend; he was a blood relative and a proper Gébler, he said, in a way that I was not. Stan could be trusted, he said; Stan was a safe bet. I wasn't.

Listening to Stan now I remembered all of this and assumed that my father must have also said to Stan what he had indicated to me. In which case, I decided (although none of this was mentioned by either Stan or myself as we spoke on the phone), Stan must know that my father would have loathed my involvement in his affairs at a time like this. Furthermore, Stan must know that my father trusted him with his secrets as he would never have trusted me, and that for this reason he would have wanted Stan to sort out his affairs.

However, my father's preferences, real or imagined, did not count here. I was family; Stan wasn't. And when there was a mess like this one, it was family the Irish state looked to.

The next day, I drove down to Dublin. The hospital was on the south side, in the suburbs. I parked and went in. There were long, echoing corridors with brightly coloured floors.

'I'm looking for Ernest Gébler,' I said to a nurse.

'What's he in for?' she asked.

'He's old. He's had a fall.'

'That'll be geriatric,' she said, and pointed the way.

I found my father in a passageway, on a gurney, in a strait-jacket. The huge cut on his cheek that he got when he fell on the electric fire was stitched with thick black thread, exactly like the stitching around the edges of the grey army blankets we had when I was a child and which gave me asthma. His eyes were black.

'Hello, Ernie,' I said.

I could only use Father when I spoke of him, to others.

'Who are you?' I heard. I saw the speaker was a nurse with a tag that said Niall.

'His son.'

This was another awkward word.

'Oh, hello,' said Niall. 'Awful nice fellow, Ernest. Until this

morning, anyway. He went berserk. Had to put him in that.'
Niall pointed at the strait-jacket.

I looked at my father again. His hair stuck up; he looked
demented.

'Will he get a bed?' I asked.

'Oh yes.' When someone died, he assured me, as someone
soon would, he'd get their place.

I left and went for my interview with the gerontologist. I was
shown into an overheated room with a dead butterfly on the
window ledge.

The doctor bustled in. He was Syrian with an Edinburgh
accent. His skin was the colour of marron glacé. He wore a
signet ring which he turned on his finger as he spoke.

The gerontologist repeated what Stan had said. The accident had accelerated my father's dementia. He was now
doubly incontinent and would never speak again. It was
Alzheimer's, of course. Well, the gerontologist thought it was.
He couldn't know for certain until he examined my father's
brain, and, obviously, he could only do that after death.

'When might that be?' I asked.

In a few weeks, said the gerontologist, six months at the
very most. I should prepare myself, he continued, and I
should remember the Alzheimer sufferer had no quality of
life.

I got his drift. When my father died, as he soon would, it
would be for the best. I wasn't to hope for a miracle or pray he
would live longer. I must accept his end when it came and be
grateful.

His pitch made, the gerontologist shook my hand and fled
before I could say another word.

I went to the window and picked up the butterfly carcass. It
was cold and silky and it turned to dust between my fingers.

*

I left the room and went off to see the social worker responsible for my father. She was a woman with big earrings and a small voice in a Portakabin crammed with brown files.

'You're Ernest's elder son, aren't you?' she said.

'Yes.'

'You have a brother?'

'Yes, Sasha, my younger brother, he lives in London.'

I did not mention my half-brother, the one my father called 'the early son', the one I thought of as the first Karl, while I was the second Karl. He lived in America and, besides, I had never met him.

The social worker cleared her throat and she said, in a no-nonsense, I-won't-brook-any-argument-about-this sort of voice, 'Your father'll have to be made a ward of the court. You'll have to get a solicitor to raise a petition.'

I nodded.

'Are there assets?'

I mentioned the house with the thick walls.

It would have to be sold, she said. The money raised would be held by the state and used to pay for his care. Had I any thoughts on this?

No, I hadn't.

The decision was mine, she said. I could have him live with me, or he could go into a private nursing home. Her only concern was that he got the twenty-four-hour care he now needed. His assets would pay the bills of the nursing home.

I thought about this for a moment. He couldn't come to Enniskillen and I couldn't imagine living in his chaotic Dalkey house. It would have to be a home, I said.

So how quickly could I get him into a home? wondered the social worker.

A month, I suggested, although actually I hadn't a clue.

She frowned.

A fortnight, I said.

A week would be better, she suggested, finally.

'You're asking the impossible,' I said. 'I don't know any homes in Dublin. I live a hundred miles away, and, besides, it's another country. You're going to have to give me time.'

The social worker looked blank. I didn't mean to sound like a Unionist but I must have sounded like one to her.

My father wasn't sick, she said. He was senile and he was using up a hospital bed that a proper sick person could otherwise have had.

With my mind's eye I saw him on the gurney in the corridor. Not my idea of a bed in a ward. I said nothing, of course.

There was a queue of sick people behind him, she said, in case I hadn't got the point.

Her tone was polite and reasonable but the message was unmistakable. Get him shifted.

I found a solicitor. The solicitor suggested a home. A few days later I went back to Dublin to inspect it.

'Before us it was owned by an order of monks,' said the nurse showing me round. She ushered me through a pair of doors into a hushed room that smelt of incense. 'Our chapel,' she said proudly. The chapel was always unlocked, she continued, and guests or patients had access at all times. If Ernest needed to offer up a prayer, he could pop in here at any time, she said.

'I don't think so,' I said.

The nurse looked at me, uncomprehendingly. Surely, unlimited access to chapel was a boon? With Catholics, yes, but not my father.

'Do you know what he used to say to me?' I asked. I was going to enjoy this.

Obviously the nurse did not.

'He used to say to me, "Do you know what the greatest day in the twentieth century was?" "No," I'd say. "Well," he'd say, "it was in the early 1930s (and he would give the date which I now forget), and it was in Spain, and that was the day the Anarchists went into the jails and shot six hundred priests and nuns. Dead. And the best thing that could happen in Ireland would be to do exactly the same," he would continue. "Round up every bloody priest and nun in Ireland and shoot the lot dead!" That's what he used to say,' I said.

'Perhaps you'd like to see our garden,' said the nurse. 'Didn't you say he liked gardening?'

I saw some other homes but the Killiney home seemed the best, the nicest, the most cheerful.

'But how do I know if it actually is the best?' I asked the solicitor on the telephone one day.

What I had in mind were newspaper scare stories describing belligerent underpaid auxiliaries biffing old people.

'Ask about access,' said the solicitor. 'If you can visit any time, day or night, that's the best safeguard.'

This made sense. Nurse Hatchet might think twice before striking if there was a possibility, albeit faint, that a relative might walk in.

I telephoned the Killiney home to check the visiting hours.

'You can come any time you want,' said the voice at the end of the phone.

'Two o'clock in the morning?'

'The door's always open.'

That settled it. I put my father in the home in Killiney. I didn't have the money to pay but I told the home it would come. I would apply to make him a ward of court. The state would collect up all his money from his numerous bank accounts. The state would sell his house. The state would hold these assets and pay the fees of the home. The home agreed. It was not the first time, I am sure, they had come to this agreement.

chapter two

I got the key to Cnoc Aluin and drove down one Sunday with my family. We arrived and climbed the granite front steps. You could just see Dalkey Island from the top. We went in.

The hall was musty; books all over the floor and tools on the carved Burmese table. Jane's bedroom was filled with dozens of blankets (stacked, as if ready for a natural disaster), and my father's bedroom was a mess of clothes, light bulbs, and electric heaters, including the one he fell on. His dried blood was on the corner.

In my father's study the shelves were lined with diaries, while the desk drawers were so crammed with stationery, none would close. Manuscripts were heaped on the floor, along with hundreds of messages that my father wrote to himself in his last years: 'Get gas checked.' 'Fix roof.' 'See lawyer and make sure miserable sneak thief sons Carl and Sash inherit nothing.' This message was underlined for emphasis.

In the back sitting room lay thirty years' worth of reel-to-reel tapes of concerts recorded off the Third Programme (as my father always called it), as well as mounds of family photographs and dozens of potted geraniums. Their chalky smell hung in the air.

The basement below was like the lair of Howard Hughes during his twilight years. Stored higgledy-piggledy was just about everything non-perishable that had ever come into the house over the previous twenty years: the spare bars for the electric fires, thousands of old bottles and jam jars, and all kinds of paper, including used Jiffy bags, envelopes bundled by size, and sheets of brown paper with little spots of sealing wax dotted along the edges.

The back pantry was filled with jams and pickles, some dating from Cannon Hill Lane, in London, where we lived when I was a child.

The kitchen was cluttered with hundreds of articles on allergies and bowel cancer culled from the *New Scientist* and the *American Scientist*, more tools, washing-up basins, maps, more books, cutlery, plates, saucepans. In the corner there was a shelf with a set of small files, snub-nosed pliers, my father's shaving mirror, toothbrushes with different bristles, toothpicks – both wooden and quill – and different tubes of toothpaste. This was where he fiddled with and fixed his teeth.

Hidden somewhere in this chaotic house were his banking details. I had come to find these and then to clear the place out. These were my tasks. Once the house was empty, the state would employ an auctioneer to sell the property. But though I knew that I must start on my tasks, I couldn't.

Instead, I picked up a knife. It had a wonky handle. Suddenly, I could remember holding the same knife. I was in Cannon Hill Lane, sitting at the dining table, a plate of mashed parsnip in front of me.

'Eat your parsnips,' my father said. My mother was silent.

I forked a tiny morsel into my mouth. It tasted of tuber, wood, earth. Horrible. I made a face.

'Don't you come on like that with me,' my father said. 'Parsnip's full of iron and you won't leave the table till you've eaten yours.'

My father waited, my mother sighed. I chopped and smoothed the disgusting white vegetable, feeling the wonky handle moving in my palm as I did.

Eventually, my father said, 'Oh God,' and stamped off to his study, exasperated. My mother rushed my plate to the fire and scraped my parsnips on to the coals, where they hissed and spluttered . . .

I went up to the sitting room again at the back of Cnoc Aluin. This was the room where I always sat on those occasions when I had visited my father as an adult. It was a big square room with a fireplace.

I must gee myself into action, I thought. That was when I noticed, sticking out from the pillar of papers beside me, a sheet of stiff, yellow paper with 'Receipt for Fee of $2.00 for Performance of Marriage Ceremony' written on the edge. I pulled this from the pile and found I was holding Marriage License No. 34114, the certificate of the marriage in Manhattan, in New York City, in the State of New York, of Ernest A. Gébler and Leatrice Hart, 12 December 1950.

I knew my father had married Leatrice before he married my mother. But I had never known when. I was not told as a child. Nor did I ask.

My wife appeared, snapping open a black plastic bin bag.

'What shall I chuck? All these papers?'

That was when I noticed something else in the pile. It was an old Xerox of a mimeographed document, white letters on a black background.

I pulled it out. It was the Decree of Divorce, granted to the plaintiff, Leatrice Gébler, against the defendant, Adolphus

Ernest Gébler, in the Second Judicial District Court in the State of Nevada, on 24 October 1952 at 3.30 pm.

'Look!' I said, waving the documents at my wife. 'Now I know, for the first time, when he got married and when he got divorced. Isn't that amazing? I've had to wait until now to find out and I'm . . .'

'Thirty-seven.'

'I'm going to bag up everything,' I said, 'and bring it home.'

My wife made a face. 'Is that wise?'

Not all of what lay scattered around the house was interesting or informative. Some of it was poisonous, like the message we'd already read about the sneak thief sons. There was plenty more of the same. On the other hand, the answers to the questions I had hoarded all my life were presumably somewhere in the papers scattered about.

'All right,' said my wife, after we talked. 'We'll take it all . . .'

For several months after this, we would drive to Cnoc Aluin most weekends; we would collect papers, furniture, crockery, books, and then we would drive back to Enniskillen with them. It took a long time to empty my father's place.

We put everything that we brought north in the basement of the house where we rented the nursery. Later, we bought a house of our own and filled this with my father's furniture. I had a floor put down in a corner of the loft in the new house. I packed my father's papers into seven trunks and suitcases and I put them up there. I was terrified as well as excited at the thought of what I would find in them.

The papers stayed in the loft for seven years. Then came the day when I got them down and began to read. But that comes later in the story. Right at the very end, and I don't want to get ahead of myself; first, it is necessary to go back.

chapter three

Nothing in my family is simple or straightforward. It's always obscure, vague and over-complex. Just like everyone else's family.

What follows here is the family story as I got it from my father when I was a child, augmented by what I overheard. I was a keen eavesdropper.

'You've a talent for listening when you shouldn't,' my father once said to me. 'It's about the only thing you have any talent for.'

The Géblers were originally Armenian. Towards the end of the nineteenth century, they were thrown out of Turkey by the Ottomans. This would be my great or my great-great-grandparents. They may or may not have been Jews.

They made their way through the Balkans and up into Austria-Hungary. A factory that made musical instruments was won in a game of cards by my great-grandfather. The factory was in Bohemia, north and east of Prague.

My paternal great-grandfather married a widow (her name was Zräly or Strahli) who had a daughter; he went on to have

eight or nine children with her, one of whom was my grandfather, born 1890. He was named Adolf. His mother tongue
was German though he classed himself ethnically as Czech

Adolf was a prodigy on the clarinet. He went to the Prague
conservatoire, graduating around 1908. He started playing
engagements around Europe.

By 1910 Adolf was in England, living in Linden Gardens off
Notting Hill Gate in London. (Fifty years later, in the early
1960s, my father took me to see the house; it was a stucco
building with the paint peeling off it. 'That's the kip,' my
father said, 'where Adolf lived before my mother snared him.')

Adolf was engaged to play first clarinet for a few nights in
a production of Franz Lehár's *The Merry Widow* in the Gaiety
Theatre in Dublin.

Adolf took the ferry from Liverpool. He arrived in Dublin
in the late afternoon and went straight to the theatre. He had
made no arrangements for the night. He planned to sleep in
the theatre. This was common practice with musicians.

Adolf played the performance. Afterwards, as the public
filed out, he was spotted by an usherette going back into the
theatre.

Where are you going? she asked.

Back inside, explained Grandfather. To sleep.

The usherette offered Adolf a bed for the night; not her
bed, a bed. Although this was not seduction she was already
in love with this dashing foreigner.

Adolf said yes. The usherette brought him home and put
him up for the night. Her name was Margaret Rita Wall. Her
family were Dublin Castle Catholics. All the male Walls had
served in the British Army since practically the Norman inva-
sion. The way my father put it, all the male Walls were
uniform-mad; first they served the Crown, then, in middle
and old age, they worked as hotel doormen or railway guards,
or at any job so long as it involved wearing a uniform. My

father disapproved. Anyone who wanted to work in a uniform was degenerate, warped, and probably queer. It was a mystery why Adolf wanted to mix with this crowd. Yet two years after he met the usherette, sometime in the spring of 1912, Adolf married Margaret Rita.

The couple were not a natural fit. I could see this from the photographs my father showed me when I was a child.

Adolf, in these pictures, was a big man with big hands in working-man's shirts and big heavy boots; a sort of Proletarian Bacchus. Margaret Rita, on the contrary, was a small-busted woman with dainty wrists and tiny feet, a sparrow-sized nymph who wore flowery frocks. As my father put it, this marriage was the splicing of big Oliver Hardy to titchy Stan Laurel.

How had the usherette managed to get her claws into the young Bohemian? my father often wondered aloud. He had various explanations.

It was language, plain and simple. She had the English, he didn't. Adolf didn't know what was happening until it was too late and he was marching up the aisle.

Or it was the age difference. She was born in 1882; so she was eight years older. She had the drop on him; she was the silver-tongued seductress, Adolf the callow youth.

Or it was sex. She seduced him (that was easy) then presented her ghastly fait accompli; they had to marry because, in Holy Catholic Ireland, to take a girl to bed was to propose marriage.

Or she pretended she was pregnant which obliged Adolf to do the right thing and put a ring on her finger. By the time he found out she wasn't pregnant, he'd been caught.

Or it was just convenience. He needed a local bride in order to stay in Ireland and avoid deportation back to Austria-Hungary, while she, an ageing spinster destined for the shelf, needed a man; so they took each other.

Or she made him promises. In Europe he was minnow, one jobbing musician among thousands. In Dublin he would be a colossus astride the Irish music scene. And he did want to prosper. My father did admit that. Adolf was ambitious. In his head he was a socialist but in his heart he was venal. He wanted his slice of pie.

My father's speculations were never conclusive. Adolf and Margaret married for one or other or all of these reasons. And, in the end, what did it matter? he would ask. In the end the outcome was the same. The woman devoured the man, Margaret devoured Adolf; it was the old story that started in the Paradise, when Eve tempted Adam.

Adolf and Margaret's first child was Adelaide, known as Ada. She was born in Dublin on 26 May 1913. Margaret was soon pregnant again. About halfway through her second term, the Great War started.

Adolf Gébler, Carlo Gébler's paternal grandfather (front row, first from left), Curragh internment camp, with the camp orchestra

Adolf was now an enemy alien. He was put in an internment camp near the Curragh and so he missed the birth of his next child, my father, Adolphus Ernest Gébler, born 31 December 1914.

I was told Adolf had a good war. He was in the camp orchestra and he was allowed home to his wife some weekends ('That's typical British oppression for you,' my father would say, 'being let home like that'), and Adolf would smuggle butter into the camp when he went back. This he sold to German prisoners at a profit. Towards the end of the war Margaret got pregnant again and, in 1918, in Londonderry, Louise was born.

The Great War ended and Adolf was released. There were three more children: Olive, born in Dublin, 1920, Irene, born in Wexford, 1923, and finally, Adrian, born in Waterford, 1924.

Ireland, meanwhile, was going through a bad patch. First the Troubles (1919–21), and then an ugly Civil War (1922–23). One casualty was the Record Office, destroyed by fire during fighting between pro- and anti-Treaty forces, my father's birth certificate being among millions of documents lost.

For this reason, my father said, he never knew exactly when he was born, but his loss was as nothing compared to Ireland's loss of her entire documentary history since the arrival of Strongbow, which also went up in smoke. Not that the Irish cared. As a nation they were like the cartoon idiot who cheerfully saws away at the branch on which he sits, oblivious of his impending fall. The Irish were a great people but thick, he said.

During this period, the Gébler family lived in the southeast of Ireland, first somewhere in County Wexford and later in Tramore, County Waterford. My father was a sickly infant and child; he was always vomiting, always poorly. It was only

later that he discovered why; he was allergic to the cows' milk
he was given to make him strong and well and healthy. As
always, as he used to remark when speaking about this part of
his life, the road to Hell was paved with good intentions.

In 1925, Adolf and family went to Wolverhampton to live.
There were factories everywhere and they had been belching
their foul smoke into the air for a century and more. The
smoke was heavy with particles and these floated down and
covered every surface with a fine film of filth. It wasn't called
the Black Country for nothing.

The people of Wolverhampton were small, stunted and
stupid. But then, what else would they be? They worked in
dreadful factories, they were paid slave wages and they lived
in slum houses. Was it any wonder they had shrunk and their
brains had addled? Of course, Capitalism and the Bosses
(both always upper case) were to blame. Like Engels, in
Manchester, a century before, my father saw the condition of
the English working classes and wept. Or so he said, anyway.

I got only one story about the time in Wolverhampton
(which sometimes, when retold, was reset in Dublin, which
confused me).

One day a crate of white Rhenish wine which Adolf had
ordered arrived at the house where the Géblers lived. Margaret
put the wine in a dark part of the hall. At the time, Adolf
('Slaving to support his family,' as my father would put it)
worked in a cinema, playing music for silent films; this was a bit
of a comedown for a Prague-conservatoire-trained musician,
but what else could he do? There wasn't any other work around.

Adolf came in late and it was dark and he fell over the
crate as Margaret had intended.

'Oh ye Gods and fishes,' cried Adolf, as he writhed in pain
on the floor. (This was his catch phrase.)

Standing hidden behind a door, where she had stood waiting for this moment, Margaret whooped with joy. She had

not just felled the wicked patriarch, but hoisted him on his own petard by felling him with the crate of wine on which he had selfishly squandered the family's scarce resources. Oh, there was a God after all and he was just . . .

The story always led on naturally to one of my father's pet themes – female malevolence and how it was always a feature of his life. What perplexed him – and he could ruminate on this subject for hours – was this: having seen his mother destroy his father, why did he then marry women who tried to destroy him?

After eight miserable years, the Géblers were finally released from incarceration in industrial England. In the Free State, a state radio station had been established – Radio Éireann. The station naturally needed its own symphony orchestra. After all, almost every other nation state in the world had an orchestra attached to its national radio. The funny Czech – or was he German? – Adolf Gébler was still remembered in Dublin musical circles. He was a good player – so good a player, Adolf was offered the post of first clarinetist in the new orchestra; he said yes.

My father returned with his family to Dublin by boat. He described the moment often. As the vessel cut across the pewter-coloured Irish Sea, he said, he saw the grey buildings of Dublin and Dun Loaghaire crowded along the edge of the bay; he saw the air above filled with a haze of blue turf smoke; and he saw the lip of the green Wicklow hills lying behind. It was lovely, he said, green, radiant, paradisical.

He was glad to be back. My father was a keen swimmer and Ireland was full of water. He swam in the Liffey. He swam in the Dublin canals. He swam in a quarry in Finglas. The water was very cold up there, and he played a dangerous game. He would empty the air out of his lungs, sink down and then climb up the submerged quarry face. When he told me this story as a boy, I couldn't stop myself imagining that I was the one

Self-portrait by Ernest Gébler, taken with a home-made
pin-hole camera, Wolverhampton, 1934

climbing the submerged cliff face, not him, and that first I climbed, and then I let go and then I was sinking back through the water towards the quarry floor and certain death . . .

My father found work as a cinema projectionist. The place was filled with Liffey rats, plump from sweets and oranges. As the cinema projectionist, it was his job to kill them.

One morning, he heard scrabbling down in the orchestra pit. He fetched the monkey wrench he used for killing the rodents and went down, expecting to find a rat had fallen in there. To his surprise he found not one but seven river rats, the size of terriers, all joined, since birth, at the tail.

He jumped down. The rats raced about like horses yoked to a chariot. He killed one. Then another. Then a third. Finally, there was only one frantic rat left alive, dragging his six dead siblings behind. My father cornered the animal and, as he was about to strike, the rat cried out.

He killed the seventh animal, transferred the seven corpses to a bucket, carted them to the furnace and threw them in. Closing the fire door, he heard one of the rats scream again, as it roasted to death.

He went to the sink. He ran the cold water tap and held his wrench in the streaming water. It took a long time to get the blood and fur off the gnarled parts. This was the detail that really stuck with me as a child, and when I was alone, I would creep out to his garage. I would find his heaviest monkey wrench, and I would wonder if this was the very one he used to kill the rats.

The great joy of his job, my father used to say, was that once the film was running through the projector gate, his time was his own.

He wanted to write but he felt he was an uneducated proletarian. So, as the films spooled through, he read; all George Bernard Shaw, Maxim Gorky, Oscar Wilde and, for light relief, Zane Grey.

His family thought he was mad. None of them believed he could become a writer. He ignored them and slowly, over the years, he turned himself from an artisan into an intellectual. He began to write – articles for newspapers, then stories and plays. His work finally found its way into small prestigious Irish literary magazines.

The war came in 1939. My father thought of joining the Royal Air Force as an aircraft fitter. The RAF was the most progressive and the most intellectual of the three services, plus the new Spitfire and Hurricane engines were mechanical miracles he longed to get his hands on.

He never did join up, however, and he never told me why.

His father Adolf had bought a house at 3 Cabra Grove, Cabra Road, on the north side of Dublin. My father sat the war out here. He worked in cinemas, when he could, and he worked on a novel. He sometimes showed me the proof copy. He bound it himself in black oilskin and put a red label on the front with the details typed on. The book was called *He Had My Heart Scalded*, and it was published in London, in 1946, by Sampson Low, Marston & Co. Ltd and promptly banned in Ireland. He was quite proud of that. It had to have had something if the state wanted to stop people reading it.

Now he was an author, albeit banned, he had to write another book. One day, sometime in 1947, he found himself in the library of the Royal Dublin Society, at Ballsbridge; he was mooching around, looking for a subject to write about, when a book fell off a shelf and landed at his feet.

The book was *The Story of The Pilgrim Fathers, 1606–1623 AD; as told by Themselves, their Friends and their Enemies*, edited from the original texts by Edward Arber.

He picked it up. We also had this book at home (the actual book that fell at his feet) and sometimes, when I was a boy, he let me hold it as well.

My father took the book from the library and began to

read. The book told the story of the Puritans who sailed across the Atlantic in the *Mayflower*, landed at Plymouth Rock and established a permanent European settlement.

As my father said of himself, he had a talent for recognising stories, and this was a good story. He decided to use it as the basis for an historical novel.

He put Arber into his suitcase and moved to London. He got a reader's ticket for the Reading Room of the British Museum (where Marx worked, as he often observed, as if he and Marx were in the same business). He read and wrote. He listened incessantly to Debussy's 'La Mer'. It helped him to imagine what it was like to be at sea, at the start of the seventeenth century, on a tiny, creaking wooden ship, with no land in sight in any direction.

After two years of work in the Reading Room of the British Museum, my father had his book. It was called *The Plymouth Adventure, The Voyage of the Mayflower*. The novel was immediately bought by the American publisher Doubleday. In March 1950, Metro-Goldwyn-Mayer bought the film rights; publication followed in April, and in May it was the month's choice of the Literary Guild of America. The book was glowingly reviewed. American readers adored it. It appealed to their vanity, he said. It put them where they believed they belonged – at the centre of history, at the centre of the world. But then that was Americans for you – they were a vain, self-centred race of Imperialists.

In California, the process of turning the book into a film began. My father was flown out to Hollywood. He was not employed by MGM to write the script. Naturally, as he would always observe sarcastically when he got to this point in his story, the studio couldn't possibly trust the writer to write it. Oh no. They brought in a pro, someone called Helen Deutsh, to do that. But MGM did put him on the payroll; they employed him as the historical advisor on the picture. He did nothing, of course. No one asked his advice, nor would anyone have listened had he offered any. So he just drew his salary and kept his mouth shut. That was the studios for you. They had more money than sense, he said.

Sometime in 1951, my father returned to Ireland with thousands and thousands of dollars tied up in a handkerchief. He bought himself a minor Irish ascendancy house called Lake Park, set in the hills of County Wicklow above the village of Roundwood.

And around the same time, when he was fresh from the American west coast and laden down with Yankee dollars, my father met an American woman called Leatrice Gilbert. She came from California but in 1951 she was living in Dublin. She was the daughter of the US silent-screen star John Gilbert. This great star was a drunk, and probably a morphine addict in his day, he said. My father always emphasised these facts in his account. Leatrice was from degenerate stock. She had also been married several times before my father met her. That was another point he emphasised. She was flighty but he ignored the signs. To his cost.

My father and Leatrice fell in love and got married, not in Ireland, but back in America, in New York. A few months later still – by this time back in Ireland again – the couple had a baby, a boy; he was christened John Karl, after the great Marx. My father was happy. His cup overflowed; he, the son of a Mittel-European immigrant who spoke English badly, was now a huge literary success in America. He had a wife, an estate and a son and heir. Spencer Tracy was to star in the movie version of his novel. He, the son of a cinema accompanist and himself a sometime cinema projectionist, was about to see *his* novel made into a film. He was happy.

But what lasts? Nothing, especially when there's a woman involved, and she's rich, spoilt and American. Leatrice found Ireland damp and cold and she missed central heating.

Desperately. She wanted to go back to America, for a holiday. She wanted to warm her bones in the California sun. She wanted to show her little baby son to her horrible Christian Scientist mother. My father was a fool. Go on, go to America for a holiday, he said, be happy.

He took her to the docks in Dublin and put her on a boat. He waved her off. He expected to see her in a few months.

Six weeks later the postman handed my father an envelope. It had an American stamp on. He opened it. Leatrice had divorced him. He'd lost her and the child.

As he put it, this was the day the gate fell on him, and joy turned to catastrophe. The worst of it was there was nothing he could do. He had to accept it. That was America for you. That was emancipated American women for you. They could walk all over you and then some; as Leatrice proved. For having dumped my father, she then married some guy called Fountain. (He was a financier, who worked in Wall Street, the lowest form of humanity, my father said.) She started calling herself Fountain and, worse, she changed the name of his son from John Karl Gébler to John Robert (or Bobby) Fountain.

And why would she do that? my father would ask aloud when he got to this part of the story. It was obvious. She wanted her son who was also his son to believe this jerk from Wall Street was his father.

The whole episode left my father very angry and bitter. How could Leatrice sneak away, as if she was going on holiday, when she had no intention of coming back? How could she steal his son and then give the boy her new husband's surname. It was ridiculous. He was a Gébler.

A little later, my father met my mother, Edna O'Brien. She was in Dublin studying to be an assistant pharmacist. She worked in Magner's Chemist shop on the North Circular road. At this point Adolf re-entered the story, albeit briefly. My

Edna O'Brien at the door of Lake Park, May 1953

mother already knew Adolf. Magner's was close to 3 Cabra Grove; Magner's was where my grandfather went for medicine for his bad stomach.

But shared acquaintance was not enough to forge a marriage. Even I knew that as a boy and my father knew I knew it too. So he explained to me what happened subsequently:

when they met, he said, my mother was bookish. She wanted to be a writer. He was older, he was established, he was published; so they dovetailed together rather well. Couldn't I see that?

Oh, yes, I used to say.

He never wanted to say it was love. In his version, he was the hapless novelist snared by the literary *ingénue* rather like his father was by his mother. I never believed this. As a child I always believed it was love. I wanted to believe it was love, too. No matter what happened, no matter how bad things got at home, I stubbornly clung to the belief that just this once there was real love between a man and a woman.

My mother got pregnant. That was never hidden from me. My mother and father married on 12 July 1954. I was born a few weeks later, on 21 August. My father decided I would be called Karl, like the sainted Marx. Brendan Behan heard of this and wrote to my father. He already had one Karl, Behan wrote, wasn't that enough? My father ignored this letter and went ahead. I was called Karl.

And forty years later, the early son returned, although not in the way my father or any of us in the family would have predicted back then.

chapter four

Carlo Gébler – only a few days old –
with his mother. The writing on the
photograph is Ernest Gébler's

I was born in a Dublin nursing home and brought home to
Lake Park a couple of days later.

When I was a child my father kept an aerial photograph of
Lake Park in his study. Sometimes he would stand me in front
of it and talk about the house. I found this photograph in
Cnoc Aluin many years later and took it home. It's black and

white, about eighteen by twenty inches. Lake Park comprised of a one-storey Georgian lodge, a two-storey Victorian extension, and a yard with offices. It had a kitchen garden, and a tennis court, and easy access to Lough Dan.

This is what I know from the photograph. What I remember, on the other hand, are the dusty flagstones on the kitchen floor, the grit pricking my hands and feet as I crawled around, and the smell, at ground level, a mixture of turf and wet wood. A girl called Greta looked after me and I called her Gleta because I lisped and I named my collie Brown Dog. He smelt of meat and wet fern.

I was a sickly infant, chesty, prone to wheezes. I remember the clang of spoon in cup as my father whipped my daily tonic of raw egg and a drop of sherry, the feel of the drinking cup on my lip, and finally, the alcohol and egg taste of the slippery, frothy, faintly mucous-like drink.

When I was one or a little older, my father took me out on Lough Dan in his boat. I remember holding the gunwale and peering at the smooth still black surface of the water. It began to rain gently. There was a smell of wet wool and brackish water and tar.

My father's rod swished in the air and the line paid out, whispering as it flew. The fly landed noiselessly on the surface. All was still and silent; then, suddenly, the rod whipped backwards and forwards and there was something silver in the water, twisting and turning as it rushed towards us. I whooped with excitement.

Then the silver form was in the boat. For a moment it lay on the boards. Then it arched and leapt into the air.

Terrified, I wailed.

'Be quiet,' said my father.

I was doubly frightened. Now, on top of the leaping silver terror, he was angry.

I began to cry.

'Didn't you hear me. Be quiet,' he shouted.

Lake Park was sold at the end of 1955 and in the new year we moved to Dublin. On the day of the move, I remember sitting on the bottom step of the stairs in the hall of the new house, hearing the shouts of the removal men and the sound of furniture being humped about but paying no attention to the hubbub. I was transfixed by the fanlight over the door with its coloured panes of glass – amber and indigo, yellow and red. Staring at the glowing panes produced a strange and pleasant sensation of fizzing and popping inside me, as well as a quiet sense of elation.

Six months later, in May 1956, my mother came home with my younger brother, Sasha Marcus Alaric. Not long after he appeared, I found the newborn in one of our bedrooms, lying on the floor. He was quite alone. There was a tin bath full of water on the bed nearby. It really was too good an opportunity to miss. I tipped the water on to the baby and then threw the bath on to him for good measure. Then I fled.

Later, I was recalled to the room, where I found my mother cradling a damp mewling infant wrapped in a towel. I was very surprised to find he wasn't dead.

The address of our new home was 29 Garville Avenue. I have an old drawing of this house that my father made in purple crayon on American quarto typing paper. The drawing is dated January 1957. I found it tucked inside volume eight of his Encyclopædia Britannica. He did love to leave paper in the oddest places.

His drawing shows the house was a classic late-Victorian or early-Edwardian Dublin town house. It was square, detached, with a chimney at either end of the roof. The front door was in the middle, with steps leading up to it, pillars on either side and windows above. In the front garden there was a path, a birch tree, a cedar and a hydrangea bush.

In his drawing my father has also included other details from our life then; Brown Dog, here called Fleabite, and his treasured silver-grey Railton motor car. (This was a sports coupé, hand-built in Cobham, Surrey, just before the Second World War, and called, from its registration, Z6 201.) And he has included me, now two-and-a-half. I wear a romper suit with a hood. I am not Karl any more; now I am Carlos. Oddly, my father makes no mention in the illustration of my brother.

A year later, 1957. I was three. It was summer and a blanket of muggy air lay across red-brick suburban Dublin. Suddenly, it went dark inside our house and thick, heavy spears of rain began to fall from a lead-coloured sky. The electric lights were turned on. My throat hurt and I was hot.

'Come with me,' said my father.

I followed him into his study. He produced a thermometer.

'Don't bite this,' he said, sternly.

He slipped the cold finger of glass under my tongue. I decided to ignore what he said. I closed my jaw and the tube snapped.

My mouth was suddenly full of shards. My father shouted. I spat and frantically brushed the splinters away.

'Get out,' my father shouted, when my mouth was clear.

I went off but I couldn't keep away; I went back to the study, though I knew I shouldn't.

I found my father kneeling on the floor, a square of cardboard in each hand and a silver puddle of mercury in front of him.

'Why do you always do exactly what you've been asked not to do?' I shifted in my sandals from one foot to the other.

'Haven't you got anything to say? No, of course you haven't, because there's nothing going on, up here, is there.' He tapped his head with one of the pieces of cardboard.

He went back to the silver puddle. As he went to lift, the mercury slithered away from him.

'Damned child,' he muttered, 'damn bloody child.'

One year on, 1958, and once again it's the summer. I was in the garden of the house in Garville Avenue, standing by one of the flowerbeds.

A round stone lay on the turned-over earth. I picked it up. It was cold, grey and smooth. I had just learnt how to throw. I reached back then flung my arm forward.

The stone made a noise like a smack as it hit the window.

My father raced out.

'I'll teach you to throw stones.'

My mother appeared.

'He just threw a stone. I'll teach him to throw stones.'

My father fetched his toolbox.

'Come on,' he said. I followed him inside the house and up the stairs to the half-landing. There was a neat hole in the middle of one of the panes in the window.

'You can stand there and you can watch. I'll teach you to throw stones,' he said.

Rather than remove the broken pane and put in a new one (too costly and too complicated), my father opted for a nut-and-bolt repair. The idea here was to hold the hole tight between washers and so prevent cracks spreading out from it across the pane.

He found a bolt of the same diameter as the hole. He slid the bolt through the hole, dropped several red washers down the stem, then put a nut on the end.

As I watched the nut creeping slowly along the screw towards the washers, I began to feel very tired and very bored. My back began to ache and my legs began to sag. It wasn't long before I wanted to run down the stairs and burst out into the garden.

'Can I go now?' I asked, finally.

'No, you cannot. You'll stay till I finish. I'll teach you to throw stones.'

While the nut travelled down the bolt, he told me some home truths. That's what he called them. I was a vandal and a thug, he said. That was why I threw stones and broke windows. He said I got this from my mother. There was something wrong with her. This, in turn, was something to do with her father and drink. Grandfather O'Brien was a mad alcoholic.

At first, when he started talking my father was angry. However, the longer he spoke about the degenerate genes passed from my grandfather to my mother and then to me, the more gleeful he became.

chapter five

I stood outside the downstairs lavatory in 29 Garville Avenue. I heard the cistern flushing inside. The door opened and an old man appeared. His hair was white and grey and his face drooped around the mouth. He looked a bit like an old dog. He smelt of old cigar. This was my father's father, Grandfather; his name was Adolf.

Adolf turned on the tap and washed his hands.

'A musician should always use a linen towel,' he said. He began to dry himself on the white hand towel. 'Never use cotton. Too coarse.'

Adolf didn't talk like we talked in Dublin; he talked in a funny foreign voice. He was from Bohemia, Czechoslovakia, a place which, at the time, meant nothing to me.

Now his hands were dry he showed them to me. They were old, bent and brown. The fingers looked like twigs on a witch's broomstick.

'Got to keep the hands good for playing the clarinet,' he said. He wriggled his fingers. Then he walked off down the corridor. I followed.

Adolf found my father and the two men began to talk. I

hung around, taking care I wasn't spotted. So long as I kept out of sight, I knew my father wouldn't shoo me away.

After a while I heard shouting, wailing, and then the words San Francisco and California. It took years of eavesdropping before I got the background . . .

During the 1940s, to augment the meagre salary paid by Radio Éireann, Adolf and Margaret began to take paying guests into their house, 3 Cabra Grove. These were mostly itinerant musicians, mostly German. Adolf loved having them about the house, and he loved talking German, his mother tongue. Of course, it was hard work having paying guests. Margaret complained a lot. After the war finished, Adolf located a housekeeper, Marianne, in Austria and brought her to Dublin to help his wife.

Marianne was also a German speaker. Adolf fell in love with her, and she with him. In 1950, Margaret left the family home and went to live with her daughter, Louise. Tongues wagged. Someone in the family reported Marianne to the authorities as an alien. (My father believed it was Ada, Adolf's eldest daughter.) An expulsion order was raised against Marianne. My father got this quashed.

Margaret became ill and returned to the family home, to her husband and the housekeeper. Then she got really ill and went to hospital and died on 17 December 1956.

Further accusations were bandied about. Once again someone went to the authorities and told tales. (My father believed it was Louise.) This time it was alleged Adolf had poisoned his wife in order to marry his mistress.

On police orders, an autopsy was performed. The dead woman's stomach was pumped out and the contents minutely examined for signs of poison. Nothing unnatural was found because nothing unnatural had been fed to the deceased. At the inquest, the verdict returned on Margaret Rita Gébler was death by natural causes.

Adolf, though exonerated, was crushed by everything that had happened. Some of his own children had reported him and caused all this trouble. Furthermore, he had heard on the grapevine that for a while, after the post-mortem, the Irish state had briefly considered deporting him. And after all the years of service he had rendered Ireland and the Irish? He had

Adolf Gébler and Marianna, just after their marriage in 1957

slaved to bring them culture and this was how they paid him back? It was unconscionable, he thought, and he was hurt. Deeply. He decided to go abroad to start a new life with Marianne. And that was what Adolf had come to the house to tell his son, my father, Ernest. This was what he meant when he said San Francisco and California. He was leaving Ireland and that's where he was heading . . .

What I didn't know then was that we too would soon be on the move. We were also emigrating. We made our move in November 1958 . . .

On the morning of the day in question I was standing with my brother on the pavement outside 29 Garville Avenue with the cedar tree behind. It was misty and cold and the dark Dublin earth in our front garden smelt strongly of cat.

A neighbour woman came up and saying, 'Here,' she handed each of us an Irish ten-shilling note – each note was red, slightly greasy and creased with lines like the back of an old man's neck. Ten shillings was a lot of money – I knew that. The money was a sure sign, I thought, there was something going on, something very important but not necessarily very nice. In fact, most probably it was not nice.

A huge lorry appeared and all our furniture was carried out of the house and loaded inside. The doors at the back of the lorry were closed and the lorry drove off. We went to a relative. I was given a stuffed toy dog. I understood this was to compensate for Brown Dog who wasn't with us and who I gathered I would never see again. He'd gone to a farmer in Wicklow.

Next thing, it was evening and we were on the side of the dock. There was a huge boat tied up, seagulls clamouring overhead, people crying all around us, and the salty smell of the sea in the air. I climbed up a swaying wooden gangplank and felt, through the soles of my shoes, the wooden strips that were nailed across to stop passengers slipping. Later still, in darkness now, I went back down the same swaying gangplank with my mother and my brother. Then I was on a dimly lit platform and there was a train standing waiting, with wreaths of steam hissing from the engine. The air was wet and smelt of coal. We got into an old-fashioned carriage with a corridor and piled into one of the separate compartments. The train pulled away. I lay across the seat that was covered with red scratchy material and fell asleep. When I woke up it was light outside, and the skin of my chin and cheek, where it touched the seat while I was asleep, was hot and prickly.

We went to the dining car. The windows were spotted with soot, little blobs of compressed powdery filth. The steward, a man with blue tattoos on his arms, forked pieces of bacon from a black pan straight on to our plates. Then he gave my brother and me half a dozen miniature jars of red and green Robertson's jam to take away with us.

As a child I had a keenly developed sense that everything that happened signified either good or bad and I was always examining whatever was happening to see what it said about what lay ahead. When I got the ten-shilling note I had worried it foretold something bad was going to happen; but now, the marvellous little jars of jam changed that. Surely, I thought, this gift was a sign that a wonderful adventure was about to start.

We arrived at Euston, got off the train and caught a taxi. We drove then for a very long time. Eventually, the taxi stopped and I got out. We were halfway up a hill. On one side stretched a damp green common; there was a path leading to a building that I would come to know as the pavilion; below this there was a huge burnt-out tree with branches that went straight up into the grey sky like outstretched arms; opposite the common there were pairs of suburban houses running in both directions for as far as I could see. This was Cannon Hill Lane where we had come to live.

My father stood at the door of the nearest house. It had a bay window and a garage at the side. While my mother paid the taxi driver, I watched my father watching us from the door. He looked grumpy. He did not like to see her spending money. I already understood this.

I darted in past my father, scuttled through the house, and emerged into our new back garden. There was a small lawn studded with worm casts, a couple of flowerbeds, and dusty concrete paths.

At the back of our garden I could hear something that sounded interesting. I went and looked over the fence. I saw a man with his hair combed back and a pointed face. He was small and thin. He was piling bits of wet wood on to a bonfire.

'Hello,' he said. 'It's Guy Fawkes . . . you excited?' Guy Fawkes did not exist in Ireland so this meant nothing to me. 'We're having a bonfire tonight,' he added, 'and fireworks.'

On cue, a rocket whooshed and exploded overhead. Marvellous little balls of green and red light rolled across the sky. The man chuckled. 'Someone can't wait,' he said.

He went back to building his bonfire. I drifted off. I heard a blackbird chirping, then the roar of turning pedals and the clatter of a moving chain. I turned and saw my brother on his tricycle pedalling down the path, his bare thin legs moving like pistons.

That was when I realised I was quite wrong on the train when I got the miniature jams and I thought this was the start of a wonderful adventure. No, I was right when the neighbour woman gave me the ten-shilling note outside our old house in Dublin and I knew something was wrong.

I stepped back to let my brother pass. At the same time I felt the tubes in my chest swelling up and then the drone as air tried to pass up and down the restricted passageways.

I sucked again, very hard; my wheeze became a roar. I felt breathless and dizzy.

My brother passed. I put my hands on my knees and locked my arms to support my chest. What was called my chestiness or bronchitis or asthma was back. It usually came from dust or blankets but today, I noticed, it came because I was sad.

chapter six

I was asleep in the back bedroom of our new home. My mother woke me early. There was something we had to do and we were late. We dressed, then put on our coats and hats. She opened the front door and we hurried out into the smog.

My mother rushed down the hill. I had to trot to keep up. The pavement was slippery. The smog muffled the usual morning sounds of husbands calling goodbye, banging their front doors shut and whistling as they walked off to work. The silence was eerie. Suddenly, a car crawled by, the two white discs that were its headlamps like twin suns.

At the bottom we turned into Cherrywood Lane. My mother continued walking as fast as before. Several minutes later we passed through a dripping gateway. I was breathless and I had a stitch.

Next thing, I was in a classroom. There was a smell of polish and Plasticine. There were little girls in dresses and little boys in shorts. Each child was scratching away with a bit of white chalk at a slate.

A woman teacher in a purple woollen skirt and a jersey gave me a slate and a piece of chalk. She told me to sit on the floor. Then she crouched down beside me. She seemed nice. She tugged at the pearls around her neck. I noticed my mother was gone but I didn't mind. The teacher wrote Karl Gébler (I was back to my original name, apparently), and the date. She showed me how to hold the chalk.

I began to copy what the teacher wrote. Then I stopped and put the chalk in my mouth. It was dusty and it sucked all the spit in my mouth.

'Right,' said the teacher, 'we're going to play shop.'

A girl called Wendy was chosen as shopkeeper. She put on a brown coat and stood behind the counter in the scaled-down shop in the corner. I bought plastic tinned peas, bread, cornflakes and butter. I paid with a plastic threepenny bit.

Suddenly, a boy hit another child. Then the assailant lay on the floor and began to scream while the victim whimpered. A man with bandy legs and a crooked nose appeared. This was Mr Woodall, the caretaker. He picked up the bad boy and carried him to the nurse in the sick room.

Later, a boy vomited. He went to the sick room too. Mr Woodall sprinkled sawdust and sand on the sick, then scooped up the mess with a wide flat shovel. Afterwards, he mopped the floor using hot water cloudy with Dettol.

'Gather round, boys and girls,' said the teacher, 'and sit on the floor.'

She opened a book and began to read. Her English voice was clear and smooth. The story was about a family of tiny people, Pod, Arriety and Homily. They lived in an old house behind the wainscoting. They were called Borrowers because they borrowed things from the big people, things like drawing pins, pencils and paper. As the teacher read, I saw the Borrowers inside my head.

As soon as I got home, I ran into the dining room and scooted under the sideboard. I had noticed the wainscoting was loose here.

'Hello,' I called through the gap at the top.

My mother came and asked what I was doing.

I explained the Borrowers were in there and I was calling to them to come out and play.

It was a month later. I stood in the room where the Borrowers lived, looking out the French doors at the vine that grew under our verandah; its twisted stems and branches were red and flaky like dry onion skin.

The smog under the verandah was like steam and I could see through it. Further away the smog was like a solid grey wall and it hid our lawn, our flowerbeds, and the houses behind us.

I turned. In the corner of the room there was a Christmas tree in a pot with red paper wrapped around it. I shook a branch and small green needles cascaded to the floor.

I gathered these up and threw them into the coal fire burning in the grate. The needles crackled as they burnt and a lovely smell came.

I shook the tree and tumbled another shower of needles to the floor.

'What do you think you're doing?'

My father stood in the doorway.

'How many times do I have to explain? Don't touch the tree.'

I sat down on the floor. The linoleum was cold through the seat of my shorts. I lifted up the present that I knew was mine. Something rattled inside; it was a nice sound.

'Why can't you leave things alone instead of always fiddling and poking and touching?'

I put down my present.

'You give me the pip.'

He went away and I heard him go into his study.

I stared at my Christmas present. One day I would get to open it, and at last that day came.

'Open it,' my mother said.

I pulled off the paper and found a cardboard box with a picture on the front; it showed a steam engine racing through the country with smoke trailing back from the funnel into a magnificent blue summer sky. I floated the lid up to reveal a clockwork railway set.

I slotted the lengths of track together, hooked the locomotive to the carriages, wound the engine, put it on the track and set it going. As the train went along the track, came round, passed me, went on, passed and went on, engine whirring, wheels clicking, I knew there was nothing else in the world as beautiful as this.

'Come on,' my father shouted. 'No more hatching. Fresh air for you.'

In the hall we put on our scarves; mine was loose and ragged when I finished, his was neat and tight.

'Do your scarf again,' he said.

Without lining up the ends I retied it.

'You clot.'

He redid it, then fluffed it up like his.

'Next time, do it properly,' he said, 'or not at all,'

He opened the front door. I saw a thin lead-coloured smog outside. I realised then it was just us; somehow my brother and mother had escaped our afternoon walk.

I went down the path and out of our gate.

'Stop at the kerb,' my father called.

He came up behind me; we crossed together and began to walk up the path across the common. The dead tree drew my eye. It was like something from a First World War battlefield. I longed to talk about that war, or any war, but my father wouldn't be drawn on the subject; he said war was for ninnies.

We came to the pavilion, a two-storey brick building, with

a long sloping roof and a wooden verandah. This was where the park keepers went; it was also a tea house in the summer.

We circled the whole common and arrived, at last, at the black pond at the bottom of Cannon Hill. On the muddy bank, a huge swan waddled up to a boy who held out a piece of bread.

'That's asking for trouble,' my father said.

Suddenly, the swan lunged for the bread. The child jumped back. The swan began to beat his wings, fiercely.

'Those wings'd break your arm,' my father said. 'Let that be a lesson; don't ever feed swans.'

At the end of the pond there was a run-off, separated from the pavement by a wall. Two Teddy boys sat here, smoking.

We passed them and stopped at the kerb. While my father stood listening for cars, a butt flew by – it missed me by inches – and landed in the gutter. I wondered would my father turn and order whoever threw it to pick it up. It would be just like him. I began to feel anxious. There were always Teddy boys on this wall; what would happen, I thought, if he got cross now and then I met them on my way home from school, when I was alone?

But he said nothing. We crossed and started up the hill. As we went I felt the tubes in my chest closing and soon I was wheezing loudly.

'You're sick again,' said my father, shaking his head. He was annoyed but he was trying not to show it.

chapter seven

All through that first London winter, from the end of 1958, when we arrived, through to the spring of 1959, while I was at school in the daytime, my mother wrote in the bedroom at the back of the house that I shared with my brother. There was a bay window with a wide ledge that she could use as a rest for her typewriter. Sometimes, when I came home from school, I would find a pile of manuscript paper on the ledge. I also remember that she would write in the tiny box-room at the front. I knew my father wrote and got money for what he produced and I assumed my mother was now doing the same thing.

One hot afternoon, it was now June or July 1959 and I was coming up to the end of my first year at school, I left school, as usual, at the end of the day. I went across the playground, the school buildings to one side, the playing fields to the other. The infants, like myself, were let out of class a little before the rest of the school.

The caretaker's house was in front of me with the school gates beside it. On the far side a crowd of mothers waited for their children.

I went through the gate. I did not expect anyone to be there. I could walk home by myself and usually I did. Then I heard my name called. I looked and saw it was my mother in a summer dress, cream-coloured with flowers printed on it. She gave me a big wave. She ran up to me. I knew at once she had news and I could tell it was good news, not bad news.

She said she had just sold *The Country Girls*, the book that she wrote over our first winter in London. A publisher would publish it. She told me the name, which meant nothing. The publisher would pay. She named the figure. This also meant nothing to me. She would have money, she said, and because she had money, she would be able to buy me whatever I wanted. Now this I did understand.

There was an ice-cream van parked at the kerb. What did I want? she asked. The van was white with words and pictures painted on the side. I could have anything, she said.

I wondered what my father would say? He did not allow us to have ice creams or lollies. He said they were packed with refined white sugar. This stuff caused constipation, neuralgia and rotted the teeth. I decided to say nothing. Why bring him up? Why remind her of his rules?

We joined the queue and, after a while, we reached the window. The smell coming from inside was chocolate and cardboard.

'What do you want?' the ice-cream man asked.

I ordered a King Size 99 with double Cadbury's Flakes, red syrup and hundreds and thousands. The ice-cream man looked at my mother. She nodded.

The man held a cone under a nozzle and pulled a handle. The ice cream came out like rope. When the man had filled the cone he added the Flakes, one on either side like horns. Then he sprinkled hundreds and thousands over the top. Finally, he added red syrup. A drop went on his finger. He transferred the cone to his other hand and wiped the finger on his apron. Why didn't he lick his finger instead? I wondered. There was no accounting for adults. They never seemed to mind passing up sweet things.

My mother paid. We walked away. I pushed the Flakes down into the cone with my tongue and began to lick.

The sky was dark blue above me and paler blue further off. The street smelt of tar. Somewhere, someone pushed a lawn mower and I heard the stop-start, start-stop of blades churning. I heard the clasps on my sandals jingling too, a light, tinny, summery sound.

When I reached the edge of the cone it was soft with my spit. I nibbled the soft cone away. Now came the best part, warm 99 and cold Flake mixed together. I ate steadily until I was left with just a thimble of cone. I popped this in my mouth. My 99 was gone.

The timing was fortunate. In only a few yards, Cherrywood hit Cannon Hill Lane and we would turn up the hill for home.

My mother stopped me. With her handkerchief she wiped around my mouth. I put out my tongue and she swabbed it with her hanky. Superimposed on the taste of ice cream and chocolate was the taste of clean cotton.

My mother put away her handkerchief.

We climbed the hill, every house like ours, same gate, same path, same bay window.

Halfway up, we came to 257. I followed my mother along the path. Creeper cascaded down the front of the house. She put the key in the lock and opened the door.

I went in, ran through the house and straight out the kitchen door. I didn't stop until I felt the yellow, dusty concrete garden path under my feet. There was a small flowerbed beside me, filled with snapdragons.

I crouched and squeezed open a purple flower. Inside, the mouth was dark at the rim, but gradually it grew lighter in

colour towards the base. The stem at the bottom was white
with a yellow sticky top.

'Come here,' my father called.

I ran in mock eagerly. I knew this pose was my best pro-
tection. I found my father at the kitchen door. He was in
slippers, old corduroy trousers, a white vest and striped
braces. These were working men's braces, he said, and they
came in a box with pictures of men at work, braces stretched
over their working backs as they baled hay and dug ditches.

I noticed the dusty smell of the vine overhead mixed with
the sharp petrol smell of the liquid he would smear over his
corduroys with a rag to clean them. He disapproved of dry
cleaners; they all overcharged for doing next to nothing and it
was easy, he said, to clean one's clothes oneself.

'Put out your tongue,' he said.

His eyes were dark but not quite black. This was not his
cross face; this was his face on the way to being cross.

I put out my tongue. I felt a flush of heat spread across my
face, a sure sign of guilt. Would he see and then interrogate?

Miraculously, he did not notice. He bent down and peered
at my tongue instead. Then he bent forward and sniffed my
mouth.

I stood utterly still, my face red and hot. I steeled myself.
The question I dreaded was coming, Have you eaten an ice
cream?

What would I say if he asked me?

If I said yes, well, he'd explode.

If I said nothing, that would be tantamount to saying yes
without actually saying yes. That would make him explode
even more.

However, if I denied it, if I said no, I didn't have an ice
cream, he'd explode still more. And that would be worst of all.

My heart raced. My legs which I was trying to hold stiff and
still began to tremble.

I made a decision.

If he asked me I would say yes. I would say, Yes, I had an ice cream. Mama bought me one.

He would shout, then. But not as much as he would shout if I said nothing, or worse, if I said, all innocent, No, I didn't have an ice cream at all.

I heard my father swallow. I heard him say, 'Tut-tut.'

I waited.

He turned away and walked back across the kitchen. He was not going to ask the question. Thank God, my mother cleaned away all the evidence with her handkerchief.

I watched him disappear into the hall and then into his study. I was safe. I had got away with it.

That same summer, 1959, we went on holiday to Cornwall, to somewhere near Penzance. When I returned to school in September I had a new teacher. She was called Miss Huggins and I liked her a lot.

We went back to Cornwall in January the following year, 1960, to get away from the smog and the damp and the misery of a London winter.

After a couple of months we went back to Morden.

One evening, shortly after we got back, my father called me into his study. I found him at his desk feeding a piece of paper into his typewriter. A book lay open beside him. It was *The New World, The First Pictures of America*. This was one of many books on America that he had dating from when he wrote *The Plymouth Adventure*. I had looked in it before and I noticed now, with a quickening pulse, that the book was open at a picture of an Indian, his head split with a cudgel, his brains in a pool on the ground in front of him. He was a camp guard, my father had explained once, who fell asleep at his post. This was how the lackadaisical were punished, he added, in those days. He appeared to approve.

There were several other fascinating drawings in the book. I had been particularly struck by the picture showing how one tribe treated the corpses of their enemies who had fallen in battle. They removed the arms, legs and scalp, then they shot an arrow either up the anus or into the penis.

'Can I see?' I asked automatically, pointing at the book.

'No,' he said, which in a way was a relief. Though I loved to look through this book, at the same time it repelled and frightened me.

My father typed the date (it was early spring 1960), and then a letter in which he explained he had decided to send me to school in long trousers because of my weak chest and my recurring bronchitis, although it was against the rules.

He took the note out of the typewriter and put it in an envelope.

'Give that to your teacher,' he said.

I went upstairs to my bedroom. My new long trousers lay on the window ledge. They made my legs feel funny when I wore them. I slipped the note in the pocket. I definitely didn't want to lose that.

The next morning, as I went through the school gates, I met Mr Woodall. In the middle of his vast nose there was a hole leaking wet. I was told it was a Jap bayonet wound that never got better. That was Jap steel for you, added the boys who had told me this.

'You've been away a long time,' he said. 'Where you been?'

'Cornwall.'

I walked down to the infants' playground. I saw several old classmates but no one spoke to me. Eventually, an older boy came up and stared at me.

'Who are you?' he asked, finally.

'I'm Karl Gébler,' I said.

The name meant nothing. The boy went away. I realised no one remembered me because I'd been away for so long; in turn, this led me to wonder if Miss Huggins had forgotten me too? I had certainly not forgotten her. She had raven-black hair and her hands were always warm.

The bell sounded. I filed along the corridor and turned into my old classroom.

'Hello,' Miss Huggins said from behind the desk.

She saw the long trousers but she said nothing. She took the note.

The roll was called. Then Miss Huggins wrote the date on the board, turned to the class and said, 'Karl Gébler is back from Cornwall. Will you please welcome him.'

It was after Easter, 1960. It was a cold afternoon, and I was on Cherrywood Lane, walking home. My brother would start school in September and then I would have someone to walk with, but today I was alone.

I approached the corner where I would turn for Cannon Hill Lane. The Teddy boys were usually to be found sitting on the balustrade wall across the road, but unusually, this after-noon, rather than facing me, they were standing on the wall with their backs towards me.

My first instinct was to hurry by and head up the hill for home. I hated passing them; I could never stop my face red-dening or my knees trembling and I was certain the Teddy boys could see that. At least with their backs turned, I would be spared that indignity today.

But then curiosity got the better of me. What could they be doing? I wondered. Behind the wall lay the pond and the far bank of the pond was fenced off for nesting birds. Teddy boys got over there sometimes and then the park keepers would go over and chase them away. Was that the reason for this excite-ment? The green uniforms were chasing the drape coats through the undergrowth where the birds nested?

I went to the kerb. I was forbidden to cross Cannon Hill

Lane without an adult. My father considered it a main road. It was certainly busier than the suburban streets along which I went to and from school.

I knew my father watched me through binoculars when I was on the common but he never watched me, at least as far as I knew, on the way home from school. I decided that if I went over, I probably wouldn't be seen.

There was no traffic. I darted across.

On the other side I saw something lying in the gutter. It was a second before I realised it was an inside-out pair of long grey, flannel trousers, similar to those I now wore to school.

I went up to the wall and as I went I realised the Teddy boys were not shouting across at the the bank but down into the run-off under the wall. This was a semi-circular concrete well about eight feet deep. Usually, the run-off was filled with twigs and mud and sometimes pond water. But today in the bottom of the run-off there stood a boy in white underpants, and black socks and shoes. He wore the blazer and the tie of the local grammar school.

'I'm going,' said the boy in the run-off.

'The fucking monkey wants out,' someone shouted. The Teddy boys scratched their armpits and made chimpanzee noises.

'You've had your fun. I'm getting out.'

The grammar school boy grabbed the lip at the top of the run-off and began to walk his feet up the wall.

'Back in your cage,' someone shouted.

A big brown bottle came from above. It hit the grammar school boy on the mouth. First, there was a smack, and then a sound like a twig breaking. The grammar school boy sank down on to the run-off floor. The bottle smashed beside him. White beer froth and shiny glass shards spread everywhere. The grammar school boy sat quite still for a second. Then blood came out of his mouth and his nose and he spat something on to his palm. It was a tooth.

The Teddy boys laughed. Someone started throwing orange peel. The grammar school boy covered his head with his arms.

I looked up and saw I was standing beside the peel thrower. He saw me look up and he looked back at me

'What are you fucking looking at?'

My legs trembled and I shuddered. The Teddy boy saw this and smiled.

'Fuck off, you yellow-bellied cunt,' he said, cheerfully.

I dashed across the road without looking and began to pant up the hill towards home.

chapter eight

Everyone in my class got a present at the end of the summer term from Miss Huggins. I got a pencil with a rubber in the shape of a troll that fitted over the end.

'It's rubbish,' said my father when I got home. 'It was probably made by blind orphans in Bolivia whose parents were murdered by the CIA.'

He had read something about this in a magazine and he began to tell me about it. I didn't listen. I was immensely proud of my present.

Later that summer I went with my brother to County Clare to stay with my mother's people, my pious Catholic grandmother and my allegedly genetically degenerate grandfather.

Our Morden house smelt of anthracite dust and the sulphur my father sprayed on the grapes under our verandah to keep the flies away. The Irish house smelt of Seville marmalade, bicarbonate of soda and my grandfather's Gold Flake cigarettes.

In Morden, my father didn't even like me playing with a stick that looked like a gun. He said all war toys were shoddy, cheap, plastic, and a waste of money. He said they were all made by slave labour in Hong Kong. He said they encouraged children to identify with the military killing machine. He said the child who played with war toys in Morden today was happy to go to the Congo as a mercenary and slaughter Blacks tomorrow. So, in London, we didn't have war toys.

In Ireland, on the contrary, it was liberty hall. We were free. We made spears and swords out of ash sticks. We made Webley revolvers and Winchester repeating rifles out of broom handles. We made pea shooters from old lengths of copper pipe we found in an outhouse and for projectiles we used my grandmother's pie weights. We made catapults with Y's of beech and strips of inner tube. But no matter how hard my brother and I tried, no matter how inventive we were, everything that we made looked handmade. Which it was. Nothing had the high-production finish or the gloss of a proper war toy bought from a shop. It was unfortunate: here we were, free to play war, but we lacked that vital ingredient – the shop-bought war toy.

We decided to try magic. We would make a direct appeal; not to God but to the Powers. The Powers existed only in Ireland and they lived only in special places. For example, there was a fairy ring behind the farmhouse and there were Powers in there. However, because of the proximity of this place to the farmhouse, we felt the Powers in there must be weak. Happily, there was a second ring at the bottom of the avenue near the road. It was a perfect circle of beech and oak trees with wild irises growing in the spaces between the trees. Furthermore, we had noticed that even in the worst of storms, the cattle *never* went in here. Never. There was something about this ring that the one closer to the house definitely did not have. Even our animals recognised this.

So off we set. As we tramped down the avenue, we were in the normal everyday world of grass, birdsong and cattle dung.

But once we stepped over the irises, with their long pointed leaves which scratched our bare legs like the point of a pin, and slipped between the massive, mossy trunks of the trees, we were in a different world. It was incredibly dark for a start; it took ages for our eyes to adjust to the gloom. It was also very quiet, so that familiar sounds, like the rasping bray of our donkey on the lawn, appeared to be much louder in here then when we heard it outside. We had noticed exactly the same effect in chapel. The peal of a bicycle bell outside the chapel doors sounded abnormally insistent and shrill, whereas when you heard the same peal out on the village street, it didn't. And like the chapel, with its incense and hymn-book odour, this tree ring also had a special strong smell: it was a mixture of chalk and wet and mould; it also smelled a bit like the Indian meal my grandmother mixed with milk and fed her chickens every morning. This combination of darkness and silence with strong woodland smells affected us in the same way the church affected us; the tree ring made us feel subdued and reverent; it awed us.

In the middle of the trees stood a heap of lichen-covered stones. This was the altar. Obviously. A stone had fallen out and left a hollow and this was where we placed our offerings. These were a brown Irish penny with a chicken on it, a headless toy soldier, a broken set of rosary beads, a Lady Finger's biscuit, and an old light bulb from the milking parlour. Then we knelt on the brown carpet of beechnuts and, until our bare knees could stand it no longer, we begged the Powers to grant us one wish: a double-barrelled shotgun with a spring mechanism that fired cork plugs for each of us. Now we were in Ireland we wanted to play at Flying Columns.

When we went to bed that evening, it was still light. In summer it didn't get dark until well after ten. The blinds were drawn right down to the windowsills and the slanting sunlight that fell on them from outside made them glow, while

around the edges, where the sunlight was able to get in, there
were threads of bright silver.

I lay in bed beside my brother, waiting for sleep. I could
smell the plastic pail where we peed at night. It was under our
bed. The pail was empty and had been washed but no matter
how often it was washed, the brackish smell of salty pee
always lingered.

A picture of the Crucifixion hung on the wall immediately
above the bed-head and I saw it upside-down above me.
There was Our Lord, his arms and legs extended as far as they
would stretch. Huge nails (hideous, crooked, like tent irons)
had been driven through his skin, bones and sinews, and into
the wood behind. His whole weight was supported on the
Cross by these three pieces of metal. His skin was purple and
deathly and his eyes were wide and terrified as he stared
towards heaven and the God who had abandoned him. Where
the nails went in and where the thorns of his Crown pierced
the skin on his forehead, the dark red blood looked like blobs
of sealing wax, I thought. Parcels and sealing wax were very
much on my mind. If our wish was granted, it would have to
come in a parcel.

We went back to the ring the next day. Our offerings were
gone. We knelt and prayed. We went back again the day after.
On the night following our third visit, my brother woke me in
the middle of the night. He had something to show me. He
lifted the blind and I stared out into the velvety darkness and
saw three silver-fringed figures hovering outside: a blind fox, a
bat and a fairy in a pointed hat. Here it was – the sign for which
I'd been waiting. I knew at once we needn't go back to the ring.

Some days later the post van pulled up and the postman
fetched two long parcels out of the back. The brown paper
seams were indeed sealed with blood-red blobs of wax. One
parcel was addressed to Master Carlos, the other to Master
Sasha Gébler.

We carried the parcels into the kitchen, slid a bone-handled knife into the seams and lifted off the blobs that held the brown paper in place. Inside the paper skin, we found two long cardboard boxes, each with a stylish picture of a shotgun on the front. We lifted away the cardboard lids and, lo and behold, inside each box we found a spring-loading double-barrelled shotgun of the type we coveted. There was also a note from my mother. My grandmother read it out. My mother said she had bought the guns on impulse. She hoped we liked them and we were not to bring them home to Cannon Hill Lane but to leave them in Ireland. Yes, I said, and shrugged. I knew what this letter meant. Grandmother had written off to her. But the guns would have come even if my grandmother hadn't written. The Powers would have seen to it. I was certain.

I unpicked the string that attached the cork plugs to the gun barrel ends (this was a ridiculous feature – the whole point of a gun was to shoot where one wanted, without hindrance) and hurried outside to kill a few Tommies, or perhaps one of my girl cousins.

One afternoon, my father showed up at my grandparents' house in Z6 201, the silver-grey Railton. My grandmother must have known he was coming because she hid our shotguns before he arrived.

My father had come not so much to see us as to inspect the Model-T Ford that he kept in one of my grandfather's outhouses. We went up to look at it after tea. It was a small black car which sat up on blocks, its roof spotted with hard, white bird droppings. I knew it well: I had often sat in the front seat and pretended to drive it.

'That was the first car your grandfather ever owned,' my father said, opening the driver door and peering in. A smell of old wood and dry leather came from inside.

'Was this Adolf's car?' I asked. This was a new and fascinating piece of information.

'Not his actual car, you clot. Listen. Adolf's first car was a Model-T like this but this is not – please, pay attention – the one your grandfather *actually* drove. Understand?'

The inspection over, we drove Z6 201 to a special place on the Bog Road where the blackberry bushes were particularly good. My grandmother had given each of us a glass jam jar to fill. These had red rubber seals around the top, a hinged lid and a steel mechanism to clamp the top closed.

I went to a bush and started to pick. For every one berry I picked, I ate two or three. These blackberries were warm, ripe and sweet.

Finally, we finished picking. The jam jars were full and the tops were closed. My father opened the passenger door of Z6 201 and tipped the seat forward. As I climbed in, I was met by a wave of heat. The interior was like an oven.

I lowered myself down on to the back seat but didn't let my bottom or my bare thighs touch the roasting leather. I lifted myself away from contact by keeping my arms straight and levering my body up. Years of cold lavatory seats had made me an expert in this.

My father fired the engine and we set off. We went down an old road full of ruts and holes, with high hedgerows on either side. These kept us in the shade, mostly, but every now and again we would pass a gap and bright white sunlight would flood the car. My father drove slowly, with his eyes screwed up. He had forgotten his sunglasses and he was anxious the road might damage his suspension.

In the back, the car rose and fell, and I went up and down with it. A warm wind blew in though the open windows. The afternoon air smelt of grass and fern, bog and bog water. I felt my stomach flutter. I felt full, then I felt light, then I felt full again. The taste of blackberry and spit, mixed with the chops and boiled potatoes that I had eaten for lunch, rose into the back of my throat, then slid away down towards my stomach, then rose into my throat again . . .

'I'm going to be sick,' I cried.

There wasn't time to stop and get out.

'Get your head out the window,' he shouted.

Lurching forward, I felt the vomit coming, and I knew I couldn't stop it. If I closed my mouth, it would just come out of my nose. So I let it come . . . It was a pink, pulpy mash of blackberry and saliva, mixed with lamb chops and potato. It shot forward and crashed on to the top of the door and then began to pour down the gap in the top of the door through which the window glass had disappeared.

'Get your head out,' my father shouted,

But before I could, another column of vomit shot out of my mouth and hit the top of the door again.

My father threw open the door. I jumped down and ran to the verge. A little more sick came up – but only a little – and plopped on to the spiky grass at my feet. The bulk of my vomit, I realised, was on Z6 201.

Back at my grandparents house, my father wound up the window. My blackberry sick, purple and puce with hairy lumps of fruit and seeds suspended here and there in it, was smeared on either side of the glass.

'Oh, you stupid child.'

My father took off the inside of the door. My sick had got all over the springs and levers that moved the glass panel up and down. It took ages to clean and the smell of my sick lingered in Z6 201 for days afterwards. Even in London, weeks later, it was still there, faintly.

At the end of the holidays I acquired a small plastic pistol that shot a dart with a sucker on the end. Perhaps because it was small and inoffensive, my father allowed me to bring it back home. This was some consolation for having to leave my shotgun behind in Ireland.

One wet afternoon I got permission to go into my father's study.

I sat on the sofa and fired the dart at various targets.

Then I began to think about Adolf Hitler. My father had told me that he had killed himself by firing a bullet into his mouth. I assumed the bullet went down his throat and into his heart. That was why Hitler died. So what would happen, I wondered, if I fired the dart into my mouth?

Idly, I pulled the trigger. I felt the dart on my tongue as it shot in. Then I felt it in my throat. I felt hot and dizzy suddenly, and terrified. The rubbery taste of the dart was never so strong as it was now. I retched but the dart did not come out. It was stuck, I realised, in my throat.

I reached with my hand across my tongue. If I didn't do this right, I'd push the dart further down my throat. It would go into my heart. Who knows what would happen then.

I felt the knobbly bit at the end of the stem. I pinched it between finger and thumb and pulled slowly. The dart came forward like something coming out of mud. I felt the sucker drag across my tongue. The taste of plastic was all over my mouth.

Had I wanted this dart to go all the way down? I wondered. I shivered and I didn't answer the question. I was attracted but also repelled by the idea, just as I was attracted and repelled by the picture of the American Indian with his brains in a puddle in front of him, or the picture of the butchered, mutilated bodies of dead warriors with arrows shot into them.

chapter nine

I went back to school in the autumn 1960. My new teacher wasn't like Miss Huggins. Miss Sherringham was tall and thin, with bright blue eyes and straw-coloured hair. When I got my sums wrong she would slap me on the legs with the long ruler she used to draw lines on the blackboard.

Early in 1961, I got sick again. I was back in my bed in Cannon Hill Lane, three pillows piled under my head. I breathed shallowly, sipping the air. With each breath my chest droned and I felt a pressing, squeezing pain in my lungs.

The gas fire was on. I heard it hiss. My father walked in rubbing lanolin into his hands.

'Is the bed hot?' he asked.

He reached down and felt the corner closest to the gas.

'That could catch fire,' he said.

He heaved the bed back from the gas and left. I heard him go downstairs.

I looked straight ahead. The bay window was in front of me with its wide painted ledge. My mother didn't type here any more. Now there was a hut at the bottom of the garden and she went down there to write.

There was a dense smog outside. It was so thick I could see neither our neighbours' houses nor the sky.

I heard the doorbell. The front door was opened. Someone came in. There were footsteps on the stairs and the doctor came in, carrying his black bag, followed by my father.

The doctor sat, took my wrist and began to count.

'Open your mouth,' he said.

He pushed my tongue down with a flat piece of wood and looked into my throat. The wood was rough. I thought a splinter would go into my tongue. The flat bit of wood was taken away. I swallowed. No splinter. The doctor prodded under my chin with his thick fingers.

'Chest,' he said,

I undid my pyjama top, then lifted up the hated girl's bodice that I always had to wear now in the winter. I felt the cold disc of the stethoscope touch my chest just below the collar-bone.

'Breath.'

I obliged.

'Lean forward.'

He listened to my back.

'Button up.'

I lay back and pulled the pyjama tunic closed. Just sitting up had taken so much of my energy that I didn't have the strength to button it up. It would be a while before I could manage that.

'Bronchial infection,' the doctor said.

He went out and my father followed.

Time passed. My father came back with a brown bottle and one of our big spoons. It was yellow in places where the gilt was worn away.

'Right,' he said, 'this will make you better.'

He tipped up the bottle over the spoon. A thick, heavy pink liquid glugged out slowly.

'Open your mouth,' he said.

The spoon felt enormous as he pushed it past my lips. The pink medicine slid on to my tongue. It tasted of fish and something bitter, like the molasses we put on our toast.

I made a face.

'You're going to have another and I don't want any whining.'

Another helping went on to the spoon and from there into my mouth.

I fell asleep later and when I woke up the curtains were drawn. My brother lay sleeping in his bed. He turned and the springs whispered. The gas fire was still on, low, and I saw the flames reflected on the ceiling.

The pain in my chest was worse than ever. It felt like two big cuts and it was as if grit was being rubbed into them with each breath.

My father came in with three saucers and a ridged bottle with a label stuck on the front on which he had drawn, by hand, a skull and crossbones in ink.

He unscrewed the top and tipped the bottle over a saucer. A clear liquid poured out. Its smell was vile and sharp.

'Never swallow this,' he said. 'It's ammonia. It's to clear the air. Hopefully you'll wheeze less.'

One saucer went on my bedside table, a second on the window, and a third on the mantelpiece.

My father sat on the side of the bed.

'I can hear you downstairs,' he said. 'Even with the study door closed. I can hear you wheezing over the sound of the typewriter.'

His voice was quiet and nice. He wasn't cross.

'You may get worse before the medicine gets you better. Meantime, you have to help yourself. You have to tell yourself you're not going to be sick any more. You have to say to yourself, over and over, I'm not going to be sick, I'm not going to be sick, I'm going to breathe properly, I'm going to breathe properly, my chest is going to open, I'm going to get better, I'm going to get better . . .'

He chanted the words like a prayer. As I listened I felt myself growing calm and quiet and still. I also got the strange feeling that I was not in myself but above and looking down on myself.

'Do you understand?' he continued. 'You just say the words to yourself, like that, in your head, over and over and over and over again, and eventually what'll happen is you'll believe the words and you'll get better.'

He looked at me. The electric light shone from the landing behind so what I saw was only the outline of his head, not his face.

'Try,' he said.

'I am not going to be sick.'

He nodded.

'Go on.'

'I'm not going to be sick, I am going to be better, my chest won't hurt, I'll breathe again . . .'

'That's it. It's called auto-suggestion, self-hypnosis.'

'What's that?'

'Just close your eyes and do it.'

I closed my eyes and began to repeat, 'I'm not going to be sick, I'm going to be better . . .'

I felt his hand on my forehead. He rubbed my scalp through my hair, timing his movement to my words. He smelt of lanolin and Heinz vegetable soup, which was the smell of his skin.

'I'm going to get better, I'm going to get better . . .'

Several minutes later I felt a funny feeling inside my chest. Deep down in the constricted tubes, I sensed the tissue shrinking back towards its normal bore.

I fell asleep.

When I woke up I did not open my eyes. I lay very still and listened. I heard the gas fire and my brother murmuring in his sleep. I heard a bin lid going back on a bin outside.

I could taste the ammonia in my nose and throat. It was like the taste of the stuff my mother put in the toilet.

Then I listened. I was still wheezing, but not as much as the night before. I wasn't better but I saw that I could resist the illness by chanting words in my head like my father had shown me.

'I am not going to be sick,' I started, 'I am going to be better . . .'

chapter ten

Carlo Gébler (left) with his younger
brother Sasha, in the back garden of
Cannon Hill Lane, Morden, 1961

I was in the hall, downstairs. Our house was unusually quiet. My father's study door was propped open with a brass statue of a bald man sitting on a rock, his heavy head resting on a hand while he pondered. My father looked like the statue when he sat and wrote.

I peered round the lintel. My father's chair in front of the desk was empty. I crept in. Although it was summer the stove was lit. The coals in the grate settled with a murmur.

I went to the tallboy. It was in the space between the study door and the glass-fronted bookcase.

I opened the third drawer up from the bottom. I knew just how to lift and pull without making any noise.

I got the drawer halfway out. There was a wonderful smell of oil. I saw my father's gun. It lay on a square of brown wrapping paper. The metal parts of the gun were black yet shiny. The handle was a deep brown with a touch of yellow.

Because toy guns were strongly disapproved of by my father this made them all the more interesting, and real guns doubly so. And here was the real McCoy, and if my father wasn't in his study, and if I was extremely quiet and extremely careful, I could actually play with it.

I lifted out the gun. The handle had hundreds of criss-cross lines. These should have made it rough but it was smooth. It was cool to the touch, too.

I pointed the gun at the common beyond the bay window. My father kept it for killing rats, he said, which was why, though I was discouraged from playing with guns, it never struck me as strange that he had a gun of his own; today, however, it wasn't rats I had in mind but another target.

Keeping my voice quiet so as not to be heard, I went, 'Bang. Kepow. Pouff,' and, in my mind's eye, one Teddy boy after another dropped dead, shot in the heart, by me, with my father's gun.

'What the hell do you think you're doing?'

I jumped with fright. I was caught by the one I most feared being caught by. I dropped the weapon and it clattered in the drawer.

'Can't you keep away from that?'

I felt everything tightening in the middle of my body. It was like lemon juice going on a cut, except the feeling was deep inside, somewhere behind the stomach, not outside.

'How many times have I told you, that's not to be touched. It's not a plaything. It's a weapon.'

My father went to his desk and sat down. I wanted to run but that would make this worse.

'Come here,' he called.

He wasn't speaking in his angry voice. This was his quiet voice, the one he used to administer a dressing-down. I preferred angry; it was quicker and, in the end, less awful.

'Come on,' he said again.

My face reddened; it always boiled up like this before an ordeal. It was a sign of my weakness and I could not bear him to see it. I also knew there was nothing to be done. I couldn't hide, or run.

'Don't dilly-dally,' he said, calmly.

I crossed the study and stood as far behind his chair as I dared in order that he should see as little of my face as possible.

'What am I going to do with you?'

I said nothing.

'I despair. You're such a stupid boy. It's not as if I haven't told you what's right and what's wrong. But do you pay attention? Of course you don't. You just plough on, going your own sweet way, isn't that right?

'I've told you not to sneak in here. I've told you not to open the drawer. I've told you not to touch the gun, haven't I? A hundred times, a thousand times? But you just ignore me, don't you?'

He looked out the window.

'But then why should I be surprised? This is what you're like, isn't it. You're just, well, stupid. I can tell you things till I'm blue in the face, but you won't listen. You're incapable.'

There was a very long silence.

'You don't want to listen, don't listen then – it's your own lookout. See if I care. But don't turn round to me when you're an adult and say, Oh, Father, you didn't warn me. I'm warning you now, do you understand? And you do know what's going to happen eventually, don't you?'

I knew where this was going from when he'd talked like this before.

'You think you're "it", don't you? But you're not and you should never forget that. When you forget these things, that's when life comes and punches you in the face.

'You know about my early son, yes? I've never kept him a secret.'

I nodded.

'Do you know why I've never kept him a secret?'

Another pause.

'Because I lived through the 1930s. I saw enough lies then to last me the rest of my lifetime. Too many lies give you cancer.'

I didn't understand but I nodded anyway.

'One day, and you'd better be ready for this, my early son will come home. He'll get away from that woman, his mother, and he'll come here. When he's grown, he'll obviously want to know who his father is. Why wouldn't he? We'll become friends.'

I shifted from one foot to the other.

'Between the first-born son and his father there's something special. Can you understand that?'

He took the tube of lanolin from the desk and unscrewed the white cap.

'I can never tell if you understand or not.'

He squeezed a worm of cream on to his palm, and began to rub it into his skin. If he didn't put on lanolin, the skin dried and cracked.

'It's going to be hard for you. Of course it is. Who wouldn't be hurt by the arrival of his better older brother. Oh, it's going to be tough. But I wouldn't be a responsible father if I didn't warn you, would I?'

I said nothing.

'I don't want you turning round when you're grown up and saying to me, You never told me. You never said he was better and cleverer. That's why I'm telling you now. And I'll go on telling you. I don't want you to be ignorant. I don't know if you'll listen. Judging by your recent performance you seem to be incapable of listening. But I'll keep trying. I'll keep my side of the bargain even if you won't.'

He paused.

'One day, although I'm sure you won't believe this now, you're going to thank me. By telling you the truth, now, I'm making it much, much easier for you later on.'

He got up and went and got the gun. He came back to the seat. He broke the gun in two and squinted up the barrel. There was a spiral inside. When the bullet went along the barrel the spiral made it turn. I knew this. He'd let me look up the gun once or twice when he'd cleaned it.

'Go on, get out,' he said.

It was early summer, a Saturday morning probably. We were in the kitchen, the three male Géblers. The light was green; it was stained that colour by the leaves of the vine growing under the verandah outside. My mother was writing in the hut at the bottom of the garden. She wrote stories for a magazine in America called the *New Yorker*. She wrote for newspapers in Fleet Street. She was also writing a novel, her second. This was *The Lonely Girl*, also called *Girl with Green Eyes*.

Out in the hall the letterbox made a noise. As the flap opened back, the noise was gentle; as the flap snapped back, the noise was loud. A second later something landed softly on the brown dusty mat.

My father sat on a high stool at the breakfast counter. He bit off another mouthful of burnt toast soaked with olive oil. This was his standard breakfast.

'Get the post,' said my father to my brother. My father's lips were shiny with oil.

My brother ran off and came back with the post. My father put out his hand and took it. The post was one item; it was *Time* magazine, folded in two, with a brown paper wrapper around the middle.

Time was American. 'I read *Time*,' my father used to say, 'to see what a mess the Americans are in.' Or sometimes he said banjax instead of mess to make me laugh.

My father turned *Time* over in his hand. There on the front of the brown wrapper was his name – Ernest Gébler – and our address. He read the address to himself as he chewed.

I wanted the wrapper to draw on although usually it went to my brother. My father said he was better at drawing than me but I believed the true reason he always got it was that he didn't get ill, he was never in bed for days at a time, and he didn't seem to annoy my father like I did. He also shared with my father an interest in machines and engineering. For all these reasons my father simply liked him more, I thought.

I smarted with the injustice of this as I stood in the kitchen, but I said nothing; instead, as I waited, a new feeling came. Perhaps, just this once, I thought, my father would take off the wrapper and hand it to me. Just like that. Without me asking. It would be a sign he really did like me.

'Can I have the paper from *Time*?' said my brother.

My father ran the bread knife along the gummy join. The wrapper fell away. My brother took it and ran to the dining room next door.

'Put a mat under the paper,' my father shouted, 'I don't want the pencil going through to the wood.'

As this was a house rule, my brother hardly needed reminding.

'Can I look at the Encyclopædia Britannica?' I asked.

He nodded.

I slipped away to the hall and turned into the study. I passed the tallboy (the gun drawer was closed) and reached the bookcase. I turned the key in the lock and opened the glass doors. The Britannicas were on the bottom shelf; they were brown books with gold writing on the outside.

I took the one from the far right-hand end, carried it to the sofa and sat. It fell open at the map of the United States, where I always opened it.

I stared at the page. America was divided up into states and each was a different colour: either pink, yellow, purple or green.

I wondered where the early son lived. That's why I always looked at this map. To see if I could tell, just by looking, where he lived. But the map didn't tell me. And it never would.

I began to turn the pages. After America came South America and then Australia. Eventually, I came to a map of the world. The words 'Trade and Shipping Routes' were written at the bottom.

On this map the different countries of the world were different colours like the different states were different colours. China was yellow. Australia was pink. America was green. England was red.

The countries of the world were connected to each other with thick blue lines. These were the sea lanes along which ships went with freight. The thickest of all was the one between the United States and England.

I ran my finger on this line. I tried to imagine the early son going from where he was to where I was. It was awfully far; in fact, it was so far I felt certain, as I always did when I looked at this map, he'd never come.

That was a cheering thought, as was the one that followed. Why was a name given? I asked myself. I knew the answer. A name got given after someone died. Karl Marx was a man who lived a long time ago. Then he died. Later, the early son came along and my father gave him the name, Karl, because my father liked this man Marx. He said he was an important thinker. Then my father lost the early son and I came along and I was Karl (and still was officially, though my mother preferred Carlos and Carlo). The early son hadn't died, I knew that, but he was so far away (which I could see looking at the map), he was as good as dead and *that* was the reason my father used Karl again for me.

This thought cheered me up. It always cheered me up. I closed the atlas, put it back on the shelf and locked the doors of the bookcase.

chapter eleven

A publicity photograph taken in 1961
for the publication of Edna O'Brien's
The Lonely Girl (later re-titled *Girl
with Green Eyes*)

M iss Sherringham did not give anyone a present on the
last day of the summer term in July 1961. She simply
told us to work harder, wished us a good summer and
watched us file out the door. I was delighted the summer
holidays had come. I had not liked Miss Sherringham and
now I knew I would never have to see her again.

A day or two later I was mooning in the hall at home when my father came out of his study.

'Right, no more hatching indoors for you,' he said.

I followed him outside and through our gate.

'Mind that,' he said. The dog mess on the hot pavement was brown and curved. There were small black flies crawling on it.

'Bloody dog owners,' he said, 'letting their dogs foul everywhere.'

Dog mess was a pet hate. Often, on our walks, if he saw an owner waiting while his dog strained to do it, he would start a sarcastic running commentary:

'Oh, don't you bother to clean up afterwards. What's a dog turd here or there? They only make children blind.'

Dog owners never liked this. Occasionally I thought there might be a fight but there never was. He could talk to people in such a way they almost got to the point of fighting but never quite did. He always felt good after these tangles I thought, while the dog owners always felt bad . . .

I stepped over the brown mess carefully and stopped at the kerb.

'Now,' said my father, 'what next?'

A policemen had recently spent an afternoon with Miss Sherringham's class and I had learnt the drill off by heart.

'"Before you cross,"' I recited, '"stop at the kerb, look right, look left, look right again, and if all is clear, it's safe to cross."'

I went to step out into the road. His hand gripped my left shoulder.

'Where are you going? You haven't looked!'

It was true: I was so pleased I had managed to recite the drill correctly, I had forgotten to do it.

'You're not thinking,' he said, 'you're not concentrating.'

I looked down the hill and saw some Teddy boys on the wall at the bottom. As I turned to look up the hill, I noticed the burnt-out tree, and that one Teddy boy was standing and watching while a second climbed in through the hole a few feet up the side of the trunk. Then I noticed a van parked on the grass. This was so intriguing I forgot my drill.

'What are you staring at now?' my father asked.

I couldn't deny it. 'That van,' I said.

'How are you going to manage in life if you can't even concentrate long enough to cross the road? Go on. Buzz off . . .'

He pushed. I ran across the hot tar, my sandals sticking as I went, and jumped up on to the grass on the far side. The ground was very hard.

'You can go up to the pavilion or down to the pond,' he shouted, 'but you stay in front of the house. Stay in sight.'

I knew the rules. He'd sit at his desk, his binoculars in the brown velvet-lined case beside him. Every now and again he'd scan the common, and if he couldn't find me, I'd get a dressing-down later.

He turned and walked into our house. I felt better now he was gone. I ran down to the van. The back doors were fixed back and a big white wall was stretched across the end.

'Hello.' It was the van driver. 'Here for the feature?'

I didn't understand but I nodded anyway.

'Three o'clock start,' he added, mysteriously, and disappeared through a door at the side of the van.

A woman and two girls, both eating Mivvis, came up. The woman put up a deck-chair facing the white wall and sat down. The girls sat on the grass beside her, also facing the white wall. Why? I wondered.

I went to the door through which the driver had gone.

'*Whistle Down the Wind*, it's a good one,' he said, from inside.

He clicked a switch and a machine started. There was a deafening racket.

I trotted off towards the pavilion; I passed a steady stream of people coming the other way, many carrying deck-chairs, blankets and cushions. One woman even had a Li-lo. As soon as I got to the pavilion I began to climb the steps. If my father saw this and asked me later I'd tell him I'd gone in for a glass of water.

As I got to the top, the pavilion door burst open and a park keeper rushed out. Strapped on over his green uniform was a big brass tank – water sloshing inside – with a hose attached.

The park keeper clumped past in heavy boots and raced away. I turned and saw he was heading towards the burnt-out tree. Smoke poured out of its hollow middle and rose up into the sky. I guessed the Teddy boys I saw earlier must have lit a fire inside. They were always doing that.

I went through the doors. Inside the pavilion there were tables with green baize tops and the long humming refrigerator. There was also a boy and I heard him say to the woman serving, 'Wafer, please.' I had arrived at the perfect moment.

The woman went to the refrigerator. It had heavy rubber sliding doors on the top. She slid one over and lifted out a block of ice cream.

I hurried over and peered down into the refrigerator. A wall of cold rose to meet me. I felt it on my cheekbones. I breathed in.

I stared at the white ice stuck to the refrigerator walls, then at the boxes of choc-ices and Polar Bears, Lovely Jubblies and Toppers lying below. Ice, I had noticed, never stuck to cardboard but only to metal. Why, I had no idea; it was a mystery.

With a knife, the woman cut an oblong of vanilla ice cream from the block, caught the piece between two wafers, and handed it to the boy. He handed her back threepence, which she threw into a Quality Street tin.

Then she turned to me and said, 'Yes?'

I gazed at the box of Mivvis in the corner of the refrigerator. They were lolly on the outside and rich yellow ice cream on the inside. They were on my mind because I had just seen the two girls eating them. I had never had a Mivvi myself.

'Do you want something?' the woman asked.

I looked up. I often came in here to look, so she knew me. Her nose was pointed and the skin around the bottom was red and flaky. Perhaps today she'll give me something for nothing, I thought, if I just stand here and keep quiet.

'You haven't got any money, have you?' she said, eventually.

I had to answer. 'No,' I said.

She put away the ice cream and slid the rubber door shut.

I went back outside. From the top of the steps I saw the park keeper was spraying water into the burnt-out tree through the hole in the trunk.

I trotted back to the van and stood at the rear of the crowd that had formed while I was away.

A bell clanged. A fire engine appeared at the bottom of the hill. Teddy boys jeered from the balustrade wall. The crowd roared back at them.

'Bloody Teddy boys,' said the woman near me. She had lifted her dress and undone her suspenders. They were brown ribbons with a metal end and a white button. Her stockings were folded down to her knees. 'I'd like to give 'em a bloody good hiding,' she continued.

The fire engine bumped up to the burnt-out tree. Firemen in rubber coats and funny hats jumped out. They ran long flat white ropes along the ground. Then the ropes went fat and water came shooting out the ends and poured down into the tree. The column of smoke trembled, then thinned, then disappeared, and gassy clouds of steam rose instead. Then there was no steam but the firemen went on squirting water anyway. Then the water stopped and the hoses went flat again.

A fireman and the park keeper shook hands. The fire engine drove off. The Teddy boys jeered again as it went past and the fire engine rang its bell in reply.

'Excitement over,' shouted the van driver. 'Everybody ready?'

The crowd roared. The woman who had rolled down her stockings said in a friendly voice, 'Do you like flicks?'

I nodded, though I had no idea what she meant.

'Here,' she said, 'have a humbug.'

She held out a long, thin, bright silver tin. Did I dare risk a dressing-down and reach in?

'Go on, they won't bite,' she said.

I turned my back to our house to block my father seeing and peered down. The tin was filled with black and white striped sweets. I reached in with finger and thumb and out came three stuck together. Disaster. To take all three was greedy. But letting them go, I'd end up with nothing.

'It's all right,' said the woman. 'They stick together in the heat. You have them all.'

'Thank you very much,' I said, in my best voice.

I crammed the three humbugs into my mouth.

'What a polite young man you are.'

The sweets were sugary and warm and lovely. As I began to suck them the white wall went dark and numbers appeared, one after the other, from ten down, and as the numbers fell, the crowd shouted, 'Ten, nine, eight . . .'

Suddenly, music burst from the black boxes on the grass and there were pictures on the white screen. I saw a man who was the size of a real man with a sack full of kittens and he was going to drown them. Then there was another man and he was a good man and he was sick in a barn. Then these children brought the sick man food because he was Jesus and one of them was a girl with long hair and she was lovely, I thought. The sick man did not get better and policemen came and took the sick man away and the children who gave him the food were very sad.

Then, as suddenly as it had started, it stopped. There was applause.

I waited to see what would happen next. I felt sad for the man in the barn but I was more interested in the girl with the long hair. When would she come out of the van?

The woman who gave me the humbugs was crying, I noticed. She blew her nose on a handkerchief, then wiped her eyes.

She looked at me and said, 'I do like a good cry but of course you don't. It's only women who like a good cry.'

I thought about the nice girl with the long hair. I wanted to find her. On the other hand, if I stayed here, maybe I'd get another humbug.

The woman fastened her stockings and stood up. She folded her canvas chair. The tin was on the grass beside her handbag. She dropped the tin inside the bag and closed it. The brass fastener made a loud click.

All around me people were folding chairs or blankets and gathering their things. Some of the crowd were already on the path, walking towards the pavilion, or walking down the hill towards the pond.

'It was very nice to meet you,' said the woman.

'Goodbye,' I said.

'What a polite young man you are,' she said. She turned and headed for the pavilion. No more humbugs, I thought.

I waited until all the crowd were gone. The grass where they had sat was flat and dark and littered with orange peel and crisp packets, blue ice-cream wrappers and cigarette boxes.

The park keeper who failed to put out the fire appeared. He began to spear rubbish with a pointed stick and put it in a sack.

I went down to the van. 'Hello,' said the driver, putting his head out the side door. Sets of bicycle wheels were turning behind him.

'Enjoy that?' He puffed on a little hand-rolled cigarette.

'Yes.'

'I said it was a good picture; I didn't tell you wrong, did I?'

I was wondering about the girl with the long hair. What I wanted to know was, why hadn't she appeared? I put my head through the door and stared into the back of the van. This was where she should be.

'Looking for something?' asked the man.

I saw the white wall and nothing else. Nothing. But I had seen them, surely, hadn't I, the bad man who wanted to drown the kittens, the sick man in the barn who was Jesus, and the lovely girl with the long hair. I had seen them but now they weren't here. How could that be?

I withdrew my head and walked right round the van, looking everywhere. The only person I saw was the park keeper as he speared the crinkled wrapper of a cupcake.

I was back at the side door again.

'Where is everybody?' I asked.

'There isn't anybody,' said the man. 'Just me.' His face was lined, his eyes grey.

'Where's the girl?' I asked, finally.

'What girl?'

'She has long hair.'

'You mean from the film? Hayley Mills, the actress.'

He looked at me in a funny way.

'Do you want to see her?'

I nodded.

He screwed up his face in a funny way. 'You can't see her. There isn't anyone here. That was a film, you see, a moving picture. It is real people but they're not here. No one's here. A film is a picture of people but it *isn't* the people.'

I looked from his face to the screen to his face again.

'Really, there's no one here,' he said.

A flicking noise started behind. The man flicked a switch. The wheels on the machine stopped moving. Everything was quiet.

He looked at me. 'You don't know what a film is, do you?'
He got something from the table and put it in my hand.
'That's what a film is,' he said.

It was flat and black and stiff. He came down the steps to
the grass. He took the film back and held it up to the sky.

'Can you see a picture?' he asked.

At first I saw nothing. Then I saw there was something
there in the middle of a black shiny square. It was a picture of
the girl. There was another picture underneath it and another
underneath it again. The girl was there in each box.

'That's film,' he said.

The man went back into the van with his strip of film. I
realised our conversation was over. I looked down the slope
of the common at the burnt-out tree and the pond beyond.
The Teddy boys were gone.

I began to walk home. I thought about the piece of film I
was shown. So there was never really a girl with long hair
standing behind the white wall. I thought she was there but
she wasn't.

I reached the kerb. The sun was sliding towards the roof-
tops of Cannon Hill. I looked across at our house. There, on
the drive, stood Z6 201, the grey Railton. It was covered with
an emerald green tarpaulin that was tied to the wheels with
string. The doors of the garage behind were open and inside
I saw my father's new car, CDF 22, another Railton. This car
was long and black, with four doors rather than two; it was
like a car Winston Churchill or Adolf Hitler might have
ridden about in during the war. It was much bigger than Z6
201.

I looked back at the house. The diamond-shaped panes in
the bay window were in shadow. They were black like the surface of the bottomless bog holes on the bog behind my
grandparents' house in Ireland. I couldn't see if my father was
sitting at his desk or not but I waved anyway. I wanted him to

Ernest Gébler with CDF 22, outside Rockingham House, Boyle, Ireland, 1964

come quickly and bring me across the road to home. I felt disappointed; I was so certain the lovely girl was in the back of the van and it had turned out to be a trick.

In the months after *Whistle Down the Wind*, when I went to bed and I was waiting to go to sleep, I thought about Hayley Mills, as well as Wendy, who was in my class, and another girl

I liked a lot called Mary Phillpot. In my mind's eye all three
merged into one and then I lay on top of this composite and
I wriggled against her and her clothes flew off, one garment
after another, and then suddenly she was naked underneath
me, this mixture of Wendy, Mary Phillpot and Hayley Mills.
But what did I do now? I always wondered, when I got to this
point. I didn't know.

In my mind I would put all the clothes back on Wendy-
Mary-Hayley and then I would imagine the wriggling and all
the clothes flying off all over again. The hours of self-hypnosis
that I practised when I was sick had turned my imagination
into a muscular organ that could keep the images flowing
effortlessly until I fell asleep.

chapter twelve

The curtains in my bedroom hung from metal rollers that ran on a rail. The sound of these rollers careering along the track as the curtains were opened was the sound of morning to me. It was the sound that said, Get up and start the day.

That morning, the clack-clack-clack woke me. I opened my eyes and sat up. There was my mother in a summer dress, the bedroom bay window behind her and the sky, huge and blue, behind the window.

I sat up.

'Today I'm going to lie in the shade with Mary Phillpot,' I announced.

It was the summer of 1962. I was nearly eight.

I ate my lunch in the assembly hall and went outside afterwards. The sky seemed very large and the houses around the school seemed very small.

I set off across the playing fields. The sun-baked ground was hard. It had been hot for days. I was back in shorts.

At the bottom of the playing fields lay a ditch and in the bottom of the ditch was a line of concrete buildings. These were air-raid shelters. Mr Ferguson, our headmaster, told me that during the war, children and teachers hid in these whenever the Germans bombed London.

I could see several children from my class milling around the shelters, including Mary Phillpot. I was pleased because I had come here to find her. Mary wore a dress with yellow squares and white lines. She was small and slim with long hair that framed her face. She looked like a pixie.

I ran up to Mary, put my arms around her and lifted her off the ground. It was easy. Mary was very light. All the boys in the class, so long as there was no teacher around, would get Mary like this and lift her up.

Mary was so light and so easy to lift because there was something wrong with her. Her bones were hollow. Miss Rutherford, my teacher, said we were to be very careful with Mary. We must never push her over or make her cry. I liked Mary so much I would never have done this. In fact, I wanted to kiss her, although I never had.

We all went over to the shelters. Using an old oil drum, the girls got up on the roof of one. The boys lay down on the slope at the side. The girls jumped over us, one after another. This was the game.

I looked up. I saw blue sky. I saw the girls with their skirts moving out. I saw their legs and their knickers. All the girls wore either blue or grey knickers. Some of them were in knickers that were too big and sometimes, as they passed overhead, I saw the smooth place between their legs. This was part of the game as well.

After a while, Wendy took off her knickers. Wendy was bigger than the other girls in the class. All the other girls went and sat on the grass.

Wendy got up on the roof of a shelter and jumped off and

we all looked up her skirt. I saw the smooth place between her legs. That was part of the game as well.

'I've got a penny,' said one of the boys. This was the last part of the game.

The boy with the penny went over to the girls. The boy and the girls huddled together. I could not hear what they said. I lay on the grass with the other boys.

After a while, Wendy left the girls and went into a shelter.

The boy with the penny waved to us. 'Come on,' he shouted.

I got up with the other boys from my class and together we all filed through a doorway. Inside, the shelter smelt of concrete and earth and dog mess. It was quite dark. We moved away from the door so as not to block any light coming from outside. There were no windows.

Wendy took off her dress, her vest and her knickers and stood in her sandals and socks and nothing else in the middle of the floor. The boys gathered round. In the middle of her body, between her legs, there were two smooth round parts separated by a dark line. Inside, the line was red like inside my cheek.

The handbell clanged in the distance; it signalled the end of the lunch break and the start of afternoon school.

I left the air-raid shelter and began to run across the playing fields towards the school buildings in the distance. Children were running from every direction. In the winter, the roll was called inside, but because it was summer it would be called outside today. In a few minutes we would all be standing in lines in the playground waiting for our name to be called. We would be quiet, obedient, and Miss Rutherford would never guess what we had been up to in the shelter.

I was in the playground. It was still the summer but not the day we played at the air-raid shelters.

The bell rang. As usual, all the children formed themselves into lines. I got into my line and Miss Rutherford appeared with the roll.

'Aitken?' she called.

'Yes,' said a quiet little voice.

'Allen?'

'Yes.'

'Armstrong?'

'Yes.'

A child coughed. Then I heard the sound of sick landing on the playground.

I turned and saw Mary standing with her head down near her knees. There was vomit on the floor. There was vomit coming out of her mouth. There was also something thick and yellow coming out of her nose. This was like lemon curd.

'Mary's brains are coming out, Miss,' a boy shouted.

Miss Rutherford ran over. Other teachers followed. The nurse came and took Mary away. Mr Woodall came with his bucket of sand and sawdust, his flat spade, his mop and his bucket of cloudy water.

Miss Rutherford began to call out our names again. The roll call finished and we went inside to our classroom.

I kept noticing Mary's seat was empty all that afternoon.

A few days after Mary's brains came out of her nose, the entire school was summoned to the hall for special assembly

Mr Ferguson stood on the stage. He wore his black cape and his funny hat with a flat bit on top like a bird table. He always wore these on special occasions.

'Now, children,' said Mr Ferguson, 'I have something to tell you. And I'm afraid it's a very sad thing that I have to tell you.'

The hall was where we ate lunch and it smelt of the steak-and-kidney pie we'd had the day before.

'You all know Mary Phillpot, I'm sure,' said Mr Ferguson. 'Well, I'm afraid I have to tell you Mary passed away last night. She's gone very far away now and she'll not be coming back to us or our school. But we will all miss her, I know.'

Mr Ferguson blew his nose. Mr Ferguson wiped his eyes with his handkerchief. Mr Ferguson was crying.

'But we should not be sad,' he continued, quietly. 'She may have gone far away and yet she's close as well; in fact, she's just beside us. Or above us. She's in heaven, up there.' He pointed upwards. 'She can see us. She can see us right now. She is looking down on us, even now, as we remember her. She can hear what I am saying.'

As he talked about Mary and heaven, I looked at the scabs on my knees and the wooden blocks on the floor arranged like the bones of a fish.

'We are now going to say the Lord's Prayer,' said Mr Ferguson.

There was a moment of silence.

'"Our Father, which art in heaven,"' he began.

I lay on the grass near the air-raid shelters. The sky was blue. Mary went to heaven, I thought. When anyone went to heaven they looked down on us so that's where it must be. Up there, in the sky.

So if heaven was in the sky and the sky was blue, then heaven was blue. I was on green grass, with the brick orange air-raid shelters in front of me and the black playground somewhere behind me, but in heaven there was only blue. Nothing else.

So why had nobody ever said anything about this?

It wasn't mentioned in the Lord's Prayer, was it, and I'd have thought it would have been. Something like that; one would have thought, the whole place blue. It would have been mentioned, surely. So why wasn't it?

I turned this over in my mind and then, inevitably, I came to the only conclusion I could come to. No one remarked on the colour of heaven, obviously, because there was no such place. Simple as that. It was just made up.

Of course, behind the sky, there was God; yes, of course there was. He wasn't like heaven. I believed in God. If we didn't have God we wouldn't have the earth or people or anything, would we? There was no heaven but there was a God. He made us.

I continued to stare up at the sky. After a while I saw God. I didn't actually see him. I saw him with my mind's eye and then I imagined that what I saw in my head was floating behind the sky above me. God was an old man with a beard and his eyes were dark and he was grumpy. I imagined he saw that I had seen him, and then I imagined we were looking at one another.

We stared at each other for a long time. This didn't surprise me. When I thought about God this was often what happened. It had happened before, and it would happen again because that was what he did. He just watched. He never said anything, he never did anything. He just looked down from behind the sky at us; he just left us to get on with whatever we wanted to do. We could be good, we could be bad; we could live, we could die; we could be kind, we could be cruel; he didn't much care. In fact, he didn't care at all. He just watched us.

And that was that. That was how it was. And would be, from now to the end of time. There were no rewards or punishments, nothing like that. Just the silent figure in the sky, watching.

chapter thirteen

Our summer holidays had come round again. My parents went on a coach holiday to Switzerland. We went to Ireland to my grandparents' house. We came home. We went back to school. My new teacher was Miss Driscoll. I was no longer in the infant section. I had gone up to the junior section. It began to grow cold. The leaves on the trees changed colour. I was beginning to grasp that each year as it followed the next had the same rhythm. There was always a summer and then there was always a winter and then there was always another summer. And so on.

It was afternoon, sometime in the early autumn, 1962. We were on Cannon Hill Common, having our daily walk, my mother, my father, my brother, myself. It was misty and cold.

We walked towards the pavilion. Leaves littered the path; they were brown, flat and shiny with wet. The leaves on the frieze at school were shiny too but that was from the varnish the teacher put on them.

We left the path and began to cross wet ground. We went under some trees. Twigs and acorns were everywhere.

We came to a ditch. It was deep, shaped like a V, with water lying in the bottom. A railway sleeper lay across the ditch. It was a thick, heavy piece of wood and black with grease.

'Go across,' said my father.

I stepped on to the sleeper. To stop it rocking, the two ends were sunk in the earth and I crossed over easily. My brother followed.

Now my father told my mother to cross. She said she couldn't. He said she should. She said she couldn't. She was afraid of heights. She said she would fall off into the ditch. My father said she must go across. She absolutely must. He said she would never get over her fear of heights unless she went across. My mother sat down on the ground. I felt my chest hurt.

'I must not be sick,' I said to myself, 'I must be better.'

The boy I sat beside in Miss Driscoll's class was Martin Rowley. He lived in a council flat with his mother and his brother Lee. His father was in prison for bottling a man in a pub fight in Tooting Bec.

Martin's clothes smelt of tobacco and boiled meat. There was always blue dirt under his fingernails. He would dig the worms of filth out with a sharpened pencil and drop them into his inkwell, or flick them at children, shouting, 'Bombs away.'

One day, Martin whispered, 'Want to see something?'

Miss Driscoll was at the stock cupboard, with her back to us, counting jotters. She wore a dress with bows on the shoulders.

I nodded.

Martin lifted the desk flap to reveal a small cardboard box. Written along the top of the lid was 'The Battle of the River Plate' and, along the bottom, 'HMS *Ajax*'. In between was a painting of a battleship with all guns blazing. It was a plastic kit made by Eagle. I trembled with desire.

At break time, Martin hid the kit under his jersey and we went to the metal fence at the back of the playground. Children didn't come here much and so the teachers didn't either. Martin got the box out.

'Can I hold it?' I asked.

Martin gave it to me. My stomach fluttered. This was happiness, mingled with desire.

'Can I open it?'

He nodded.

I floated the lid up. Inside, I found the grey plastic parts that glued together to make the ship; they smelt of pear-drop sweets. There were also a short history of the Battle of the River Plate, including the part played by HMS *Ajax* in the attack on the *Admiral Graf Spee*, and the instructions; 'Black for the Main Gun Barrel Tips', I read. The detail was thrilling.

'Can I borrow it?' I asked.

'No,' said Martin.

'Just for the night.'

He took it back .

'It's Lee's. He doesn't know I took it. He finds it gone tonight, he'll do me.'

Lee was older than Martin.

I pleaded all break time but Martin's answer was always no. Then the bell rang and we went back in. As he sat down, Martin lifted his desk flap and put away the kit in one sly deft movement. Unfortunately, Miss Driscoll happened to turn at the same moment.

'Martin Rowley, what are you doing?' she shouted.

'He's got a toy, Miss,' a child behind called out.

Miss Driscoll hurried over. 'Open your desk.'

Martin put his arms on the desk and then his head on his arms.

'Right,' said Miss Driscoll. She grabbed Martin's ear and lifted him to his feet. Martin squealed with pain.

'In future, when I say for you to do something, you do it,' said Miss Driscoll. She lifted the flap with her free hand and took out the kit. 'What's this?'

Martin said nothing.

'It's a toy. Are we allowed toys in school?' She twisted Martin's ear but still he said nothing.

'Class?'

'No, Miss Driscoll,' the class chorused back. I did not join them.

'That's right, we're not allowed toys, are we. This is going in the stock cupboard; you can have it back at the end of term.'

She carried the box to the cupboard and locked the doors.

Martin was still standing. 'Sit down, Martin,' she called.

He sat. I heard him sniff but he did not cry.

When I got home that afternoon, I went to my father.

'Can I have a piece of wood?' I asked.

'What for?'

'To make a boat.'

'A battleship, I suppose.'

His mind-reading powers were uncanny. I said nothing.

He gave me a length of wood out of which I carved a crude hull. Then I stuck on bobbins for funnels and matchboxes for deck buildings and gun turrets. For the gun barrels, I used old matches.

Despite his aversion to war toys, my father was impressed. Perhaps this was because I had actually made the vessel myself. He sprayed the whole ship grey for me without comment. Only when he finished did I remember the instructions in Martin Rowley's box: 'Black for the Main Gun Barrel Tips'.

'Can I have the gun ends black?'

'Never happy with what you've got, are you? Always got

the hand out, haven't you? Paint them yourself if you're so desperate.'

He put my ship in the vice and painted a red line round the hull.

'Do you know what that is?' he asked.

'No.'

'Pay attention. You might learn something. That's called the Plimsoll line.'

He explained that in the olden days, ship owners were selfish and greedy. They always put too many people and too much cargo aboard their vessels. This made them so heavy the ships often sank.

Then an Englishman called Samuel Plimsoll said all ships had to have a line on them. If the water went above this, the ship was overloaded and it couldn't go to sea. Ship owners didn't like it but that's capitalists for you. The Plimsoll line saved many lives.

We filled the kitchen sink with water and launched the *Ajax*. She turned upside down immediately. My eyes filled with tears. My father made a noise; first I thought he was cross, then I thought he was laughing at me. I wanted to throw my HMS *Ajax* in the bin.

My father took the boat away and screwed a piece of metal to the hull. Then he came back and put her in the water; she floated perfectly.

He went away again. When a ship was too light it turned over; it had to be made heavier to float properly. Why was everything so complicated?

The next morning, when I met Martin Rowley in the playground, he had two black eyes and a split lip.

'What happened?' I asked.

'Lee's a fucking maniac,' was all he would say.

I stood on the chair at the sink and launched HMS *Ajax* into the choppy waters of the South Atlantic. In the ocean there were mines, submarines, ice-bergs, and of course the *Admiral Graf Spee*.

'Bang. Kepow. Pouff.' The Battle of the River Plate was raging. Suddenly, loud talking in the dining room interrupted the six-inch naval guns. I went and peered through the hatch.

Next door I saw my father at one end of our mahogany dining table and my mother at the other. He was furious. My mother was silent. She was looking at the table. I thought she was going to cry. Suddenly, my father saw my face at the hatch.

His face went dark. He got up quickly and came running over.

'Mind your own business.' He slammed shut the hatch door.

I went back to the sink and began to move HMS *Ajax* round in a circle. I tried to think about mines and submarines but I could only think about my father shouting and my mother looking at the table. I knew something was coming and I knew I would not like it. I had a feeling it would be the most horrible thing that ever happened. The tubes in my chest, I noticed, were sore, as if they already knew what I had just realised.

Later that evening I found the front door standing open. The porch light was on. I knew then that the worst thing had happened.

I ran down our path and out on to the pavement. I saw the vague outline of an oak tree. I saw light spilling from the house next door and light falling from the first streetlamp. I saw the pavement stretching away. In the distance there was only darkness. I saw no sign of anyone.

I listened hard. I heard plates rattling on a table and the laugh of a child. A train rumbled on the far side of the common. The noise was a clackety-clack that repeated and repeated, gradually fading until there was silence. I listened for another noise in the darkness, the particular scrape of her heel on paving stone, that noise that my mother made when she walked. This noise was so precise and my ears were so acute I could identify her step when I was in the house and she was halfway up the hill. But tonight I heard nothing.

I turned and went back up the path. As I stepped inside I met my father.

'What are you doing? Stop mooning. Come in and close the door.'

I closed the front door.

'She's a selfish child, your mother. I'm going to take you to New Zealand or Cornwall. You're never going to see her again. I'm going to have things the way I want them from now on.'

With his foot my father swiped away the statue of the thinking man that he used as a doorstop, went into his study and banged his door shut behind.

chapter fourteen

The following morning I got up and went to school as usual. At about ten o'clock a child came to the classroom door.

'Mr Ferguson wants Karl Gébler,' the child said, wriggling with excitement.

'Karl Gébler, headmaster wants you,' said Miss Driscoll, nicely.

I went along the corridor, the concrete floor speckled with bits of silvery mica. Why was I wanted? I wondered. I passed the sick room, with its examination table covered with coarse paper, its weighing scales and wooden contraption for measuring the height of children, the cloakroom, with its rows of hooks, huge white sinks and little drawstring bags for holding plimsolls, and several classroom doors glossy with paint, behind which I could hear teachers talking.

I arrived at Mr Ferguson's. His door was closed. There was a bench standing against the wall nearby. I always hated the spot because I had often passed children, usually boys, sitting here with unhappy faces, waiting to go in. This morning the bench was empty. A good sign, I thought.

I knocked and waited for the reply; it came and I went in. The room was square with windows overlooking the playing fields. There was a painting of Queen Elizabeth in a big coat with a cross on the front; there was also the cupboard. When Mr Ferguson had me in once for a ticking off, the cupboard's doors were open and I had glimpsed his dreaded slipper, a dark fraying plimsoll with no laces, lying on a shelf inside. This morning the doors were closed.

Mr Ferguson sat behind his desk and my mother sat opposite. I was surprised. I was not expecting this. Mr Ferguson spoke to me, not in his usual gruff way but in a different, cheerful voice. Then he smiled. I felt something wonderful was about to happen.

My brother appeared. My mother thanked Mr Ferguson. Suddenly I realised we were going off with her. Something wonderful really was happening.

Immediately outside the front doors of the school, in a part of the playground where cars weren't normally allowed, we found a taxi waiting. My mother opened the door of the cab and told us to get in.

We drove to Charing Cross station and caught a train to Kent. Here we stayed in the house of John Osborne and Penelope Gilliatt. I remember nothing of the house except long corridors and dark rooms.

The next event in the sequence that I can recall, I was in another taxi with my mother and my brother. The cab drove slowly up Cannon Hill Lane and through the window I saw the common. The leaves on the oak trees were brown and russet and tawny. The pavilion was closed up.

I listened as my mother explained that we were going home, my brother and I, but it was only for a while. We would live with our father until she found somewhere, then we would live with her. She was quite emphatic. She and our father had met somewhere, she said, a day or two earlier, and they had agreed this.

The taxi stopped. We all got out. My father appeared at the front door. I went up the path. I did not feel unhappy. There was Z6 201 under its familiar emerald green tarpaulin. There was the bay window with the diamond-shaped panes. There was the woodbine creeper tumbling down.

I stepped past my father and went in. The hall smelt of lanolin, Lapsang Souchong tea and the sulphur that he sprayed on the grapes.

I began to climb the stairs. I wanted my HMS *Ajax*. It was on the table beside my bed, near the saucer where the ammonia went in winter. I heard a noise. It sounded like the front door closing. I turned. My father had closed the front door and slipped on the chain.

My father opened the door as far as the chain would allow and shouted out through the gap at my mother on the porch step outside, 'You have legally deserted your children.' He shouted other things too that I didn't understand.

Then he closed the door and drew the bolt across the top.

A few weeks later I was on a bus trundling along Putney High Street. I reached up and pulled the red cord that ran under the ceiling. The bell rang in the driver's cab. He pulled the bus in to the last stop before Putney Bridge. I jumped down on to the pavement and my mother followed me. My mother had collected me after school and we had come out to Putney together. My brother was back at home with my father. He was ill so I had her to myself. I didn't know quite how but I knew my mother and father had come to some sort of arrangement, because now my brother and I were able to see her from time to time. This was usually in the daytime. I knew she was living in flats she borrowed from friends and that's why we were in Putney; she had the loan of a flat out here.

We walked along the pavement towards a large window with condensation on the inside. Someone had written in the wet with their finger 'Hello' and 'Come in'.

On the plastic fascia above was written 'Wimpy'. I had long wished to visit one of these places and now my wish was about to come true.

My mother pushed open the door and I stepped into a long room. All the tables had red plastic tomatoes on them. We went to the rear and sat at the table nearest the counter where the cooking was done.

The waitress took my order; Wimpy with onion, French fries and a strawberry milkshake. My mother had nothing. The cook was a black man. I watched him throw meat and onions on to the hot metal cooking plate, which was covered with a fine sheen of grease.

The food arrived. I devoured it. When I finished, the waitress came back, hands buried in the pockets of her overall. She had a pen in one pocket and she clicked it continuously.

'Something else?'

I glanced greedily at the hotplate. Did I want another? my mother asked.

'Oh yes,' I said without hesitation.

'Chips? Milkshake?' the waitress asked.

My mother nodded.

The waitress clumped away with my plate and empty glass, shouting ahead to the cook, 'Same again,' as she went. A little later she returned with my second milkshake. While I took my first mouthful and my mother thought I wouldn't notice, she quickly opened her purse and glanced down into it.

I knew at once she was looking to see if she had enough money to pay. Suddenly, I wished I could undo what I'd set in motion. But I couldn't. I could see a handful of pale onion pieces and a moist, raw red hamburger were already sizzling on the hotplate.

Later, we went to the flat where my mother was staying. It was at the top of a big house that overlooked the Thames. As it got dark, I stood at the window at the back and watched one Thames tug after another sail past, long lines of steel barges filled with coal trailing behind them.

The next morning my father collected me in CDF 22. On the drive home we did not exchange a single word. If I said anything nice about my mother he would be angry and I wasn't going to please him by saying something horrible.

chapter fifteen

Carlo Gébler and Sasha in their boy
scouts cub uniform, Cannon Hill Lane,
October 1964

I wore a navy round-necked shirt with half-length sleeves, a green neckerchief fastened with a leather toggle, and a splendid green hat decorated with yellow piping and a red badge. I was in my Cub Scouts uniform.

'Now, boys,' said Mr Lorimar, our Cub Scouts master. He had a beard and different coloured eyes, one brown, one blue.

'"Ging gang gully gully,"' he continued. He shoved a piece of card in the air. The words of the song were written out in Biro.

'"Ging gang gully gully gully gully wish wash . . ."' Mr Lorimar pointed at each word as he spoke it. 'All right? Let's do it . . .'

Later, walking home through the smog, I sang the song over and over again. At the same time I took care to avoid stepping on the cracks between the paving stones. This was one of several self-imposed laws that I made myself obey. If I failed to observe these rules I knew I would be overwhelmed by something awful, although precisely what, I had no idea.

I reached the bottom of Cannon Hill and began to climb towards our house. I didn't sing now. Getting closer to home, I knew it was important to rein myself in, to dampen down my spirits.

Reaching the gate, I saw our porch light was on. The smog nearest to the bulb was lit up by it and it looked like candy-floss. The curtains behind the bay window were closed tight. I assumed my father was inside at his desk, typing on his Remington. When I got back from Cub Scouts he was usually at work and he would send me to bed; I would fall asleep to the sound of his typewriter keys banging away below.

I went up to our front door and pushed it open. It was always left like this on Cub night. My father loathed the bell and having to answer the door; both disturbed the rhythm of his writing, he said. Several children at school had front-door keys and sometimes I wondered if I shouldn't tell my father this. He might think to give *me* a key, which I would have liked. But in the end I never had told him because, when I thought about it seriously, I realised he wouldn't trust me with a key.

I stepped into the hall and carefully wiped my feet on the mat. I didn't want to be accused of tramping in dirt which he would then have to clean up. I closed the door quietly and released the snib. There was something different about our hall, I realised, and for a moment I couldn't work out what it was. Then I got it: instead of the clatter of the typewriter coming from the study, I could hear the sound of the television in the dining room. But the television was never on at this time, I thought, never, ever. Oh, but it was now; I could hear it.

I crept down to the dining-room door and peered in. I saw my father sitting in the middle of the room in his customary sitting position; he was on a hard chair, his back perfectly straight and his feet flat on the linoleum floor. This was also how he sat when he read or typed. He was very careful with his posture because of poker back, or anchylosis spondylitis, which I knew was its proper, medical name.

My father had explained it to me many times. This was a disease to which we Géblers were particularly susceptible. It was carried in the female gene but only men suffered from it. This detail struck him as particularly poignant and significant.

The way he explained it was like this: over time, and for no reason anyone understood, tiny little fingers of calcium formed on the spinal vertebrae; after years and years, the fingers would finally knit together and the vertebrae would then form a single long bone.

There was no way to stop the fingers forming, but by sitting straight, at least he'd be locked upright if his back locked, and not bent double, like most other anchylosis spondylitis sufferers.

I too might well develop the condition, he had warned me, but he didn't think I'd fare as well as him. Given my slack deportment, he said, there was a serious danger that if I did develop poker back, mine would be the horizontal variety. The question was, did I have the gumption to avoid it? He'd

given me the information; now it was up to me to act on it. I
did try to keep my back straight when I was sitting. The trouble was, after a few minutes I always forgot about sitting
straight and slumped.

I glanced past my father at the television in the corner. It
was a square set with curved corners and big buttons. On the
television I saw the man I knew to be John F. Kennedy, the
President of the United States; Kennedy was talking into a
microphone.

'What are you skulking out there for?' my father said suddenly.

'I heard the television.'

'So?'

'I came in to see what was on.'

'Hoping for cartoons, or cowboys and Indians, or that sort
of drivel, were you?'

'No, I wasn't,' I lied. He was right. Whenever I heard the
sound of our television I always crept down in the hope of
glimpsing one of the programmes we were forbidden to
watch, like *The Flintstones*, *The 6.05 Special*, or *Rawhide*. At
school, the children talked about these programmes incessantly. I longed to join these communal discussions but first
I had to see the actual programmes.

'Do you know what's going on in the world?' he said.

'No.' He was going to chat to me perhaps. I felt cheerful,
suddenly.

'Well, if you paid attention, you might.'

'I am paying attention,' I said.

'Oh, are you. All right, tell me what's going on then? Go on.
You say you've been paying attention. You tell me what's going
on.'

Such a simple trick and I'd fallen for it. My face reddened.
He was still staring at the set, which relieved me. He wouldn't
see my red face.

'You haven't a clue, have you?'

'No.'

'Your ignorance doesn't surprise me. You evince no interest whatsoever in the world around you. Too wrapped up in yourself of course, and we know where that comes from. But I hate ignorance. It's a curse. It's been the ruin of working people for generations. Since forever. Since feudal times. Since cavemen times. Since the beginning of history.

'Well, I won't have you ignorant. For your information, we are about to blow ourselves to kingdom come.'

He paused to allow the information to sink in.

'You know what the atom bomb is, don't you?'

'Yes.'

'I thought you would, given your warped obsession with war and all things to do with war.

'The atom bomb, and the much more powerful hydrogen bomb that we use nowadays, both have the capacity to destroy the world and all of mankind, at a stroke, just like that.'

He clicked his fingers but he went on watching. He hadn't taken his eyes off the set once since I appeared. This wasn't unusual; when he watched the gogglebox, as he called it, he did so with complete attention. What was unusual was that he was talking at the same time. Normally, when he watched, there was absolute silence until the programme ended.

'Do you understand?'

'Yes.'

I knew the bomb made a big white cloud in the air shaped like a mushroom. I knew we dropped two on the Japs. Mr Woodall at school had told me. And jolly good thing too, Mr Woodall thought. The Nips got what they deserved, he said, and Reg, who was the father of our nice babysitter, Vera, he said the same, except Reg didn't say Nips. He called them fucking slanty-eyed cunts.

'In our world,' my father said, 'the rich, strong, powerful countries are the ones with the nuclear bombs, while the poor, weak, underdeveloped countries have no bomb. Typical but that's the way things are done in our world. Are you following?'

'Yes.'

'Cuba is near America. You know where that is?'

'I know where America is.'

How could I not? Hadn't I looked at the map often enough? America was where the early son lived, he who would one day replace me.

'Are you listening? I didn't ask about America. I asked, did you know where Cuba is?'

'Oh.'

'I wish you'd learn to listen. It'd be such an advantage to you.' He sighed. 'Cuba is in the Caribbean, south of the United States. Do you know where I mean?'

'Yes.'

'The Americans say Cuba's in their "sphere of influence". What they mean by that is *they* have the right to bully Cuba and no one else does.'

Suddenly, I could sense Marx and the Soviet Union were looming.

'Yes,' I said, to show I was following.

'The Americans ran Cuba for years. Bled it dry.'

'Yes,' I said again. Now I was beginning to understand; this place Cuba and the place on television were one and the same.

'This is how it happened. Try to concentrate,' he said. 'In 1959, the Cubans have a revolution. They kick out the Americans and for the first time, ever, there's a proper Cuban government running Cuba. Yes?'

'Yes.'

'What did I say?'

'A proper Cuban government.'

'The Americans don't like this. Oh no. Cuba's their "sphere of influence". Remember. They want to invade. They do invade, at the Bay of Pigs, it's botched. Having been invaded, and knowing it'll happen again, the Cubans say to the Russians, Comrades, give us weapons! Give us bombs!

'All right, say the Russians, we'll give you weapons but we'll do it secretly. But then the Americans take pictures of Cuba from the air with their spy planes.' He pointed at the television. 'That's a picture taken by an American spy plane. Those are Russian rockets in Cuba that you can see.'

I nodded although I couldn't see anything. Just a set of off-white splodges on a fuzzy grey background. This was frustrating. Why were there no sleek rockets rising gracefully towards the sky, brilliant flames flowing out behind as they powered upwards?

'The Americans, of course, are furious. They don't want the Cubans to have weapons because then they won't be able to bully the Cubans any more. So they've said that unless the Russians stop sending weapons to Cuba, and withdraw the weapons already there, there's going to be a nuclear war. And that's as far as the story has got.'

Now he turned and looked at me. 'And where are we who did not make this problem?' he asked. 'I'll tell you. We're right in the middle between Russia and America. So when it happens, we die first. We may not wake up tomorrow morning. We may all be dead. Think about it and weep: the human race is about to destroy itself.'

He studied me carefully.

'Do you understand what I'm saying?'

'Come on, get up.' Rosemary shook me the following morning, then whooshed the curtain open. Rosemary was the au pair. Rosemary was Irish. She was looking after us all the time now my mother was no longer with us.

As I swam slowly upwards from sleep to wakefulness, I remembered the conversation of the night before. Was I dead?

I opened my eyes. I saw my green candlewick bedspread and the little fluffy white bits like candlewicks that stuck up from it; I saw my bedroom doorway, and the landing beyond.

Perhaps I was dead only I didn't know it yet? No, no, I couldn't be. Hadn't Rosemary just shaken me?

No, she was dead too. What? How did that work? Perhaps, when you died, I reasoned, you went somewhere that looked exactly the same as when you lived. The one difference was that it went on for ever?

I got out of bed and went to the bay window. I looked down at the verandah roof and through the glass I saw the outline of the red vine beneath. I looked at our flowerbeds, bare grey-black earth held in crumbling yellow concrete pens. I looked at the garden fence, brown and damp with creosote. It could be a copy but it didn't feel like one. This felt like the world I woke up to every morning. So in all likelihood, I wasn't dead. In which case, did that mean no bomb had fallen? Well, not here, I reasoned, but perhaps in America it had? And if America was hit, then that might mean the end of the early son.

The television was back on that evening. It was on again the day after and the day after that. Suddenly, we went from being a house where the television was almost never on (except for approved, improving programmes) to being a house where the television was almost always on.

Finally, there came a Sunday when I knew the crisis was coming to a head. My father was in the dining room watching the news. I did not try to watch the television from the doorway of the dining room as I had done in the preceding week.

I stood in the kitchen instead and listened at the hatch. Judging by what I could hear, there was no talk, sadly, of Soviet bombs falling on America.

The news finished and my father came into the kitchen.

'What are you doing?' he asked me.

'Nothing.'

I was sitting on one of the high chairs dangling a tomato-red plastic fob watch. It had come into the house as part of a cowboy sheriff dressing-up set along with a Colt .45 pistol, a belt with a holster and bullet loops, and a silver badge stamped US Marshal. (Where this set came from, I don't know. It did happen that, from time to time, we were given toy guns by adults who didn't know my father's views, so I presume it came by that route.) The holster was in the box of dressing-up things under my brother's bed but the gun and the badge had disappeared. I believe my father threw them away. The fob, however, he liked, because it was educational. He kept it and he had taught me to read the time with it.

'Mooning is what you're doing,' he said. 'Can't you read? Or draw like your brother? Can't you use your time profitably, instead of standing around doing nothing?'

'Is Cuba all right?'

'Trying to get in my good books, are we?'

What I really wanted to know was whether America was bombed. I said nothing.

'Yes, Cuba is all right,' he said. He lit the gas and put on the kettle. The Russians, he explained, had decided not to bring any more missiles to Cuba. It was just on the news. The Cuban missile crisis was over.

The kettle boiled. He trickled hot water into the teapot to warm it. The Russians, he continued, were going to take home the weapons they had put in Cuba. There'd be no war now. He tipped the teapot over the sink. The water that came out was brown from the tannin inside.

He levered the top off the caddy, spooned dusty black leaves into the teapot and poured on hot water. The kitchen was filled with the lovely smell of tea. So America was not destroyed, I realised, and therefore the early son remained alive. Damn.

chapter sixteen

My mother went off to New York. Her books were to be published in the United States. I made no connection between her destination and the early son. It was only in connection to my father and myself and the early son that America meant anything to me.

She got back a few days before Christmas and came out to Cannon Hill Lane with toys for us from America.

My present was a helicopter. We all went out to the common to test-fly it. The ground was scattered with pearls of wet.

I set the helicopter on the stem in the middle of the launching pad, then pulled at the string that worked the gearing mechanism underneath. I felt a rush of pleasure as the blades whizzed and the helicopter rose into the air. Then there was more joy, as the helicopter moved forward, before dropping slowly back to the earth and landing perfectly.

I felt my father's stare. His eyes pressed on me, hot and watchful. I skipped away across the wet grass, retrieved my new treasure, and dropped it on to the pin in the middle of the launcher. I pulled the ripcord; the blades churned again.

The red bubble rose towards the lid of grey cloud above us. I felt another rush of pleasure as intense as the first and, at the same time, I felt my father's eyes again.

When we got back home, I put the helicopter and the pad back in the box it came in and closed the lid. When I next opened it, I would pretend I had just got the helicopter, and it was my intention to keep the box so perfect I could relive that marvellous moment when I received my gift over and over again.

I went to sleep that night with the helicopter on the table beside me. When I woke the next morning, the first thing I did was check it was still there. It was.

Later that day, as I came down the stairs, my father called from his study, 'Where's the helicopter?'

'In my bedroom,' I called back.

I had left it there. That was the safest place, I thought.

'Bring it down here to me, would you.'

I didn't want to do this but I didn't want to say no to him either. I went upstairs and fetched the box from my table and brought it down.

'Right,' he said, 'give it over.' He was sitting at his desk.

I handed him the box. He looked at the lid. Here there was a picture of a real helicopter, its blades turning, seen from above. The ground below was covered with jungle.

My father stared at the picture for a long time. Perhaps, I thought, he wanted the box in order to study the picture, and when he was finished he'd hand it back to me. Then, to my surprise, he got up, went over to the glass-fronted bookcase and dropped the box behind the high pelmet that ran along the top.

'It'll keep it safe up there,' he said. 'When you want to play with it, you just come and ask me.'

He sat down at his desk again.

I left the room.

*

Very early in January 1963, I sat with my brother in the back
of CDF 22. We drove along one empty foggy Wimbledon
street after another. Finally, in a road I had never visited
before, my father stopped. He pulled on the handbrake carefully and the spring clicked. We got out. He locked the car.

A moment later we were in a flat. It was very cold. The
windows were fogged up and there was a little pool of water
on each windowsill, fed by threads of water streaming down
from above. The yellow streetlamps outside were obscured by
the heavy condensation. When I breathed out, I saw my
breath. The flat was my mother's. She had just taken it. She
was there, wringing her hands. My parents were talking. The
plan had been for my brother and me to spend the night there
together; however, my father now mooted that I shouldn't
stay. I was wheezing, he said. It was true.

How do I get to stay? I thought. I know.

I started taking little shallow sips of air. I hoped that by
doing this I would reduce or even eliminate the dreadful
sickly drone that I could hear coming from inside my ribcage.

This ploy was hopeless, as I knew it would be. A few sips
and I was oxygen-starved. Unable to stop myself, I now
gasped and greedily tried to swallow the air I needed to make
up for what I had failed to take in. The drone became a roar.
My father heard. A decision was made. I was sick. Very sick.
I would go, with him, home. My brother was well. He could
stay. I was bitterly disappointed.

We left, went back down to the street and got into CDF 22.
What a desolate morgue, he observed, from the front seat;
cheap paint slapped over dirty walls; floors all filthy. The furniture my mother bought was gimcrack rubbish, he added.
And to top everything, he said, my mother, having paid a
non-returnable deposit of seventy pounds for this dump, was
going to have to find another place to live if she was to have
any hope of having us.

His monologue was an unsettling mixture of delight and fury. I knew he hated her and therefore he hated whatever she did. He also delighted in her failure. My feelings were the very opposite of his. Cold, yes, a bit grubby, yes, but there was nowhere I more wanted to be than the desolate morgue we had just left. I said nothing. He saw I was saying nothing. He fired the ignition and pulled away.

On the drive back to Cannon Hill Lane he drove unusually slowly. I looked out the window. The smog had thickened up while we were inside the flat. On the outgoing journey, I had seen trees, cars and houses, but now, on the return, I saw only the spectral outline of trees, cars and houses, and all the detail which was there previously was now gone.

As we drove I could feel the air going in and out of my chest. The further we drew away from where I wanted to be, the more the tubes narrowed, I fancied. This made it harder for the air to pass up and down and before very long I was making a noise like wind in a flue. It was the body in protest against what was happening.

And, if that wasn't bad enough, at the back of my throat I could also feel a sharp, piercing sensation, exactly like the feeling I got if I had lemon juice without any sugar in it. The raw feeling in the throat was a sure sign I was about to cry. Of course I knew I couldn't, I mustn't. It would provoke a dressing-down like none I had ever known before.

I dug the nail of my right thumb into the palm of my left hand. I pressed and pressed until it hurt and I kept pressing until we got home. I did not cry.

chapter seventeen

In the afternoon, as the winter dark was coming on, Rosemary was in the bathroom, bent over the bath, rinsing her hair. She was going out later.

While Rosemary filled one jug after another with hot and then cold water, and then tipped the jug over her head, my father also began to get ready. He laid old newspaper on the workbench under the verandah, carried out his best chestnut-coloured corduroy trousers, and laid them down. He pegged the trousers, top and bottom, to the bench with bulldog clips; then he carefully began to clean them with a rag soaked in white spirit. It was a white rag and as he ran it up and down, a glaze of black filth magically appeared on it, while the corduroys lightened in colour. Later, he polished his brown shoes. He sang quietly as he worked.

He was happy because he was going to see Henrietta. I had never met this woman but since my mother left Henrietta had often rung the house and I had answered the phone to her once or twice. She had a high-pitched English voice. My father called her his friend but I thought he really meant she was his girlfriend. I knew that Henrietta's husband had deserted her (deserted was the word my father used), and that she lived in the country. I also knew that Henrietta had a child, a girl of my age called Sophia. Once or twice my father had mentioned that this girl was far nicer and better-behaved and more intelligent than I was. He also said this made him wish, more than ever, that he'd had a daughter.

Evening came. I sat in the dining room with a book. Rosemary had left already. She had gone to a dance at an Irish club in Kilburn. My father was in his study. He couldn't go until Vera came.

Vera babysat us when Rosemary couldn't. Vera even used to come when our mother lived at home and my parents went out together. On one of those times something happened which I had not forgotten . . .

Vera had asked me to show her round our house. We went upstairs. I opened my parents' bedroom door, turned on the light and went in; Vera followed me. My parents' double bed was old with a round headboard. It had been Adolf and Margaret Gébler's bed before. My father slept on the right of the bed and, over the years, the action of his head, rubbing against the headboard when he was sitting and reading in bed, had rubbed away the varnish and made a black patch.

'Oh,' said Vera, stepping forward into the room.

For a second I thought it was the patch she was talking about, but then, when she said 'Saucy,' I realised it was the painting that hung on the wall above she was referring to.

The painting was of a naked woman on a couch, with her back facing outwards. She was leaning on her elbow and her hair was pinned up. There was a boy with wings holding a mirror and reflected here was the woman's face. She was sad but beautiful. The painting was called the *Rokeby Venus*.

Whenever I looked at this painting I got a fluttering in my

stomach, and now, looking at it with Vera, I felt the feeling even more strongly.

Vera tested the mattress with her fingers and went 'Oh' again. Then she lay down on the bed. Her dress rode up slightly. I saw her suspender clips, black and lacy.

'Come here,' she said.

I said nothing.

'Come on, I won't hurt, I'll cuddle you.'

I remained frozen to the spot.

'Suit yourself.'

She got up and smoothed down the front of her dress. Then she ruffled the top of my head. I took her next door and showed her the Meccano set I kept under my bed.

After that, when I thought of Wendy and Hayley (I didn't think of Mary any more because she was dead) I thought of Vera as well . . .

This evening I was so excited that Vera was coming that although I had *The Mystery of the Spiteful Letters* by Enid Blyton open on the table in front of me, I couldn't take in the words of my favourite writer.

I heard the front doorbell ring. That was Vera. Fantastic, I thought. I heard my father walk from his study to the hall. I heard the sound of the front door as he opened it. I waited to hear Vera saying 'Where's them boys?' but instead I heard a low male voice saying I couldn't tell what. Oh no.

I went and peered into the hall. I saw my father in his best tweed jacket and a green knitted tie, and I saw a man in silhouette. He was wiping his feet on the mat. The man did this carefully; he was clearly trying to impress my father. This man was not Vera but Reg, her father.

Reg stepped in, bringing the mist and cold of a winter's night into the house with him. He was an enormous man with a pot belly and a big square beard like a prophet in the Bible might have had; his hair was long as well; it was grey too and he wore it swept straight back. Reg stopped directly under the hall light; he had Brylcreem in his hair and it shone so brightly from the light that streamed from the bulb above that it suddenly didn't look like hair; it looked like he had a woman's bathing cap pulled tight over his head.

I knew Reg. He would often deliver or collect Vera in his Austin van. I had also met him in the street and out on the common. In the war, Reg was a POW in Japan. He had often told me the Japs were cruel. He told me how the Japs punished a hungry British soldier who stole rice by skinning his arm with a bayonet. 'The skin came off like a banana skin,' Reg explained, while he acted out the peeling for me. The soldier's arm, he explained, went black in the tropical heat of the jungle and then the man died. 'It was a horrible way to go,' said Reg, 'but there was always worse.' Then he told me how the Japs put a glass tube up a man's penis and broke it with a hammer and the man couldn't pee and that was a more horrible way to die.

'Vera can't come,' said Reg to my father. 'She's got to go out somewhere. Don't ask me where. She's sent me instead.'

Reg noticed me in the doorway of the dining room.

'I hope I'll do.'

He turned to my father again.

'I think I know the ropes. What time do you want 'em in bed?'

''Let's see,' my father said. 'What time do they go to bed.'

He furrowed his brow as he opened the clothes press and at the same time he whistled.

'Bedtime. Make it eight o'clock, or thereabouts,' he said, finally. 'They can read in bed for half an hour.'

My father put on his scarf, tied it and fluffed it up.

'And make them wash their teeth, will you, for God's sake, before they go to bed. Made them do it properly, too.'

He pulled on his coat and opened the front door. I saw the

sleek outline of CDF 22 parked and waiting at the kerb just beyond our gate.

'Bye,' he said.

My father went out and closed the door behind. A few moments later I heard my father start the engine and drive off down the hill. Reg unbuttoned his coat and took it off.

Now he had taken off his coat, I saw Reg was wearing a jacket-cum-cardigan with waistcoat pockets and a rounded collar a bit like a priest's dog collar. It had piping around the cuffs and big buttons down the front. It was like something Acker Bilk might have worn (and the fact that Reg, despite his bulk, bore a slight resemblance to Bilk made the comparison all the more credible). I had a good idea what Bilk wore and what he looked like because my father had several of his records, including Bilk's hit 'Stranger on the Shore'. My father often played this record on his Ferguson Radiogram and after he had played it he would usually say to me, 'My old man was a clarinetist too. Good as this one.' 'Stranger on the Shore' seemed to cheer up my father but it had quite the opposite effect on me. When I heard the slow melody played on the clarinet, I thought only of my mother. It made me yearn for her. I hated 'Stranger on the Shore'.

Reg hung his coat in the clothes press. I went back to the dining room and my Enid Blyton book. Reg followed me in a few seconds later.

'I wonder what's on the box?' he said.

I didn't have an answer to his question. How would I know?

Reg turned the Bakelite knob at the bottom of the set. There was a crackling noise inside the television as it started to come on. There was no picture yet; the set had to heat up. What a novelty, I thought. Our television was never turned on just like that.

In our house, other than during the Cuban crisis, television was always planned. Each week my father went through the *Radio Times* ringing suitable programmes in red Biro. The television was only turned on at the time that a selected programme began, and after it was over, the television went straight off again. The television was never allowed to stay on on the off-chance the next programme might be interesting. We were also forbidden to turn on the television and simply watch it willy-nilly. Mindless goggling was the quickest route to brain rot, my father said. He watched the news, *Panorama*, and what he called good cultural programmes like *Armchair Theatre*. We were allowed to watch Marx Brothers comedies, Charlie Chaplin films, and dramas from the Soviet Union. All drivel was prohibited; drivel included advertisements and anything that involved cowboys and Indians, or soldiers, or war, or spies, or any American cartoon. Drivel, of course, was everything I longed for.

With a whoosh the picture came on; it was black and white. Reg sat down at the dining table and took out a packet of cigarettes.

'Get us an ashtray, would you?' he said in a friendly way.

My father loathed smoking; he hated the stale smell that lingered in rooms where cigarettes had been smoked; but this was as nothing compared to the big problem which was – as he repeatedly told us – that tobacco caused cancer. Of course, the tobacco companies denied it (well, they would, wouldn't they, that was consumer capitalism for you), but the scientists knew better, he said. Their findings were reported in the *New Scientist* (to which he subscribed along with *Time*). He often read out articles on cancer to us at mealtimes. He also told anecdotes which he supposed would reinforce his message, one especially:

When he was fourteen, Adolf gave him the end of a cigar. My father went out into the lane at the back of the house in Wolverhampton, sat on a wall where passing toughs would see him, and set about smoking this stub.

After a few puffs he felt nauseous. Then he vomited. He threw the cigar away and fled back into the house, ashamed in case anyone had seen him. He found Adolf waiting, a smirk on his face. 'Enjoy that?' Adolf asked. That was when my father understood that Adolf had intended what happened. He'd wanted my father to be sick, so that my father would never smoke like he did.

'Clever man, Adolf,' my father would say when he told me this story. 'Of course, I took the odd cigarette at parties, when I was a young man, but I was never serious. Your grandfather had made certain of that.'

Vera smoked when she came to babysit but, knowing my father disapproved, she always smoked at the kitchen door and puffed her smoke out under the verandah. After Vera left my father always sniffed the air in the kitchen. I was sure he guessed what she did but he never said anything about it. Now, with Reg, I found myself hoping it would be the same, although if the French doors stayed closed, and it didn't seem they were going to be opened, I couldn't see how the smoke would get out.

I got a saucer from the kitchen and came back. Reg had lit up and the room already smelt. There was also the oily smell of his Brylcreem. There was a fire in the grate and I told myself his cigarette smoke would go up the chimney with the coal smoke. My father would never know; at least I hoped he wouldn't.

Reg smoked away and watched the television. I didn't go back to my place at the table; taking my book with me, I went and stood in the doorway and watched from behind Reg, while keeping my head cocked towards the front door in case my father suddenly came back. It was possible he might have forgotten something. If I heard him, my plan was to scuttle into the kitchen and pretend I was reading. Finding me reading while the television was on, I might even get into his good books.

*

'Right,' said Reg, 'come here.' I trotted forward into the dining room. There were now half a dozen butts in his saucer. He got up and carried the saucer to the fire and threw them on the embers. 'Bedtime,' he said. 'Go upstairs. Put on your pyjamas, brush your teeth, get into bed.'

I went upstairs. Reg found my brother and sent him up too. I put on my pyjamas. They were made of thick flannelette. The bottoms were held up with a white cord which I tied in a tight bow. I washed my teeth in the bathroom as my father had shown me (according to his system, one's teeth were divided into twelve sections, and each required twenty careful downward strokes that took in the gums as well as the teeth) and then I rinsed my mouth. I peed in our toilet which smelt of Harpic. I got into my bed.

'Are you in bed?' Reg shouted from the hall below.

'Yes,' I shouted down.

'And your brother?'

'Yes,' my brother shouted back.

Downstairs I heard Reg go back to the dining room. Our bedroom door was open. My bed was in front of the door. As I lay there, I looked out on to the landing and the stairwell. I saw the shadows of our banister rails on the far wall, thick and black like bars. I heard the television downstairs. This was unknown to me. When my father had the television on and it was after our bedtime, he closed the dining-room door and turned down the volume. This was so we wouldn't be kept awake, he said, but really it was so we wouldn't be corrupted. It was exciting to lie in bed now, with the sound downstairs . . .

'Come down,' Reg shouted. This was later. I put on my dressing gown and my slippers and I went downstairs.

'Come in here.'

I went into the dining room. Reg had pulled out the armchair from the corner and put it in front of the television. Reg was sitting in the armchair. I saw Reg had taken off his jacket-cum-cardigan and hung it over the back of one of the dining chairs. He was wearing a white shirt underneath. The sleeves of the shirt were rolled up.

'Stand there,' said Reg.

He pointed at a spot on the black and white linoleum tiled floor just to the right of his chair and close to the armrest.

This was odd but I saw no reason to refuse. I went and stood where he said. There were blue and black smudged tattoos on the bare forearm lying on the armrest beside me. I saw an anchor, a mermaid and various words, including Ethel, his wife's name, and Vera, his daughter's name. There was a son called Mitch, as well, but there was no sign of Mitch's name on his father's arm. Reg, Vera told me once, did not get on with Mitch. His son had been caught fighting in a pub in Balham and was now in Borstal. Suddenly, my eye slipped sideways to Reg's torso. I noticed that the belt that held up Reg's trousers was undone and so was the button that fastened the top of his trousers. I decided to pretend I hadn't seen this.

Reg was watching the television so I began to watch as well. The programme was about snakes. A man with a nice voice was talking into a microphone and there were pictures of snakes wriggling through water, rushing across sand, and creeping along branches. In one sequence, a small snake was shown attacking a bird in its nest; the snake opened its jaw wide and swallowed the bird whole. A huge bump appeared in the snake's throat. That was the bird and the bump moved because the bird inside the snake was still alive, thrashing and flapping. It was frightening and yet I couldn't take my eyes away because it was also fascinating.

I noticed Reg was fiddling. I thought he was lighting a cigarette. I glanced down and saw that no, he wasn't lighting a cigarette; he was doing something else; he was working his trousers and his underpants away from his waist to his hips and then down his thighs. I saw the skin below his belly button was very white and fatty with black hairs all over it. Then I saw the top of the hairy bush that grew between Reg's legs. The hairs were black but there were grey hairs mixed in with them.

I felt Reg undo the front of my dressing gown and then I felt him pull at the drawstring of my pyjama bottoms. I felt my pyjama bottoms fall to my ankles.

Reg pulled out his penis and pointed it up at the ceiling. It was long and thin. He began to rub it with his left hand. It went hard but it stayed thin. I felt him take my penis with his right hand and begin to jiggle it about. I felt the same feeling as I got when I thought about Hayley Mills.

On the television there were more snakes and Reg was watching. I watched as well. At the same time I wanted to run upstairs but my legs felt weak. I was trembling around the knees. I wondered if my legs would carry me to my bedroom? I doubted it. I was also frightened Reg would get angry if I ran. I thought he would tell my father some lie and get me into trouble. When I had these thoughts they weren't in the head of the me on the floor. They were in the me that was up above, floating just under the ceiling and looking down on what was happening in the dining room below.

And this me above events saw the whole scene, saw Reg sprawled on the chair, legs out, trousers and underpants around his ankles, his hand around his long red pointing penis, and myself, my pyjama bottoms around my ankles, and my smaller penis sticking out from between the edges of my dressing gown and Reg with finger and thumb ringed around the slender, half-stiff end . . .

Next thing, I felt myself being shaken and I heard my father saying, 'Come on, wake up.'

I opened my eyes. I was under my brother's iron bed, with

my brother asleep beside me. All I could make out was the
bedframe overhead and my father peering in at us.

My father pulled us both out from under the bed, and
brushed the dust off our knees and elbows. He put my
brother in his bed. He put me in my bed. I went back to
sleep . . .

A day or two later I was in the hall. I heard my father's
voice. He was in the dining room, on the telephone.

'When I got back, I found the front door wide open,' I
heard my father saying. 'I thought the house had been
robbed.'

I realised he must be talking about the night Reg was our
babysitter and what happened when he had come back. I
assumed Henrietta was on the other end because he was talking in his nice voice, whereas when he spoke to almost
everyone else on the telephone, he was brusque and abrupt.
He didn't like the telephone. It wasted time, he said; it
allowed people to blather away uselessly; and that, in turn,
was a waste of money. But worst of all it allowed people to
ambush you and get you to agree to do what you wouldn't
normally agree to do.

Myself, I liked the telephone enormously, especially at
moments like this. When my father was on the phone, I could
eavesdrop; I could glean tidbits of information and he would
never know.

I crept closer to hear better.

'I came into the house, very puzzled,' he continued. 'I found
the television was on. It was late, the programmes were long
over, and there was just that girl doing noughts and crosses or
whatever – the test card. No sign of the babysitter but he'd left
an ashtray full of butts. Fire almost out. House cold.'

My throat tickled.

'I went upstairs,' my father continued. 'No sign of the boys.
They weren't in their beds. I didn't know what to think! Were

they kidnapped? Had the bloody man taken them home with him? Had Edna snatched them? Then I heard something – the older one, wheezing. The sound came from under the younger boy's bed. I got down on my hands and knees, I lifted up the counterpane, and would you believe it? There they were, asleep on the filthy, dusty floor, under the bed.'

I gently cleared my throat in order not to cough.

'Hang on,' my father said.

The Bakelite handset went down on top of the sideboard and suddenly he appeared in the dining-room doorway.

'What are you doing?' he asked.

'Nothing.'

'Do you know it's wrong to listen to people on the phone?'

I said nothing.

'Go on. Buzz off.'

He went back into the dining room and closed the door behind him. I heard him talking on the other side of the wood but I couldn't make sense of what he said.

chapter eighteen

Rosemary's brother lived in Mitcham. He worked in a factory that made fork-lift trucks. One Sunday, when she went to visit her brother, Rosemary brought me with her. Her brother's flat smelt of sour milk and disinfectant. There was a party going on and it was crowded with people, every one of them Irish. The men were all drinking Guinness out of black bottles with cream labels, and the women were drinking Babycham out of wide glasses. A strange woman I had never met tickled me behind my knees and asked, 'Do you like butter?' Then she gave me a florin and said, 'You can buy yourself some sweets with that, can't you?'

In the corner of the lounge was a dressing table with a huge television sitting on it, and in front of the television there was a sofa. It was bottle green with high, hard armrests at either end.

The television was on (the end of a football match was showing) although no one was actually watching the set. I slunk over and sat heavily, affecting a sigh as I did. If anyone asked me what I was doing watching television without permission, my plan was to get to my feet slowly and say that I wasn't watching television, I was resting myself.

A man came and sat down on one side of me and the woman who had given me the two shillings sat on the other side of me. I felt her arm sliding around my back. Her warm breath smelt of Babycham. The football match ended.

'You'll enjoy what's coming next,' said the man. 'It's good.'

He levered the top off a bottle of Guinness. A little stub of brown tawny froth came out of the bottle mouth. He lifted it off with his finger and put the finger in his mouth.

'After the advertisements,' he said, 'it's *The Man Who Knew Too Much*.' He explained this was a film by someone called Alfred Hitchcock and that anything, absolutely anything made by him was a cracker.

The grown-ups now began to talk across me about another film. This one was called *Vertigo*. It had greatly impressed them. It was the best film this Hitchcock ever made, said the woman, and Kim Novak was the most beautiful woman in the world. I gathered this film was the story of a man who was frightened of heights. This man loved a woman, who was Kim Novak, but he couldn't save her falling to her death from the top of a tall tower because his fear made him sick.

Vertigo sounded wonderfully interesting, I thought. This film that was about to start on the television was not *Vertigo*, sadly, but the grown-ups said it was almost as interesting.

There were so many things out in the world, I thought. I wondered if I would ever have the chance to get to know them all?

I settled back on the sofa to watch. The credits came up. The grown-ups called out the names James Stewart and Doris Day as they appeared. Then the film began. In the story, Doris Day's son is kidnapped. Doris Day doesn't say much but inside, I knew, she was crying and shouting. My legs began to shake and it wasn't long before my feelings for my mother, who I missed desperately, and the story in the film, all got mixed up together. Next thing, I knew I was going to be sick. I ran to the sink in the kitchen. My vomit shot out and landed on top of several empty Babycham bottles and two heavy cut-glass ashtrays full of butts and bottle tops. I began to cry. I was ashamed and I was annoyed. Here I was in a house with a television; I was free to watch it; indeed, I was being encouraged to watch it by the two adults on the sofa, and what had I gone and done? I'd gone and been sick, hadn't I, that's what I'd gone and done.

The woman who gave me the money fetched Rosemary.

I heard the two women come into the kitchen behind me.

'I think I should take him home,' said Rosemary. 'He's probably over-excited.'

A few minutes later we put on our coats and left to catch the bus back to Morden.

chapter nineteen

On that Friday evening, when I got in from school with my brother, I found father in the kitchen, sitting at the breakfast counter. The anthracite stove in the corner was grumbling away and little puffs of smoke were forcing their way out of the slit in the chimney stack.

He looked at me as I came in. He said nothing. He wasn't cross, he was neutral, but if I made a mistake, I knew he could get cross.

'Hello,' I said.

He picked up the glass bottle with the long stem that held his olive oil and upended it over the thick, burnt, much-scraped piece of toast on the plate in front of him. A yellow thread of oil began to stream down from the eye of the dropper jammed in the neck of the bottle. As soon as the oil hit the toast he began to move the bottle and now, as if he were drawing in olive oil, he made a clockwise spiral on the surface of the toast. He always made a clockwise spiral when he put his oil on his burnt toast.

'Running off to Putney, are we?'

This was a reference to the small, yellow-brick house in Deodar Road that my mother had recently bought. Since she had bought it, our routine had changed. Now, in the week, we stayed in Cannon Hill Lane with my father and went to our school and played on the common in the evenings if they were dry, but at the weekends we went to her. Sometimes we went over on Friday evening, sometimes on Saturday morning. It varied. I knew that today, which was Friday, we were due to go to Putney that evening.

'Yes,' I said, watching the spiral growing smaller and smaller.

'I see,' he said, mysteriously.

The spiral was finished. He put down the greasy oil bottle. He pulled the egg cup of salt towards himself, took a pinch between finger and thumb, and sprinkled it on to his toast. For an instant I saw the white salt grains lying on the oil, then they vanished as they dissolved.

'Can't keep away, can you? Can't stop yourself, can you? Oh it's Liberty Hall at Deodar Road, isn't it, and you can't get enough of it, can you? You're so pathetic.' Another pinch of salt went on. 'A few baubles, a few sweets and unlimited drivel on television, and you're anyone's, aren't you? You've absolutely no gumption, have you? None! None whatsoever.'

He cut the toast in half, picked up the smaller half, bit, chewed, pondered.

'You know of course what's she's doing, your mother?'

There was a pause.

'Oh, come on, don't act stupid with me. What do you take me for? It's called corruption, you idiot. Don't you see that? She's trying to turn you into her creature. She's trying to turn you against me. It's obvious that's what she's doing and you'd have to be a fool not to see it.'

Another pause.

'Of course you don't see it, do you? You can't. You're

blinded, aren't you? Hypnotised. All you want to do is fill your belly with chocolate and get your hands on as many cheap plastic toys from Hong Kong made by slave labourers as you can. Am I right?'

There was a pause. 'Well, say something, can't you,' he said, finally. 'Show some sign, for God's sake, that you're alive or I'll have to call the doctor.'

Silence would get me into worse trouble than speaking. 'Yes,' I said.

'Anyway, I'm damned if I'm bringing you to Putney tonight. You can get there on your own steam. I'm not chauffeuring you around any more like Little Lord Fauntleroy.'

After tea my brother and I walked down the hill and crossed Martin Way to the bus stop. After a while a double-decker bus arrived. We hopped on. The bus took us up to Morden. We got off at the Underground station and went to a different stop. It began to get dark and the streetlights came on.

The Putney bus now came nosing out of the gloom with all its lights on inside.

It stopped and we got on and went straight upstairs. The upper deck was completely empty. Good. The first bus had, unfortunately, been full of passengers, which had stopped us. Now we were free – hooray.

I heard the conductor ring the bell downstairs to tell the driver to go. The bus began to crawl along Morden Road, heading north.

I squinted at the round mirror above the stairs. No sign of the conductor yet but we had to be quick. We whipped off the back seat under the emergency exit. In the well underneath there were masses of scrunched-up tickets shoved in there by bored passengers.

I squinted at the mirror again. Still no sign of the conductor. I put my hand through the tickets and felt around. The tickets rustled and scattered and suddenly I felt what I was searching for. I pushed the tickets aside and there it was, lying right in the corner, a two and six. We'd struck gold today; this was a colossal sum.

I had another squint at the mirror. I could see the conductor at the bottom of the stairs. In a moment he would grab the handrail and begin to pull himself up towards us on the upper deck, his metal ticket machine bouncing against his front. If he caught us, he could say it was his money, or that he knew who had lost it and that he wanted to return it to its rightful owner. He could try to make us hand it over. That's what happened with another conductor once when we found a ten-shilling note. We wouldn't hand it over so he told us to get off his bus. He rang the bell three times – the signal for an emergency stop. The driver pulled over – we were somewhere in the middle of Wimbledon Common and it was dark. The driver hurried round to see what the matter was. The driver and the conductor argued with each other. In the end we were allowed to stay and to keep the ten shillings but we had to sit on the long seat downstairs. This was so the conductor could keep an eye on us. It was horrible. Since then we'd been particularly careful to avoid getting caught.

We dropped the seat back in its place and threw ourselves down. An instant later, or so it seemed to me, the conductor appeared at the top of the stairs.

'Hello, boys, what's it to be?'

'Putney High Street, two halves.'

He whizzed the handle and the tongue of white ticket with blue writing all over it came out of his machine.

I paid with the two and sixpenny piece although I had the right money in my pocket.

I took the tickets and the change and the conductor went away. I turned and looked out the window. We were in South Wimbledon, and we passed one street after another of small houses made of yellow brick.

In a while we would get to the common; on one side we would see big houses behind their walls and gates, and on the other the dark empty heathland, and we would glimpse dark trees and the spectral eerie windmill. At the Green Man public house, the houses would start again and we would go down a hill, towards Putney, passing more rows of little streets of little houses, then the railway station, then Putney High Street with its shops, all shut for the night, some shuttered. Coming up to the bridge we'd ring the bell. 'Star and Garter,' the conductor would shout. We would get off and go to the sweet shop in the little parade near the greengrocer's on Wandsworth Bridge Road; here we could buy Flying Saucers, Barratt's Sherbet Fountains, Cup-Tie Chews, Fairy Milk Drops, gobstoppers, Black Jacks, candy shrimps, aniseed balls, Razzle Dazzle chewing-gum balls (grey gum surrounded with a crust of candy), liquorice pipes with red speckles on the end for embers, and liquorice laces coiled around a small red sweet, round and hard like a ball bearing, and known as David's Sling; then we would go round the corner to the little yellow brick terrace house with stucco round the windows and a flower tub outside the front door, where our mother was waiting for us, and we would settle in front of the television on which she let us watch virtually whatever we wanted, and we would chomp our way through our booty. We had two days of this freedom before we went back to Cannon Hill Lane.

chapter twenty

'Come on, you,' my father said to me.

He led me out into the garden. I saw beds of black earth, some bare rose bushes and my mother's old writing hut. This was now my playroom where I acted out scenes from Enid Blyton's 'Famous Five' and 'Secret Seven' series.

'If the world was ever destroyed,' my father said, 'and only you were left alive (God help us!), you couldn't survive, could you?'

I said nothing, uncertain where this was leading.

'Well, it's no big secret; you couldn't feed yourself, could you?'

I nodded.

'So you'd have to agree, having just admitted what you've admitted, it's time you learnt?'

I nodded again, still uncertain.

'Right, that is going to be your plot.'

He pointed to a small square of earth near the back fence.

'You'll dig it, seed it and weed it; that way you'll provide some vegetables for us to eat and learn something useful in the process.'

He fetched a spade from the garage and led me to my plot. He showed me how to turn the earth. He went off and I began to dig the patch. The earth was heavy. I took out all the weeds and stones and threw them in the wheelbarrow. The work made me wheeze.

When the plot was a smooth grey-black square of turned-up earth, my father returned with seed packets; they were old and yellow and the corners were torn. He tipped and I saw seeds in his palm, small speckles, like ground pepper grains. How could something so small grow into anything big? My father put the seeds in the earth carefully and then fetched the battered watering can and watered them.

The next day, when I went out to look at my plot to see if anything had grown overnight, I found a large toad squatting in the middle. The toad's back was gold and lumpy. Its eyes were shiny and black like the liquorice Pontefract-cakes we got every week to keep our bowels regular.

I went back to the house and found my father in his study.

'There's a thing on my plot.'

'What kind of a thing? Unless you learn to speak clearly and properly, you won't ever get anywhere in life. Hasn't that sunk in yet?'

'It's a frog,' I said, and then I corrected myself, 'no, it's . . . it's not a frog, but it's like a frog.'

'You're completely hopeless, you know that.' He stared at me with his dark brown eyes. 'Words are how we describe the world. If you haven't got the words, then you haven't got the world, have you?'

He got up, sighing. I followed him back to the garden. The toad was where I left it.

'That's a toad,' he said.

He crouched down.

'Hello, Toad. What are you doing? You're a long way from home. Come to eat all our slugs?'

He talked to the toad like this for several minutes. Then he got up and went back inside.

I remembered then that I wanted his help to move the toad off my plot in case it ate the seeds. But I couldn't go in and ask him now, could I? He'd make fun of me.

I filled the watering can and put the spout on the end. I tipped the can and drops of water began to rain down on the toad's head and back. The creature blinked but did not move.

'What the hell do you think you're doing?' my father shouted. He had seen me from the kitchen.

He came out and walked up to me quickly.

'I wanted to get the toad off,' I explained.

'By watering it. Don't be such a bloody imbecile. Pick it up.'

I trembled. Surely not with my bare hands? 'I can't touch it,' I said.

'Not by hand. You've got a brain, for God's sake use it.'

He fetched the spade, slipped it under the toad and lifted.

'See.' The toad was on the spade looking at him. 'That wasn't so bad. Nothing ever is if you use your brain.'

Suddenly, the toad launched itself sideways and landed in the flowerbed beside the fence. I let out a little shriek.

'It won't hurt, you know. They don't bite. It hasn't got any teeth. It's slugs and flies that must beware him.'

When I weeded and watered my plot over the following weeks, the toad was always there, in the flowerbed, watching. Sometimes I saw his gold back moving between the flower stalks and shrubs, sometimes I only heard him moving around. Then one day he vanished. I went on tending my plot. Finally, the day came that there was something red and bulging in the earth immediately underneath the green shoots that had shot up. I ran inside.

'They've come,' I shouted, 'my vegetables . . .'

A few minutes later my father strolled out into the garden, rubbing lanolin into his hands. Reaching my plot, he crouched down and stared.

'Oh dear,' he said finally, 'only your radishes have taken. Nothing else. I don't know, I suppose I shouldn't be surprised.'

The days grew warmer and longer. One day my father announced, 'We're spending too much money. We have to economise.' I stopped taking school dinners and started coming home every lunchtime. I always found the same sandwich waiting for me on the breakfast counter; radishes (mine) on white shop bread spread with Anchor salted butter.

After eating the sandwich I would set off for school again. As I walked down the hill I would burp. My burp would taste of radish. Then I would feel sick.

There was a big oak tree halfway down our hill and I would go behind it. I would support myself with my hands against its trunk and I would sick up my lunch. It was easy, effortless, like shrugging. My vomit was mostly white – that was the bread and radish – with little flecks of red radish skin in it.

chapter twenty-one

We got back to Cannon Hill, after school, and marched up the path. I pushed the door, expecting it to be on the latch. To my surprise, the door was locked; this was untypical.

Perhaps our father had gone away? I thought. It was not an unpleasant thought. And if he had gone away, I knew exactly what I'd do, even though neither my brother nor I had any money. We'd just walk back to Putney, following the route the buses took.

However, just to be on the safe side, I rang the bell anyway. I heard the peal inside, then silence, then my father's footfalls.

The door opened back, and there he was, suddenly, in front of us. I noticed, at once, the black stubble on his face. This was not unusual. He often didn't shave. Then I noticed his red eyes. Something was up.

There was no sarcastic greeting. Nothing. He stepped aside. We stepped inside. He went straight into his study and closed the door. I went down to the kitchen. Rosemary was at the sink carefully washing lettuce under the tap.

'Hello,' I said.

She said nothing, just went on waggling a green leaf in the stream of flowing water. I assumed my father had imposed what he called a silence period. These were times when no one was allowed to speak. We had silence periods in the car, frequently, but it was not unknown to have them in the house as well.

I heard something coming from the study, a faint, mysterious noise. I went back to the hall and stood near the study door. Again, I heard this noise coming from the other side of the wood. What was it? I took me a while to realise. It was my father crying. Perhaps he was sorry about Mother, I thought, and then I rejected the idea. Of course not, I thought. So what was this about? I had no idea. I went out into the garden to await developments.

'Boys,' he called later. 'Supper.' It was evening now. Rosemary had gone out somewhere. We filed into the dining room and I sat in my place on one of the hard chairs and my brother sat opposite in his. My father sat with his back to the piano that he never played because he didn't know how. His eyes were worse than when I came in from school. The rims were raw red and the whites were bloodshot. On the table there were hard-boiled eggs and a tossed green salad and slices of thick brown bread spread with runny butter.

'Your grandfather died,' he said and blew his nose. A telegram had arrived the previous day, he explained, which was Sunday, from Marianne, my step-grandmother, in San Francisco; it said Adolf died Saturday. I was in Putney at my mother's.

So that's why he was crying, I thought. He was gone, dead, the man called Adolf, the one who advised me in Dublin years before, in his funny foreign voice, to always use linen towels.

I knocked my egg on the plate, cracking it open. Then I

pulled away both the shell and the hard white elastic membrane beneath that fitted the egg like a sock. When everything was off I looked at the flesh of the egg; it was white but there was blue in it as well.

'Tell me about Grandfather?' my brother said.

My father began to talk. Adolf was great man, he said. He was a gifted musician and a charismatic teacher who worked tirelessly all his life to bring culture to working people. Throughout the time he was in the Radio Éireann orchestra playing first clarinet, he was also working for the Irish Transport and General Workers Union, nurturing and rehearsing the union's brass and reed band; his work bore fruit; in 1949, he led the band to victory at the All-Ireland Feis Ceol.

However, Adolf never received the credit that was his due, neither from Radio Éireann, nor the union, nor his adopted country, Ireland. His life was a struggle, artistically and financially, and he was undermined, at every turn, by a succession of appalling women.

Only in his last years, with Marianne, did Adolf know any happiness, by which time, it was too late: Adolf was old and dying by then. And now Adolf was dead. He would never come back. Never. And my father would never know his like again. Never. It didn't bear thinking about, my father said. It was a tragedy.

I was bewildered. I'd already heard the set-piece stories about Adolf; how the clever Bohemian came to Ireland, got snared by the usherette, got interned in the First World War, played piano in silent cinemas in the English Midlands in the 1920s, and returned to Ireland, in triumph, as the newly appointed first clarinet with the Radio Éireann orchestra.

I had also overheard my father complain – just once or twice – about Adolf's drinking and about Adolf's refusal to teach him a musical instrument. It annoyed my father that Adolf happily taught his girls, Ada, Olive and Irene, but not him, and him the eldest, the first-born son, and surely, as such, deserving of a musical education.

However, set pieces and these modest criticisms aside, my father did not discuss his father. Until now that is, when suddenly here he was talking about Adolf non-stop, and in a way that was quite out of character.

When my father talked about other people he usually talked about their faults or their mistakes. There was almost nobody in the world who didn't have something wrong with them. The exceptions were George Bernard Shaw, Vladimir Ilyich Lenin and now, apparently, Adolf Gébler.

How had I failed to grasp this until now? Unless of course, I thought, nibbling my egg, my father didn't mean what he was saying. He was just making it up because Adolf had died. I had noticed adults did do that.

It was a thought I wished I hadn't had.

I separated the radishes from the lettuce on my plate. I would not eat them.

When a father died, I heard my father say, it was terrible for the son left behind. Did we understand this?

Oh yes, I said.

He hoped we did. He hoped we did.

I could sense the real feeling behind his words. No, I was wrong. He did mean everything he said. He wasn't making this up.

When I lay in bed later, I thought about my father and these feelings he was showing that I had never seen before. This, in turn, made me wonder what I would feel if he died. I didn't take me long to realise I wouldn't feel a great deal. In fact, the truth was, I would be glad. If he died, then my brother and I would have to go and live with my mother, full time, and I wanted that very much.

This thought left me very uneasy. What if he found this out?

He would say I really was my mother's creature and, as he had always known, I really did have her degenerate genes.

He would say I was a father-hater.

He would say I was mentally defective because I already knew I would feel nothing in advance of his death.

I would have to be careful, I thought, that he never guessed the thoughts that I had and yet, even as I thought this, I also knew that he knew everything that went on in my head. Of course he knew I didn't like him. And what was more, he knew, I knew, he didn't like me. The truth was out. There was no point trying to pretend otherwise.

chapter twenty-two

When I came from the verandah, I saw Rosemary in the armchair in the corner of the kitchen. She had her arms on the anthracite stove beside her, and her face pressed into them. The stove was cold because my father had decided, as another economy measure, that this summer we wouldn't light it. The stove produced our hot water, so when we washed now it was always with cold water.

I stood and looked at Rosemary; suddenly, her body quivered and I realised she was crying. Perhaps my father had asked her to go, I thought, as he'd hinted he would. But I knew better than to ask outright. Where grown-ups were concerned, patience was the only course.

After a bit Rosemary realised I was on the kitchen step.

'Let's go for a walk,' Rosemary said.

We went out on to the common and walked up to the pavilion.

'Do you want something?' she asked.

This was a first. Usually she never offered sweets or ice creams or lollies because my father forbade them. Yes, she was probably leaving, I thought.

Of course, I said.

We went into the dark, dusty interior. She bought me a choc-ice.

'Let's go behind the pavilion,' she said.

I agreed. If my father happened to look through his binoculars now, he'd see me with a choc-ice, and I didn't want that.

We went and sat on a bench with names, dates and obscenities carved into the slats. I began to nibble at the hard chocolate casing. This was a delicate operation. I didn't want the coat shattering and tumbling away.

'I'll miss you,' Rosemary said, and she squeezed my hand. 'I'll come back and see you, I promise.'

Now I knew for sure; yes, she was leaving.

I smiled. I knew she meant what she said; I also knew it would never happen. Adults were always making promises which they meant when they said them but which they always forgot about later.

At the end of the summer term, 1963, Miss Driscoll gave everyone in her class a Scooby-Doo set as a farewell present. Inside the package there were different coloured lengths of plastic piping from which a nimble-fingered child could plait such things as keyrings, purses and bookmarks. Scooby-Doo was for girls. I was disappointed.

'Instead of drifting off, try to concentrate!'

My father sat on the tall chair at the breakfast counter. I stood beside him.

'If you don't stop mooning and start paying attention, you'll be sunk. The world's fed up with dreamers.'

He tapped my forehead sharply with two fingers.

'The world only wants those who can see and think clearly.'

I nodded to show I understood.

'With no Rosemary here any more to wait on you hand and foot, you're going to have to start pulling your weight.'

'Yes,' I said.

'And as it's school holidays, we're going to have a new morning routine.'

He took the fob watch from the wireless, the one he'd used to teach me the time.

'You're nine, aren't you?'

Almost. I would be nine in August, a few weeks away. I would have my birthday in my grandparents' house in County Clare. Meantime, my brother and I were with him. My mother was away. A camping holiday in Wales before we went to Ireland, with my father and my brother and my best friend Aidan Varma, was also in the offing.

He turned the knob and whizzed the hands around the face of the fob.

'Before I go to bed I'll set this.' The arms stopped. 'What time is it?'

'Eleven.'

'So, you wake, you dress, come down, you see this, and then, when it's eleven, this is what you do . . .' He explained what to make him for breakfast and that I was to wake him when it was ready. When he had finished he said, 'Let's see if you've got it. What have I asked you to do?'

'Make tea and toast.'

'What tea?'

'Lapsang Souchong.'

'How do I want my toast?' he asked.

'Burnt.'

'And?'

My mind was a blank.

'God help me, does anything ever sink in? Scraped! You brown it and scrape it three times. Then you put on the olive oil.'

'And a pinch of salt,' I added.

'And a pinch of salt. Very good. Then you come and wake me and I come down. I don't think you're capable of bringing up a tray yet.'

There was a silence.

'And there's to be no going out in the mornings when I'm not up. Understand? You are not to leave this house. It's a dangerous world outside; the roads are full of criminal drivers. I'm not having you exposed to any risks. Got that?'

I nodded.

'So what did I say?'

'Sash and I are to stay in.'

'When?'

'When you're sleeping.'

'What else?'

'No noise.'

'That's right. And no television,' he added.

I saw the television through the hatch. Since I wouldn't touch it, let alone turn it on, without permission, I hardly needed reminding now.

'In the mornings,' I volunteered, 'we can read or do woodwork.'

He nodded. I was about to slip away but he stopped me.

'Do you know why I sleep late? Because I work at night. And why is that? Because I can't work in the day. And why is that? Because you and your brother are inconsiderate clots.

'Have you any idea of the noise you two make and the disruption you cause? No, of course you haven't. You've been spoilt by your mother. Well, all that's over. God help me, but if it's the last thing I do I'm going to knock her nonsense out of you. There'll be no more Liberty Hall here. It's time you and your brother knuckled down. I'm fed up to the back teeth with the way you have the hand out all the time and take everything for granted. Be clear. Growing up starts now.'

chapter twenty-three

I woke early. It was the morning of the day when we were to leave for our long-promised camping holiday in Wales. I was excited (Aidan was definitely coming) and I wanted to be off, even though I also knew I would probably not enjoy myself all that much.

Since my parents' separation nine months earlier, my father's antagonism towards me had grown more pronounced. I dimly realised this was because he was angry with my mother and what he perceived as my siding with her. Then, when Adolf died, I saw how glad I would be if my father died too, because then I would have to live with my mother and that was what I wanted. However, there was one final complication: my wish that he love me had also grown more and more acute since the separation. I longed for his love, and I longed to have with him what I thought other boys had with their fathers. I didn't know anything about this from direct experience. We didn't socialise. I never saw other fathers and sons. My idea of fathers and sons came entirely from novels, especially those of my favourite author, Enid Blyton.

In her books, fathers always were absent. Important business so often seemed to take them away, freeing up their children to have wonderful adventures. Yet these Blyton fathers were also forceful, affectionate and totally committed to their children and, at the end of every book, they always rode in to rescue their children at the eleventh hour. Something like that, I thought, would suit us; there'd be distance, yes, but huge warmth at the core and no more sarcasm or hard words.

In my mind, this holiday that we were about to have and my secret yearnings had meshed. I'd got it into my head that once we were in Wales he would start to like me and my company and we would enjoy warm relations exactly like in an Enid Blyton story.

At the same time, I also knew I would never get what I wanted. Yet knowing this didn't diminish my desires in the slightest. My realistic assessment and my hopes lived side by side in my thoughts, neither compromising nor undermining the other.

I got up, washed and dressed. Then I went down the stairs, taking care to avoid the boards that creaked, and crept to the kitchen. The light that came in through the back door was stained green by the leaves of the vine outside.

I sat on a high stool. On the breakfast counter were two bowls of Bemax (one for my brother, one for myself), which my father had left out before going to bed earlier that morning, and a bottle of liquid paraffin. This was for the constipation that we would suffer, inevitably, when we were camping. An old silver dessertspoon lay nearby, the gilt worn away in spots and the alloy underneath showing through. It was the same spoon he used in the winter to give me my chest medicine.

I took the spoon and half filled it with liquid paraffin. Although I detested the stuff, I would take it. When my father came down, the first thing he would say to me would be, 'Did you take your liquid paraffin?' If I hadn't but said that I had, he would know; he always knew when I lied. The only thing to do was to take it.

I fed the spoon into my mouth. The edge was sharp and I felt it scrape my upper lip. I tipped it. The liquid paraffin rolled off the spoon and spread sluggishly across my tongue. It was a dense, heavy liquid. It tasted of fish and cod liver oil. I swallowed and although most of the paraffin went down, it left a film behind, all over the inside of my mouth.

I took a scoop of Bemax with another spoon and crammed it in my mouth. After a moment or two, the taste of fish was gone, absorbed by the dusty wheat.

I glanced at the wireless. Where was the fob? Not there. I looked around the countertop. Not there either. My father, I decided, must be waking himself with his enormous alarm clock, as he would do, from time to time, when he had an important appointment.

After breakfast I washed up in silence, dried and put away in silence. I was desperate to start the holiday but there was nothing to be done to speed matters along. I would just have to wait until he woke.

I went out to the garden and set up one of the deck-chairs that had come with us from Dublin. I took a book with me, *The Enchanted Wood* by Enid Blyton.

The sun rose and towards midday one of the upstairs windows at the back banged open. His bald brown head shone in the sun as he leant out the window.

'Carlos,' my father called. Though I was still Karl at school I was Carlos at home now.

'Camping's off,' he continued. 'It's too late. It's almost midday. We'll never get packed up and off to Wales. You shouldn't have let me sleep in.'

Apparently I was wrong assuming he was getting himself

up. Yet, I wondered, how was I meant to wake him without the fob to tell me when. I was a creature of habit who didn't know how to show initiative.

'I'll ring Mrs Varma and tell her we're not going today,' he said, and with that he shut the window and vanished. I stared at the pebbledash, blinding white in the sunshine, then turned and looked at our fence, greasy with creosote. I knew that I must not dwell on the news that we were not to go on holiday. If I got sad my lungs would seize up and then we would never go on holiday and then he would never start to like me.

So I bent open my book and threw myself into the world of Jo, Bessie and Fanny, the Faraway Tree, Saucepan Man, Moon-Face and Silky the elf.

The next day my father reversed CDF 22 from the drive and parked it in front of the house. The camping gear was piled in the hall. My father told me to carry everything out.

'But don't go near the car,' he added, 'and don't touch the running board.'

This was a critical moment. Our departure was almost within sight. I must not talk or lark about. I must not annoy him or touch CDF 22. The car was a thoroughbred and I was an unruly lump. I mustn't put my paws on the upholstery or bend the fender.

I shuttled between hall and kerb with the gear. With each journey we moved a step closer to the holiday and the closeness I dreamt of.

When I got all the stuff out, I stood on the grass to watch him packing. A smell of cellulose paint and rubber wafted from the boot.

'Is that the best you can do?' he asked. 'Gawp?'

I stepped back to our gate. That satisfied him. He loaded the boot with the same customary care that he did everything.

I began to wonder if the job would ever be done? At this rate, it would be evening soon, and we'd have to put off going for another day.

But then, suddenly, it was done. He dropped the boot lid and turned the key in the lock.

'Check the house,' he said.

I ran upstairs and flushed the lavatory. I gave the bathroom taps a turn. In my bedroom I checked the brass flange on the gas fire was in the off position. My father rattled the French doors in the room below.

'Stop dawdling,' he called. I ran out to the car.

'Don't touch the running board,' he shouted as usual.

I climbed in the back and sat on the slippery leather seat beside my brother. My father got in. He checked the route plan; this was a detailed list of the roads, roundabouts and principal towns on the way to Wales; it was written on the back of an old envelope that was clipped to the driver's side sun visor with a clothes-peg. He started the engine.

We drove up our hill and turned on to Parkway, and some minutes later we pulled into a street off Worple Road, Raynes Park. The houses were small, red brick, Victorian. The people here did not have as much money as those who lived in our road.

My father stopped. We were at the house of my school friend Aidan Varma. I went to the door. Mrs Varma appeared in a sari and gold jewellery. The Varmas were Christians from India. My friend Aidan came out carrying a small holdall that didn't seem to have much in it. The running board was re-negotiated again and, at last, we set off properly on our camping holiday.

By tea time we were parked on a lay-by along the A40. The Primus was pumped but refused to light. The nozzle was blocked.

With barely concealed delight, I produced the pocket

camping stove I had got, from Milletts near Wimbledon station, for just such an emergency. I assembled four flat pieces of metal into a square, put a methylated spirit fuel block in the middle, and lit it. My father put the kettle on.

A few minutes later he was sipping tea. I watched him carefully as he drank. He said nothing. He finished the tea and flicked the dregs into the hedge. Should I have produced my emergency stove? Did he think I was showing off when I got it out? I tried to see if his eyes had gone small and dark and angry. But I saw nothing.

Our campsite was in Wales, outside Abergavenny. It was a beautiful summer's evening when my father nosed CDF 22 slowly through the gate. Shadows from the trees lay across the grass and clouds of midges danced in the air; in the distance, a Welsh river raced past.

There was also a wooden hut with notices pinned up and a hand-painted sign that read 'Administration'. My father pressed the horn.

The door of the hut flew open and someone bounded out. He wore sandals and a shirt covered with badges. At first, with the sun in my eyes, I thought he was a Boy Scout. But when he got closer to CDF 22, I saw he was an adult. Then he lowered himself to my father's window and I saw he was a man, about my father's age, with a creased face. He wore spectacles with round metal frames.

'Hello,' he said. He sounded like Charles Hawtrey in *Carry On Nurse*, which I had seen earlier in the summer. (Since *Whistle Down the Wind* I had seen quite a few films at the travelling cinema on the common.) My heart sank. The man was what we called a nancy, or a fruit, at school. My father didn't use that word; he called them homosexuals or sometimes queers, and he loathed them.

'The name's Presley,' continued the face at the window, 'but

just call me Willy.' My face went red. His Christian name was
the worst imaginable.

My father paid for our pitch and we drove off.

A few minutes later, as we struggled with our tent poles, he
cleared his throat then began to speak.

'That fellow Willy,' he said, 'the one in the hut, do you
know what kind of a man Willy is?'

'No.'

'Oh, come on, you lot, use your brains. God help me but
I've explained about that type of man often enough before,
haven't I?'

There was a silence.

'Does nothing I say ever penetrate your thick skulls? Are
you retarded or what? Yes, I think you are. I think you're
incapable of taking something in and retaining it.'

Out of the corner of my eye I saw Aidan looking at the
grass. I assumed his father talked to him like this too and he
was simply waiting for my father to stop so he could get on
with putting up the tent.

'No child should go near that kind of man,' said my
father. 'Do you hear? He's the type who hangs around men's
lavatories and interferes with children. You are not to go
near him and if he offers you anything, if he offers you
sweets, anything, you come and find me right away, do you
understand?'

Later, when my father went off to get water, we sang
together, myself, my brother and Aidan:

> 'My Uncle Billy
> Had a ten-foot willie,
> He showed it to the girl next door.
> She thought it was a snake
> And hit it with a rake
> And now it's only four foot four.'

We lay on the ground and laughed. When my father came back with the gallon can full of water, we stopped laughing and got up and went back to tightening the guy ropes.

I fell asleep that night to the sound of rushing Welsh water but when I woke it was to the sound of voices, guttural and angry.

I put my head through the tent flap and saw two women. They wore mini-skirts and shoes with heels, which had sunk into the soft ground. I listened to their angry exchange and I picked up their story. They were both from Birmingham. They lived on the same estate and their families had been feuding for years. By chance they had arrived at the campsite at different times during the previous night, each having chosen the site without knowing the other would be there; then they had woken to find one another, and neither was now prepared to leave. As they talked the women referred to their menfolk, husbands and older sons, currently sleeping but easily roused.

My father came out of his tent; it was larger than the one where I was sleeping with Aidan and my brother. He lit the Primus (he had cleared the blockage with a needle the night before) and put on the kettle. It was Czechoslovakian, decorated with flowers and birds. He always bought Eastern European goods, where possible, in order to support socialism.

In the distance, the women stopped arguing and went their separate ways. I realised the feuding families were camped one on either side of us. We were in the middle.

'Oh God!' said my father, who had now taken in the situation. 'The lumpenproletariat.'

After breakfast, my father said, 'Right, time to do your business, boys.'

My father believed regular evacuation of the bowels was essential for mental and physical well-being, and, conversely, that a constipated child was a poisoned child. He said all food must be masticated properly before swallowing (twenty chews to every mouthful). This ensured stools that moved smoothly through the body. Processed foods and sugars were forbidden because they produced hard stools that then wouldn't shift from the bowel. These stools stayed in the system and leaked their poison back into the body.

His ideas came from *The Culture of Abdomen*. I had sneaked a look at this book once or twice. It was filled with line drawings of the lower abdomen and passages (underlined by him) that praised the Turkish Squatter over our European Crapper.

He wasn't happy unless we did our business every day. Each evening, before supper, he would smell our breath for the tell-tale odour of constipation. He said it was a smell like rusting metal. (Sometimes I would sniff at rusting metal to see what he meant but I never got the hang of what he was on about.) If we were constipated he got us moving with liquid paraffin. If this didn't work, we got a hot-water enema.

The campsite latrines were over by the administration hut. We hadn't visited yet (we'd just peed behind the trees the night before) but my father had taken a look and found they were dirty and unsanitary. There was also the Willy problem. The latrines, presumably, were where Willy did his lurking. Because of dirt and danger, my father said he had decided that rather than use the latrines, we would cross the river and do our business on the bracken-covered hill on the other side.

We washed our breakfast things in river water that was brown with peat. Then we each pulled some lavatory paper off the roll, stuffed it in the pockets of our shorts, and took off our plimsolls.

My father said he would stay and mind the tents from the

warring families. I guessed he was going to a proper lavatory later. I kept this thought to myself.

We stepped in to the river gingerly. We began to cross. The water was fast-moving and very cold. In the middle, where the river was deepest and fastest, Aidan Varma lost his footing. He put a hand out to steady himself and let go of one of his plimsolls. It plopped on to the water and was carried away at enormous speed. We watched the blue-black shape grow smaller and smaller; then it vanished from sight. We heard my father on the bank behind us going, 'Tut, tut.'

We reached the far side and separated. I found a place and made a hole in the sandy ground and squatted down. I was surrounded by ferns. I smelt their distinctive odour and stared at the hard, crinkled, cardboard-like edges of the leaves. I heard Aidan hopping through the undergrowth on a single plimsolled foot.

When I finished I wiped myself. Then I buried everything and went back to the river and washed my hands.

We reassembled and crossed back over.

'Put something on your feet,' my father ordered Aidan.

'Can't,' he whispered.

The plimsolls were all he had. He tried my spare shoes. Too big.

'How could you come camping and not bring spare footwear?' my father demanded. 'Are you an imbecile?'

Silence. Now I realised what I should have guessed when I first saw Aidan's holdall. Never having been camping and not knowing what he'd need, Aidan had brought next to nothing.

'I suppose,' my father said, looking at me, 'as a stupid boy, it naturally follows you'd have a stupid friend like Aidan.'

He was annoyed because now he would have to buy Aidan shoes.

'I'll go and try and find it,' I offered.

'Don't be ridiculous. It'll have washed out to sea by now.'

I set off. After a few minutes, I met a fisherman coming my way. He wore rubber waders up to his armpits, and carried a rod on his shoulder like a rifle.

'Lost something?' he asked. He could tell I had from my face.

'Yes.'

He swung the rod forward. The plimsoll hung from a feathered hook.

'A miracle I caught it,' he said.

I thanked him and hurried back. I was happy. I foresaw a wonderful moment ahead. When I returned with Aidan's plimsoll, my father would say 'Well done'. He would throw his arms around me. Perhaps this was that moment when he would start to like me?

In the event, my hope remained just that – a hope – because when I got back, war had been declared. The Birmingham families were down at the river's edge, hidden from view because they were below the level of the bank but quite audible. They were hurling rocks at each other and, judging by the cries I could hear, the hit rate was quite high.

I sat down on the ground-sheet behind my father. I didn't want to be in his line of vision in case he said something sarcastic. Screams mingled with the sound of rushing water came from the river. Occasionally, a rock appeared in view, flew through the air, then disappeared again. In medieval times, I remembered, tourists often gathered near battles to watch or listen. I knew this because, despite his disapproval, I had read up on war in his Encyclopædia Britannica when he was asleep in the mornings.

A boy with a bleeding face scrambled over the bank and ran past.

'Why have I come?' my father muttered. 'This is awful!'

Willy came and separated the warring parties. Fathers and sons clambered up from the river and shuffled past us. I saw thin men in wet clothes, with blood on their hard faces. This was not the end of their war. This was a temporary truce. I knew that. The battle would recommence, the faces said, when Willy wasn't around.

A little later, rain began to pour from the sky. I watched thick, heavy rods of wet hurling themselves at the ground. Before long, sheets of water covered the campsite and the swollen river started to roar.

We retreated into the bigger tent, the one my father slept in, and lay back on the ground-sheet. I watched the rain drumming on the canvas, and listened to the water as it sheeted off the fly. The light was green in here, like the light in our kitchen.

We all grew bored and restless, and my brother ran a plimsoll toe idly along the canvas overhead. Suddenly, where his touch had glanced past and, in so doing, undone the waterproofing, water began to pour in.

'Didn't I warn you not to touch the inside of the tent, you stupid boy!' my father shouted. 'You've ruined the waterproofing.' I was glad it wasn't me he was shouting at.

A saucepan went under the drips.

'That's it. I've had enough,' my father said later. 'You wanted this holiday; right, boys, you're welcome to it. There's plenty of food. There's fuel for the Primus. The pitch fees are paid. You can fend for yourselves.'

He pulled on his raincoat, put his clothes in the boot of CDF 22, and went to a hotel in Abergavenny.

In the days that followed it went on raining and the warring factions went on fighting. Days and nights were punctuated by shouts and curses and screams of pain. The police came twice, an ambulance once. We huddled in the tent, read Enid Blyton and Richmal Crompton and ate baked beans which we heated on my emergency stove. I took advantage of my father's absence to use it at every opportunity.

Once, my father took us to his hotel for lunch. In the dining
room there was a fire and horse brasses on the walls. I had
mushy peas and mashed potatoes covered with gravy made
from lamb fat.

Then, a day or two after our lunch, the clouds cleared and
the sun appeared. The wet ground began to steam and the
river subsided from a roar to a chatter.

My father came at tea time with his fishing rods. In
Abergavenny he had heard the river at the campsite was
excellent for brown trout. A perfect summer evening was in
the offing. It was too good to be true – of course it was – and
within minutes the Birmingham families were back at war.
This time they didn't fight down by the river's edge; this time
they fought on the campsite itself, and soon rocks were flying
backwards and forwards.

My father went off to get Willy. No sooner had he gone
than my brother picked up a boulder and hurled it at the
driver's door of CDF 22. There was a thump as metal buckled
and black cellulose paint came away in huge flakes.

We chased across the site and arrived breathless at the
administration hut.

'Father!' we piped. 'Quick, you'd better come.'

We led him back to the car with long faces and showed
him the damage.

'The families,' we explained and looked suitably frightened.

He turned and began to walk in the direction of a knot of
men who were fighting and jostling. Then he thought better
of it and came back.

'Pack,' he said, and within an hour we were on the way
home to Morden.

chapter twenty-four

It was autumn. My brother and I were back to our routine; school days, we were in Cannon Hill Lane with my father; weekends, we were in Deodar Road with my mother.

It was a school day, afternoon. Climbing Cannon Hill Lane, I noticed the mounds of leaves heaped on the common. The park keepers had been busy.

I went through our gate, my brother following. I pushed open the front door and went in. I was surprised to see my helicopter lying on the carved, glistening Burmese table just inside.

'Can I play with my helicopter on the common?' I called to my father in his study. If I was really lucky, the helicopter would land right on top of one of the piles and the blades would scatter leaves everywhere.

I reached for the box, its scuffs and tears covered with Sellotape that was yellow and brittle with age, though the stirring illustration on the front (a helicopter flying over Vietnamese jungle on a mission to kill Viet Cong, my father insisted) was as bright as when my mother gave it to me.

'What are you doing?'

My father was suddenly at his study door. He was not in his usual clothes. This afternoon he wore a good cotton shirt, his chestnut-coloured corduroys and a knitted tie. He had shaved and his smooth chin shone like the table top. There could be only one reason why he was dressed this way: Henrietta. I was aware that she still rang from time to time.

'Did I say you could take your helicopter?' my father asked. He spoke quietly yet he was on the way to being cross.

I said nothing.

'Yes or no, answer me.'

There was no way out. 'No,' I said.

'If I didn't give permission, then why are you taking it?'

I let go of the box.

'You'd better say goodbye.'

I did not understand. Goodbye? We'd only just got in.

'Don't be so stupid, act your age.'

Suddenly, I knew to whom I was to address my farewell; not to him but to it, my treasure.

'It's going away,' he explained. 'You don't need it any more. It's cluttering up my study. You've had it long enough. So look on it one last time and say goodbye.'

'But I love my helicopter,' I said.

'Oh yes, I know you do. And I know all about your addiction to toys and guns and plastic, not to mention sweets, comics, drivel on television and the rest of the rubbish Capitalism throws in the way of unsuspecting idiots like yourself and which your mother encourages you to gorge on. I know all about your addictions *and* where they come from.'

This was a reference to my mother and her side of the family. She was a fame addict, my father said, and behind her stood my grandmother, who was a God addict, and my grandfather, who was a drink addict and a tobacco addict, and behind him were his parents, my maternal great-grandparents, and they, in turn, were drink addicts who died of sclerosis of the liver. Half my genes came from these addicts; my father was trying to save me from them, he said from time to time, but he seriously doubted that he could.

'You know,' he continued, 'it's time you learnt to think about other people for a change instead of thinking about yourself all the time. You've got everything you want but very few people in the world have everything they want.'

The clock ticked at the bottom of the stairs. 'Did you hear me?'

'Yes,' I agreed. This was leading somewhere I wouldn't like.

'Those who haven't got should get what they want, sometimes, shouldn't they? And those that have got should give what they have, sometimes, to those who haven't, isn't that so?'

'Yes.'

'In the country, there is a good child and her mother who has been deserted by her husband. They have no money for clothes, let alone toys. Don't you think a lucky boy like you who's got everything, a workbench and tools, a whole common, a library in Morden, a warm house and a loving father who gives him three meals a day, not to mention his mother's in Putney, stuffed with any amount of junk, don't you think he should be able, just for once, to say, I have everything, let those who are more deserving have one of my toys?'

'But I want to keep my helicopter,' I said, faintly.

'You're a spoilt brat, aren't you? Look, I'm tired of talking to you about this. It's going, all right. It's going to go a child who unfortunately lost her father, unlike you. I thought, I hoped, you'd surprise me and show a little grace but of course you haven't. Yet why am I surprised? How could you? You're incapable of generosity.'

He gave us supper in the kitchen early. With autumn looming the stove was back on and the smoke that leaked from the stack formed a blanket around the light bulb.

After dinner, while I was washing up, I heard him reverse CDF 22 out of the garage. A moment later he was back in the hall.

'Is the gas off?' he called.

I looked at the cooker. All the jets were out.

'Yes.'

'You're not to answer the door or the telephone. Don't leave the house. Bed at eight o'clock.'

'Yes.'

'And wash your face,' he said. 'And tell your brother to do the same.'

I heard the front door close. I heard the engine of CDF 22 as he drove off down the hill.

I dried my hands on a tea towel and went out to the hall. The helicopter box was gone from the table.

chapter twenty-five

That evening, coming into the house after Cub Scouts, I heard the television. I peered into the dining room and saw the screen filled with a talking face. My father was not sitting, as usual, with his back straight but slumped sideways. He pulled out a huge handkerchief and blew his nose. Something was up. Was he sad about Adolf again? I wondered. But he hadn't mentioned Adolf for ages.

On the television was a picture of the United States President (I remembered his face from the Cuban missile crisis), then an open car speeding along a road, crowds, the president waving . . .

'They shot him,' my father said. Then he wiped his face. My father was crying, if I wasn't mistaken.

I slipped away to the kitchen. From here I could overhear what went on in the dining room without being accused of trying to sneak a look at the gogglebox.

I listened. I heard the forceful voices of people talking on television. I heard the strangled noise of my father crying. But why was he sad? I could understand him crying when Adolf died. If my mother died, I would have cried. But this I could not grasp. On the rare occasions when he had spoken of Kennedy, it was to say he was an idiot, a fool and an Imperialist. Now, suddenly, the president was dead, and my father was weeping for him.

In bed, later, I thought about what I had seen. Why did my father cry? I thought long and hard but I could not explain it.

This set me thinking about what else I didn't know about. There must be much more, I decided, but I would never know the other things in his head because he would never tell me about them. This made me sad, and I felt the tubes in my chest narrowing.

'I will not be sick,' I began to recite, 'I must not be sick . . .'

chapter twenty-six

One day, early in February 1964, I came home to Cannon Hill Lane from school to find a young man sitting in our kitchen. His forehead was huge and shiny and he had a slick of hair that flopped sideways across it. This was Stan. His mother was Olive Davies, my father's younger sister. She had married a man in the furniture business and emigrated to Canada. I couldn't remember ever meeting her. Whether this was because she left Ireland before I was born, or because she was never invited to visit us, I didn't know. I assumed the latter. My father talked about his siblings incredibly rarely, and when he did, he nearly always spoke badly of them.

Stan Davies, or Gébler-Davies as he later styled himself, had ambitions to write, and he had come to live with us in order to learn the secrets of the literary business from my father. I had no idea how this idea arose but I had a strong sense it wasn't going to work.

Stan moved into the boxroom where Rosemary had slept when she lived with us. The house was suddenly very happy. There was laughter over dinner, and afterwards there was whiskey and talk of books. My father praised Stan extravagantly. Stan, he said, had left the philistine wilds of Saskatchewan and come to old Europe to rediscover his roots and find himself as an artist. My father approved. Hugely. He told Stan he had no doubt that he could write. Stan simply had to do as my father had done when he was a cinema projectionist. He had to read, and he had to read a lot, Shaw especially, because there was nobody to beat the master. At the same time, my father said, in his most imperious and dogmatic tone of voice, Stan had to practise and practise and practise his craft; write and rewrite and rewrite, again and again and again. That's how he had made himself a writer – by hard practice – and that was the only way Stan would make himself a writer – by hard practice.

I observed Stan listening as my father spoke. He held his head sideways and made little movements with his mouth. I thought Stan disagreed with absolutely everything my father said but that wisely he decided to say nothing.

One afternoon, Stan took me to Regent's Park Zoo. It was cold, wet, and my trouser legs flapped in the wind. We went to the children's enclosure, filled with llamas and sheep. A donkey bit a boy and the boy wailed, 'He nipped me, he nipped me,' more in surprise than pain.

Stan soon had enough of this. 'Come on,' he said. We went to a café, the windows steamed up on the inside. Complaining of a headache, he drank one cup of tea after another while munching Anadin.

Later, at Baker Street station, he bought me a toffee apple. I licked the gorgeous red glaze then cracked it like an eggshell.

'You won't mention this to Ernie, will you?' said Stan.

'No,' I said. What did he think I was?

On the escalator, hot air rose from below, bringing with it the Underground smell of scorched oil and hot metal.

'Promise you won't to say to Ernie about the toffee apple?' said Stan, again.

An advertisement on the wall showing a woman in a brassière flashed past. Some wag had drawn spectacles around her eyes.

'Of course I won't.'

'You're sure?' Stan continued.

'Yes,' I said, emphatically.

Stan turned and looked ahead. The escalator mechanism clattered under my feet. How could he doubt me? Then it occurred to me: he was frightened of my father, just like everyone else. My sense that his staying with us wasn't going to work intensified.

A few days later, when I came in from school, my father came out of his study.

'Stan's still in bed,' he said, grumpily. 'Go and see if he's all right.'

I went up and knocked on the boxroom door.

'Yeah,' Stan shouted.

'My father asked me to ask if you're all right?'

'I'm fine. Just tired.'

'Ask him if he's getting up,' my father shouted from below.

I swallowed. How did I do this without making either man angry?

'My father wondered if you were getting up?' I said, very politely.

'Yeah, I'm getting up in a minute.'

'You'll be getting up in a minute then,' I said, so both men would hear. 'Do you want anything?'

'A kick up the arse,' my father hissed from below and stomped off.

I went downstairs again. I found my father in the kitchen feeding anthracite from the battered scuttle into the stove.

'Well. Did he show himself to you?'

My father's mouth had shrunk and his eyes were black. I said nothing.

'He'd better be down soon, or else.'

My father banged the lid back on the stove, and Stan appeared, bleary, unshaven, yellow grains of sleep around his eyes.

'Hello,' he said, sleepily.

'It's after four in the afternoon,' my father said. He went into his study and closed the door sharply.

'What's the matter with him?' muttered Stan. He lit the gas and set the kettle on the ring.

'I don't know,' I said.

I liked our visitor. He had improved my father's mood, but I realised that was over now. That evening, there was no laughter at dinner and there was no book-talk afterwards, either.

Over the following days the atmosphere grew worse. My father began to mutter things. Stan was bone idle. Stan never washed up after himself. Stan was dull and ungracious and bad-mannered and depressing. Stan was one of those types who wanted something for nothing. Stan was going to eat us out of house and home. Stan was a leech.

The final rift was coming, and I was filled with a sense of dread. I hated confrontations. They made me wheeze.

A few days later, coming into the hall with my brother after school, I heard my father calling from the study, 'Come here, boys.'

We pushed open the door and entered his lair. My father sat at his desk, typing. The curtains were pulled and the electric lights were on. 'Stan's gone to Wimbledon,' my father said. 'He's gone to see about a job in a jazz shop, amazingly. When he comes back, you're not to let him in, do you understand?'

So the end had come, at last.

We agreed, my brother and I, we would not answer the door.

Abruptly, my father got up and went into the hall. He drew the bolts shut and put on the chain.

About an hour later I heard the creak of our gate. It had to be Stan. I was in the hall, sitting on the stairs.

'Under the table,' my father growled from the door of his study.

I clambered under the ornate Burmese table. Loops of grey cobweb hung down underneath.

I heard a key slipping into our Yale lock, then an exclamation of surprise. The voice was unmistakably Stan's.

The letterbox creaked. I saw the upraised flap, and the eyes looking in. I ducked back.

'Hello,' Stan called through the slit. 'Anybody there?' He sounded puzzled. I wanted to shout, 'We're here, Stan. Father's locked the door.'

With my mind's eye, I saw Stan on our doorstep, peering through the letterbox, and then I saw myself running to my father and piping, 'Open the door, it's Stan.'

The muscles in my calves began to tremble as if this scene was real.

'There must be someone in there,' Stan shouted. 'Open up.'

He didn't sound surprised any more; he sounded angry.

'Come on.' He kicked the door. I could be trapped here for ages, I realised, and suddenly I desperately wanted to pee.

The letterbox sprang shut with a bang. Our gate squeaked. Silence.

It was twenty-six years before I heard Stan's voice again.

chapter twenty-seven

It was early morning. The house was quiet. I was in the kitchen. My father was asleep. I had taken my liquid paraffin. I had eaten my Bemax.

I went out to the hall, to the grandfather clock. It had a round cream-coloured face with numbers written in black and the clockmaker's details under the spindle; Fengley Bros., 5 Crow Street, Dublin.

It was nine o'clock. I went back to the kitchen and checked the plastic fob. It was set to noon.

'Let's go to George's,' said my brother, who was sitting at the table.

George was a school friend who lived in Eastway, round the corner. We could be there and back long before twelve.

'All right,' I said blithely, but my heart was beating.

We put the front door on the latch, went out and closed it behind. To anyone passing, our door would appear closed.

We walked to George's and rang the bell. His mother answered. She wore a summer dress. It was not summer but it was well on the way.

'Come in,' she said.

We played with George in the garden but every few minutes I would run into the kitchen and ask his mother the time.

'Have you got to be somewhere?' she asked, eventually.

'We've to be home by twelve, latest.'

'Tell you what,' she said. 'When it's nearly time I'll tell you.'

But a few minutes later I was back.

'Don't worry,' she said.

Later she called us in. On the dining-room table I saw three glasses of orange squash and a plate of Jammie Dodgers, white rounds of shortcake with red hearts in the middle.

'Don't worry, it's not time yet. Help yourselves.'

George took a glass of squash and began to drink greedily. I did not move; nor did my brother.

'Go on,' said George's mother.

'We're not allowed squash or biscuits with jam and sugar,' I said.

I didn't want to risk my father smelling my breath, because if he did, then he would discover where we had been.

George's mother squinted at us. It occurred to me, dimly, that she felt sorry for us.

We said goodbye and walked down the hill to our house. As soon as we got inside I re-engaged the lock and closed the door tight. Our father was still upstairs in his bed. We had got away with it.

I made his breakfast, then went up and knocked on his door. Nothing. If I let him sleep on he'd be furious. I opened the door.

Inside, the room was dark. It smelt of lanolin and vegetable soup and corduroy. He sat up slowly, sleepily, blinking.

'It's the time on the fob,' I said.

'Pull the curtains.'

Outside there was a grey sky.

'Ah, the English spring,' he said, grimly.

I glanced at the Rokeby Venus and went down to the kitchen. I heard the lavatory flushing above. Then he came in and ate his toast and drank the tea without talking. I was not surprised. Since my mother went, whole days could go by and he would not say a word.

When he finished eating, he filled the sink with cold water and took off his vest. He bent forward and put his head right underwater. I saw bubbles coming up. I saw his vertebrae sticking up under his brown skin. I looked for signs of his anchylosis spondylitis but each vertebra, as far as I could see, was separate from the next.

He came up from underwater, dripping and gasping.

'That's the way,' he said, reaching for a towel and drying himself.

He opened his eyes; they were slightly bloodshot.

'That's how to wake up and get alert. Take it as a tip from your old man. If you could learn to listen, you might amount to something one day. On the other hand, it's more than likely that you won't.'

He pulled on his vest and sauntered out whistling. Why did he say that? I wondered. Suddenly, I felt certain he knew we'd gone to George's house, even though I was also absolutely certain he had been asleep all morning and he couldn't possibly know. It took hours for the panic that swept through me to subside.

chapter twenty-eight

Around this time my mother bought a tall red-brick house with a long narrow garden that ran down to the Thames. It was in Deodar Road where she already had her small terrace house, so when she moved it was only a matter of driving two hundred yards down the road.

With the new house came a change in our routine; on Monday, Wednesday and Friday nights we stayed at Cannon Hill Lane; the rest of the week we stayed in Deodar Road.

It was the afternoon of one of our Morden days. When we got in, my brother, as usual, slipped silently upstairs. I loitered in the hall wondering what to do. I noticed the bad-egg smell of sulphur.

'Is that you?' I heard my father calling jovially from the verandah.

I went through the kitchen and out the back door. I found him standing on his sturdy, paint-spattered stepladder. He had acquired the steps, he told me, when he was a cinema apprentice in Wolverhampton more than thirty years earlier, and they were still going strong on account of how he looked after them. Why appease Capitalism, he used to say, by not looking after something and throwing it away, when with a little effort one could make most things last?

'Don't breathe in,' he ordered.

He had a brass contraption in his hands. He plunged the handle and a fine spray of sulphur dust squirted out of the nozzle and coated the tiny hard dark grapes that had just started to show on the vine.

'Hello,' he said.

He sounded unusually cheerful.

'Come and meet someone,' he said.

I followed him into the garden. The deck-chairs were set up; one was empty but the other had a woman sitting on it.

'This is Phyllis . . .' he said.

Her hair was wavy, her face was wide and her arching eyebrows were painted black. She wore a polo-neck and black ski-pants, the stirrups hooked under the soles of her flat shoes.

'. . . Though I'm renaming her Jane,' my father continued.

'Hello,' she said, blushing as she shook my hand. Her voice was strange.

'Don't worry, she talks funny,' my father continued. 'That's because she's from Yorkshire. Now where's that brother of yours? Sash?' he shouted.

That evening Jane cooked; we had lamb chops. My father talked endlessly about his novels and my mother's much greater success despite her mediocre talent. In his view, success was in inverse ratio to talent. Jane laughed a lot.

I washed up with my brother. Then we listened to *The Goon Show* on the wireless in the kitchen. When the programme finished, my father sent us to bed. Later, I heard him and Jane leaving the house. He was going to drive her back to her room in Sydenham. Much later, I heard him coming in again . . .

Over the following weeks, signs of Jane began to appear – her eyebrow tweezers, her coat, her yellow Marigold washing-up gloves. Then, one day, I noticed my father's bedroom door standing open. This was unusual because, since Jane appeared, he had taken to keeping it closed. I peered in and noticed a bag on top of the wardrobe.

I could hear Jane and my father laughing in the garden. As long as I was quick, I thought, I'd get away with this.

I carried my bedside table into my father's bedroom, and used it to climb up. I reached down the brown canvas bag and unzipped it. It was filled with women's underwear and a huge bundle of sanitary towels bound together with a rubber band.

I put the bag back and carried my table away. Once I was back in my room, I felt my heart beating quickly. It was partly due to what I had done but mostly due to what I had discovered. On the nights when my brother and I were in Putney, I realised, Jane stayed with my father. Though I had always known my mother and father would never live together, there had always been a little bit of me that had hoped they would someday, despite also knowing this would make us all miserable. Now that I had looked in the bag I knew for certain this would never happen.

My heart pounded. It was going to take a long time to slow down.

'Oh, Ernie,' I heard Jane shouting in the garden, 'you're the funniest man in England who isn't writing books.' She said this a lot over the coming months. It became her catch phrase.

chapter twenty-nine

I was on the common, heading towards the pavilion. It was a cloudy summer's day. I saw a woman coming towards me. I realised it was Vera. She hadn't been to babysit for ages.

'Vera,' I called out. I was pleased to see her and I hoped she was pleased to see me too. Perhaps she would be so pleased she would buy me an ice cream, which I could then eat behind the pavilion where my father wouldn't see.

Suddenly, two Teddy boys (both young men of about twenty) got up from a bench beside the path and ran up to Vera. One put his hand up her skirt. Vera squealed, and tried to squat down.

I froze. I hoped this was just a bit of larking about and that the Teddy boys would soon go back to their bench, leaving Vera free to talk to me.

But instead, the Teddy boys began to run Vera across the grass towards the burnt-out tree. From where I was it sounded as if Vera was laughing, but then again she could have been shouting angrily. It was hard to tell.

Suddenly, one of Vera's shoes came off. She pulled against the Teddy boys as if she wanted them to stop so she could go back for it. The Teddy boys wouldn't let her. They kept yanking her forwards.

When they got to the bottom of the burnt-out tree, the two Teddy boys lifted Vera up and shoved her through the hole head first. Then they scrambled up and went through the hole after her. It happened incredibly quickly. Then all was still. Then a bit of cloth came flying out of the hole, and landed on the grass.

Why don't I bring Vera her missing shoe? I thought. She would need her shoe, wouldn't she? Of course she would. And maybe that way I could get to talk to her.

I went across the grass and picked up the shoe. I walked down to the burnt-out tree. A pair of knickers lay on the ground, white and scrunched up. Inside the tree there was shouting and laughing. It didn't sound nice. I lobbed Vera's shoe in through the hole.

'What the fuck was that?' shouted one of the Teddy boys inside.

He stuck his head out of the hole.

'What the fuck did you do that for?'

'It's, it's . . .' I said.

I wanted to say, It's Vera's shoe, in a lovely cool, clear voice, but the words wouldn't come.

'Who is it?' shouted the other Teddy boy; this was the one I couldn't see.

'It's a boy.'

'What the fuck is he doing here?' the one inside shouted.

'I'm fucked if I know.' The one with his head sticking out now looked at me. 'Were you on the path just now?'

'Is that you, Karl?' Vera called from inside the tree. She called me Karl.

'Yes,' I said.

'Tell him to fuck off,' said the Teddy boy inside.

'Karl, go away,' said Vera, 'go on.'

She sounded sad but I couldn't be certain. She also sounded emphatic.

'You heard, fuck off,' said the Teddy boy looking at me, 'or I'll kick your fucking balls in.'

'If he has any,' said the hidden one.

Suddenly, I felt very frightened. I turned and ran back to the pavilion as fast as my legs would carry me. I dashed up the steps and flew through the door.

Inside, I looked around wildly. My plan was to find a park keeper and tell him the tree was on fire. But the place was empty.

'What do you want?'

The voice came from behind the counter. It wasn't the woman who usually served, the one with the sharp nose and the flaking skin. It was a boy, just a couple of years older than me. I doubted he'd know what to do if I said the tree was on fire. And I couldn't imagine, either, explaining to him what I thought was happening, let alone the two of us going down to the burnt-out tree and challenging the Teddy boys.

'Nothing, thank you,' I said.

I sat down near the door and looked out. I saw the tree in the distance and the treacle-black pond beyond. Perhaps I was overreacting? This was something my father often said of me. My mother had recently explained to me what grown-ups did when they made babies. Perhaps, I thought, when grown-ups did the grown-up thing, they always shouted and appeared angry. Anyway, there wasn't anything I could do now except sit.

So I sat and I waited. After a while the Teddy boys climbed out and Vera climbed out after them. She picked up her knickers from the grass and went behind the tree where no one could see her from the road. She reappeared a moment later, smoothing her dress. Then Vera and the Teddy boys began to walk away towards the pond. They went together. They seemed not to be shouting or arguing any more. They seemed to be quite happy to be with one another. At least as far as I could tell they were.

I got up and went down the steps. I could still see Vera and the two Teddy boys in the distance. There was no accounting for adults, I thought; one minute they'd be crying and the next they'd be laughing. It was so confusing.

chapter thirty

'Right,' said Miss Crawley, my new teacher, 'who wants to go to grammar school?'

I shot my arm up. I heard rustling behind as all the other children in the class did the same.

'Oh, so we all want to go to grammar school, do we? Well, how do we get to go to grammar school? We have to sit the Eleven-Plus, don't we? If we pass, we go to grammar school. And if we fail, we go to secondary modern. Does everyone understand?'

I sat at a desk at the front. Miss Crawley was only a few feet away. She was a small woman with a large bust. Her hair was grey and wiry. Her cheeks were red with purple veins in them. The veins had a wiggle to them, just like her hair. Miss Crawley taught the Eleven-Plus class; it was the first day of my last year at junior school.

'Are we all prepared to work?' asked Miss Crawley.

'Yes, Miss Crawley,' the class thundered.

'Good, I'm glad to hear it. If you want to get anywhere in life, you have to work at it. If you're not prepared to do the work, then you never get anywhere.'

Miss Crawley stared at us. Her eyes were blue and very bright. Miss Crawley had a reputation. She didn't send naughty children to Mr Ferguson. She slippered them herself in front of the class. We were all frightened of Miss Crawley.

'And I'm not prepared to waste my time on children who aren't prepared to do the work. Do you understand?'

'Yes, Miss Crawley.'

'Good. We will start with a test.'

Miss Crawley unlocked the cupboard and folded back the doors. On their insides, both doors were covered with photographs of the Queen and the Royal Family. Miss Crawley was a monarchist. She had been known to take favoured children to Buckingham Palace to see the Trooping of the Colour. The shelves of her cupboard were filled with textbooks and jotters, dip pens and bottles of ink.

'Monitors,' Miss Crawley shouted, as she pulled out a sheaf of papers.

The two girl monitors scrambled to their feet and ran up to her.

'Hand these out,' she said, dividing the papers into two piles and giving a pile to each of the girls. 'No one is to look at the paper until I say,' shouted Miss Crawley.

The monitors rushed around putting an Eleven-Plus test paper face down on each desk.

'Right, have we all got a pencil?'

We all held up our pencils.

'When I say "Start", you will turn over the paper and read it – I hope you got that – you will read it – and then you will answer the questions. When I say "Stop", you stop. Understand? Right. Start . . . now.'

I turned over the paper and began to work through the questions. I found it difficult, particularly the mathematics questions.

'Right, stop,' bellowed Miss Crawley.

The monitors came round and the papers were collected.

After lunch, Miss Crawley strode into the class with the test papers in her hand. She threw the papers down on her desk with a bang. We were already quiet. Now we were silent. Miss Crawley was furious. Her blue eyes had gone very dark.

'Karl Gébler,' she shouted. 'Go to the back of the class. Go on. Go to the back now. You can sit there.'

She pointed at the desk in the corner by the window at the very back. This was usually the desk for those boys who couldn't read or add up. I would never have sat at this desk. I always sat at the front in the place where I was now. I liked school. I was keen.

'And you,' Miss Crawley shouted at the boy whose desk was now apparently to be mine, 'get up and make room for Karl.'

The boy stood up and I slid into his seat. The wood was warm and slippy.

'And wipe that horrible smirk off your face,' she shouted at the boy. 'You didn't do much better than Karl Gébler. You were only third from the bottom. So you can go in that desk there.' She pointed at the desk two in front of the desk where she had put me.

Miss Crawley rearranged the entire class according to their results. The girl who scored the highest mark took my old desk in front of Miss Crawley.

chapter thirty-one

I sat at the dining table doing a practice Eleven-Plus paper, the *Wimbledon Borough News* spread below to stop my pencil scoring the table top.

When I finished the pencil was blunt. I went to the kitchen where Jane sat knitting in the easy chair she had installed in the corner. A sheep's heart simmered in a saucepan, and there was a strong, meaty smell. Jane lived with us now and slept in my father's bed every night.

'Are those Eleven-Plus questions you're doing for home-work?' Jane asked as I sharpened my pencil.

'Yes,' I said.

A thin spiral of wood squeezed past the blade and dropped into the coal-scuttle where it lay like a worm. This was the late autumn of 1964.

'Go and get them.'

I made no move. This could only lead to trouble.

'I'm a teacher. I teach it.'

She said this in her most reasonable voice. I could not refuse.

I fetched the paper.

'Pencil,' said Jane.

I handed my pencil to her. She began marking. She made more crosses than ticks. When she finished, she handed me back my pencil with a smirk, got up and dashed into the study shouting, 'Ernie, you're so right, you know.

'I don't know why I don't believe you,' I heard her continue, 'when you tell me things. Look at his Eleven-Plus test paper. He's got at least half wrong. He's never going to pass, he's stupid.'

I didn't hear what my father replied.

Jane put her head out the doorway and called, 'Lay the table.'

Later, we took our usual places at the table. I had my back to the fire, my brother was in front of the sideboard, Jane was in my mother's old place, and my father sat at the head, his back to the piano.

My brother and I each had a sheep's heart on our plates. They were fist-sized and browny red, apart from the white tubes hanging out of them. My father and Jane had pieces of dark beef with thin red juice oozing from the meat.

I cut off a piece of heart and put it in my mouth. The flesh was tough but flaky. Next I tried a piece of tube. At first, as I chewed, I got a taste of the vegetable stock. When I'd squeezed out the stock taste I was left with a strong taste of wet dog and old iron. The texture of the tube was rubbery.

I took the tube out of my mouth and put it on the side of the plate.

'Doesn't he like it?' said Jane.

'Don't you like it?' said my father.

'It's too hard,' I said.

'Ah diddums,' said Jane, 'too hard for you? Cut it up, shall I?'

I ignored her and sliced off another piece of muscle. I put

it in my mouth and chewed belligerently to show I didn't
need her help. But in the end I couldn't swallow it and I had
to take it out.

When the meal was over there were bits of tube all along
the edge of my plate.

'Instead of always being on the take,' said my father,
addressing my brother and me, 'why don't you two make
yourselves useful and clear the table.'

Jane and my father went through to the study. I scraped my
plate over the fire. The rejected bits of tube landed on the
embers, hissed and steamed but did not catch fire.

Jane didn't like me, I thought, because my father didn't
like me. He didn't like me because, as he said, I was my
mother's product (rather as if I was made in a factory). In me,
I understood, he saw her whom he hated.

It was also true, however, there was something about me
that had always irritated him. From as far back as I could
remember I annoyed him. Even if my mother were still living
at home, and even if she hadn't written novels that were much
better than his, he'd be down on me. It was just how things
were.

The next morning, before I left for school, I went to the fire
to see if the heart tubes were intact but I saw the grate was
filled with ashes. In the end, everything got reduced to ash, it
seemed.

chapter thirty-two

It was damp, misty, and wet dripped from the school gate. 'Hello,' called Mr Woodall. Every morning, without fail, Mr Woodall was to be found standing here, greeting children as they passed.

'Hello, Mr Woodall,' I replied.

In the middle of his long, pale, crumpled face, the weeping wound on his nose was like a lump of wet sealing wax.

'Good luck,' he said, 'with your Eleven-Plus.'

I walked across the slimy playground. A dark blue E-type Jaguar was parked near the front entrance. I ambled over. There was an animal crouched on the bonnet, coiled and ready to spring. This was Miss Crawley's car. It could do a hundred, or more. Or so she said. It was rumoured in the school that Miss Crawley had several convictions for speeding on the Kingston bypass.

I peered in through the back window. The seats were blue leather and shiny. On the back window ledge there was a battered shortbread tin with a picture of Queen Elizabeth and

Prince Philip on the front. Once upon a time, Miss Crawley
always left her car open. Then a boy in the year above mine
called Beverly (known as Bev since his full name – though no
one would have ever dared say so publicly – was really a girl's
name) had opened the car during break and emptied the tin.
At the next assembly Mr Ferguson said, 'I'm saddened and
appalled at this incident, especially as the stolen sweets were
distributed around the playground. Everyone who took a
sweet is as much to blame as the individual who broke into
Miss Crawley's car in the first place – whoever that was.' I
hadn't been offered a boiled sweet but my ears burnt with
shame anyway. If the chance had arisen, I knew I'd have taken
one. Despite Mr Ferguson's plea, no one ever told on Bev; the
consequences would have been too dire. Bev would have
killed the tell-tale.

I walked around the Jaguar, admiring the dashboard and
the steering wheel with its little indentations for fingers like
the dips between vertebrae.

Miss Crawley, I thought, had come to school early that
morning in order to check everything was ready.

This was an idle thought, but no sooner did I have it than
I was filled with dread. In a short while, I realised, I would go
into the room where Miss Crawley was probably straightening
desks at that very moment, pick up a pen, and start the
Eleven-Plus exam.

I wanted to pass. Everybody said grammar school was
better than secondary modern. Grammar school boys were
polite and got good jobs. Secondary modern boys were yobs
and ended up in the factories on Martin Way.

And if I passed, what would happen at home? My father
wouldn't be able to say any more I was stupid because I had
degenerate genes. He would have to say I was clever. He
might even say he was proud of me.

What I did in the next couple of hours would transform

his opinion or confirm it. And I desperately wanted to transform it. My stomach trembled and fluttered with these thoughts.

I walked down to the entrance where children from my class stood waiting. Two girls were exchanging Scooby-Doo good-luck charms.

After a while the door was unlocked from inside and opened back by Miss Crawley. She rang a handbell and we all formed a line. Miss Crawley wore a blue sailor's dress with a white collar. There was rouge on her cheeks; it was red, thick and dusty and it covered the little blue twisting veins that lay under her skin. There was lipstick on her mouth; this was red as well and it looked wet and sticky. She smelt of perfume and she had varnished her nails red. This was the biggest day in her year, Miss Crawley always said.

'File into the assembly hall,' Miss Crawley called.

We passed in, one after the other, and began to walk down the corridor. I heard the scuffing of our feet on the wooden floor and the tick of the electric clocks that hung on the walls. As it was Eleven-Plus day, we were the only children there that morning. The rest of the school was kept home, until breaktime, so that we could work undisturbed.

We passed Mr Ferguson's office and the bench where naughty boys sat when waiting to be slippered, and came to the assembly hall. There were two large doors with brass handles. The child at the front stopped and everyone stopped behind. We were all shy and nervous of going in.

'Go on,' Miss Crawley shouted from the rear. 'In you go. Don't be frightened. There's nothing in there will bite you.'

The child at the front swung open the doors and we all marched in. It was a big room with a stage at one end. It smelt of pastry, polish and leather. The vaulting horses stood in the corner and there were several rows of desks with chairs laid out. I found the desk with my exam number as I knew I had to. Miss Crawley had run us through the drill several times over the preceding days.

The invigilator appeared. He was a wiry old man in a black suit and a black tie. He looked like an undertaker.

'Good luck, boys and girls, do your best,' said Miss Crawley gently. I had never heard her speak like this before. She nodded and left the room. The smell of her perfume and her make-up lingered.

'I will hand out the first of two papers,' explained the invigilator. 'These will be placed face down in front of you. When I give the word, and not before, you will turn your papers over and you will start. You will answer all the questions. When I say stop, you will stop.

'There will then be a short break. You will then return and you will do your second paper.'

A paper appeared on my desk, face down. It was not quite white, more cream.

'You will now start. Turn the papers over and begin.'

I turned over the paper and began. I managed the questions on the first page but then the questions became more difficult and I began to struggle.

The break came and we were sent out to the playground. It was still misty and cold. I went down to the fence where Martin Rowley had shown me the HMS *Ajax* kit. I began to cry. After a while I heard footsteps. I wiped my face and turned and saw it was the school nurse. She wore her blue uniform, her blue cape, her blue nurse's hat and flat black shoes. She carried a large thick white plate covered with quartered oranges.

'Have some,' said the nurse.

She offered the oranges. I took a quarter. I put it in my mouth and began to suck. The juice was tart and the peel was bitter.

'It can't be as bad as all that,' said the nurse.

I put the orange peel on the plate and took another quarter.
'Just do your best,' said the nurse.

I was doing my best but I knew that my best was not good
enough. Even if I could answer all the questions on the next
paper I knew I had failed.

chapter thirty-three

I made a wigwam frame out of bamboo canes and covered it in brown paper. I stiffened the paper with yacht varnish. I was immensely proud of my creation.

'Why don't we play in the wigwam on the common?' I suggested to my brother. My mother was away in America again and we were staying in Cannon Hill Lane all week. It was a warm evening, May or June 1965. Three or four months had passed since the Eleven-Plus. The results would not arrive until the end of the summer and I did not let myself think about them.

'All right,' my brother agreed.

I went upstairs and got the holster from the dressing-up box under his bed, the one that came with the plastic fobwatch, and then, because I didn't have the gun, I got the monkey wrench from the garage (the one I thought my father killed the seven rats with) and I put it in the holster. Then I buckled on the holster. It sagged nicely because of the weight of the monkey wrench, and I could almost believe I had a real gun.

I went to the door of my father's study. He was working at his desk. Jane was not at home.

'We're going to play in the wigwam on the common.'

I was allowed to cross the road on my own now. I would be eleven in August.

'All right. Be sure you observe your road drill. I'll be watching you through the window,' my father said.

We went out to the kerb. I looked ostentatiously left and right. We crossed the road. I looked back. My father was bent over his typewriter.

We began to amble towards the pond. There was a nice level stretch of ground under a chestnut tree. I decided to set up the wigwam here, under the green spreading leaves.

We played and time passed. Then, suddenly, I saw a boy striding towards us across the grass. I recognised Bev. Though he'd since left my primary school and gone to secondary school, I'd not forgotten him. Besides his facility for getting everyone into trouble, he was also a bully. His favourite pastime had been taking infants down to the basement boiler room and burying them in the coal slack. Once, one of his victims passed out from lack of oxygen. An ambulance came and I, along with several other children, had watched, amazed and appalled, as the unconscious child, his face completely black with soot, was carried out of the boiler room on a stretcher. Bev was slippered by Mr Ferguson for this crime. The infant lived, we were told, but he never came back to school.

'Hello,' I called, as Bev drew close. I'd never had any trouble with Bev. I'd always made certain we were on good terms. Bev had short hair and a freckled face. The skin around his eyes appeared swollen. Bev hadn't changed except that he was far bigger than when I last saw him.

'What's up?' said Bev, acknowledging my greeting. He smiled dimly and then, without warning, he kicked the side of the wigwam. The stiff brown varnished paper tore with a horrible wrench and suddenly there was a gaping hole through which I saw bare bamboo rods.

'What did you do that for?' I asked.

'Oh stop it,' Bev shouted, 'or you'll annoy me.'

Bev laughed then. How could he laugh like that, I wondered, having just wrecked my wigwam?

Then a cold, clean, clear thought came into my head.

'I'm going to get you,' I said.

I knew exactly what to do and I knew, having decided, I must not think; thinking would just inhibit me; I must just act, immediately, or I would not be able to carry out the beautiful plan.

I began to unbuckle my holster and at the same time I ran towards Bev. Bev began to jog in a circle around the wigwam. He moved like one who was confident he could handle whatever I threw at him. Then he laughed again, a big, hearty, full-chested laugh. He was happy. He was ecstatic. He kicked the side of the wigwam again, making a second hole.

I had undone the holster now. I took hold of the belt ends and ran up behind Bev. Then I swung the holster with the wrench in it towards Bev's back. The holster caught Bev between his shoulder blades. Bev let out a cry of surprise mingled with pain. He thought I had only a light toy gun in there. He didn't know I had the wrench.

'What you do that for?'

I swung again, much harder than before. Bev's stride faltered. This was so unexpected. I hit him a third and a fourth time.

Bev veered sideways and ran towards the pond. I hurried after him. I swung the holster at his feet. I caught his ankle. He tripped and toppled forward on to the hard ground. Now I had Bev at my mercy.

I swung the holster with the wrench at Bev's head. I caught him on the cheek. Bev let out a cry and covered his face with his hands. I hit him again and again and again and again, always on the head or the neck or the shoulders. At first when I hit Bev he screamed. Then something seemed to go out of Bev and the noise that came out of him instead was like a sob. Then the sobbing stopped and it was a whimper. Then the whimper stopped and Bev wasn't making any noise any more. The only noise now was the noise of the holster with the wrench as it hit him on the head. The cold, clean intention with which I started was still with me. I would kill him. He would never kick my wigwam again. I was aware of my brother standing under the chestnut tree several yards away and watching what was happening.

Then, to my utter surprise, I felt arms close tight around me, followed by the sensation of being pulled backwards. I saw a pair of green sleeves. Curiously, it was exactly the same colour of green as the uniform worn by the park keepers. Then I realised it was a park keeper who had grabbed me from behind.

The park keeper shouted, 'Let go of the belt.'

I let go and the holster fell to the ground.

Bev lay still at my feet.

'You all right?' the park keeper asked Bev.

Bev moaned and muttered, 'Yes.'

'What's your name?' the park keeper asked me.

'Gébler.'

'Where d'you live?'

I pointed at our house.

'Number?'

I told him.

'You'd better go home.'

I rolled up the torn wigwam, picked up the holster and wrench, and, accompanied by my brother, I walked back to the kerb across from our house. I called and waved across. My father looked up from his desk. Then he bent down and resumed his work. I looked up and down. I saw the road was clear. I crossed the road with my brother and went into our house. I did not tell my father what had just happened.

That evening, someone knocked on our door. I went and opened the door and found a policeman. He wore a white short-sleeved shirt and blue serge trousers. He cradled his hat under his elbow. I looked down and saw the handle of his truncheon, with a leather wristband on the end, sticking out of his pocket.

'Go in the kitchen and wait,' my father said from behind.

The policeman and my father went into the study and the door was closed. I heard their voices through the wood but not what they said.

After a while the study door opened again and my father and the policeman came out into the hall. They went to the front door. The policeman said goodbye and left. My father went back into his study.

I sat on in the kitchen. I dangled the toy fob watch, swinging it backwards and forwards, then stared at the painting beside the hatch of a woman on the beach, her lustrous black hair spread on the sand behind.

'You'd better come in here,' I heard my father calling, finally. 'I want a word with you.'

I went to the study door. It was open but I knocked anyway. My knees were shaking. I wanted to pee.

'Come in,' he said, grumpily.

I went in.

My father sat at his desk. Beyond the bay window stretched the common. I saw the pavilion and the burnt-out tree.

I waited. Now my father would tell me what the policeman had said. When boys were naughty at school, Mr Ferguson gave them the slipper. I wondered if the policeman or my father would tell Mr Ferguson what I did to Bev, and if I, too, would then get the slipper as a punishment? As I stood waiting I grew more and more certain that this was what would happen. It was a frightening idea.

But my father said nothing at all. He just went on staring at the common. Then he began to write something on his typewriter and I was left standing in the middle of the floor. Perhaps he had forgotten me? I thought. The clock chimed in the hall. I looked first at the striped braces that ran down his back, then at the common where the shadows of the trees slowly lengthened across the grass, then back at his striped braces again.

Finally, he spoke. 'If you don't mind your P's and Q's,' he said, 'you're going to end up in Borstal.'

He didn't sound annoyed, but as I couldn't see his face, I couldn't be certain.

'Do you know what Borstal is?' he asked.

I didn't know exactly what it was. I also knew better than to say I didn't know. He loved it when I showed my ignorance. So I said nothing.

'It's where they lock up juvenile delinquents,' he said. 'Those boys who hang around the bottom of the road, they're the type who get locked up in a Borstal. You wouldn't like to be locked up with the likes of them, now would you?'

'No.' I said this quietly. It was true. I wouldn't want to be locked away with the Teddy boys. It was a dreadful idea.

This answer seemed to satisfy him. 'Go on,' he said, 'get out.'

chapter thirty-four

I was in Putney; we were on holiday and this was one of the days when we were due to go to my father's. My brother was sick so I knew I would have to go there alone.

'I won't go,' I said to my mother.

'You will go,' she said.

She brought me to Wimbledon station and put me in a taxi. She told the driver the address and paid him the fare.

Some minutes later the taxi pulled up outside the Cannon Hill Lane house. The driver reached round and opened the door. I got out. The driver said goodbye and began to write something in a book. I went up the path and rang the bell. The door swung back almost at once and there was Jane. Had she been hovering inside, waiting for me to arrive? I wondered.

'What's that?' she asked. She pointed at the taxi; the driver had finished writing in his book and now he was turning his cab in front of us.

I said nothing.

'Come by taxi, did we?' she continued.

I felt my face go red. I wished now I'd waited until the taxi had gone before ringing the bell.

'Don't pretend you didn't come in a taxi,' she said.

I saw I had no alternative. I nodded.

'Come all the way from Putney, did we, in that taxi?'

'No, just Wimbledon station.'

'Oh, just Wimbledon station.' She lowered her broad face so that it was level with mine. 'And I suppose if your mother hadn't sent you in a taxi, you wouldn't have come to see your poor old father, would you?'

This was true.

'You know what you are? A horrible, dirty, treacherous, unloving little boy. He's done everything for you and you've done nothing in return, nothing. You just take, take, take. It's like he says; always got the hand out, haven't we? You are a truly horrible little boy.'

I left myself and rose up; from above, I saw myself with my red face, and Jane with her arching eyebrows and lips like lengths of plug wire.

I saw myself starting to cry, quietly. I saw Jane smirking. But this wasn't the victory she thought it was. She didn't know I had gone to a place far beyond her reach.

'Anyway, as you're here, you'd better come in,' she said.

She stepped back into the hall. I slipped back into myself. I felt shaky. I swallowed to try and stop myself crying. I rubbed my sleeve over my eyes. I stepped into the hall. There was a powerful smell of sulphur.

'Bring him through,' I heard my father shouting. He sounded cheerful.

I went down to the kitchen. My father was rinsing sulphur off the bunches of black-blue grapes he had just cut from the vine.

'Grape juice?' he asked.

'Yes,' I said. I liked grape juice.

He filled the glass reservoir of the blender with grapes and flicked a Bakelite switch. The propeller whizzed inside. The fruit sank downwards as it was sliced up, then bubbled and frothed upwards. My father turned off the machine. He strained the juice into a glass and handed it to me. I drank. The grape juice was warm and thick. It tasted faintly of chalk. I finished the glass.

'You'd better show him the letter,' said Jane.

'Oh yes, the letter,' said my father. 'Do you think it'll upset him?'

I had a good idea, I thought, what this was about.

'Upset him,' said Jane blandly. 'I don't know, what do you think?'

My heart began to race.

'I don't know,' said my father. 'You're the teacher, you're the expert.'

'Depends if he knows what stupid is, or not?'

'Well, if he doesn't, he'll certainly know after he's digested the contents of this.'

Now I knew for certain what they were talking about.

My father took an envelope from the top of the wireless and handed it to me.

'Go on,' he said, 'open it. Face your future, go on, take it on the chin.'

I pulled out the letter that was inside. I unfolded the letter. I saw by the address at the top that it was from the Local Education Authority. The letter said I had achieved a 'D' in my Eleven-Plus. I had failed.

'You'll have to go to the secondary modern in Wimbledon,' said my father.

'Oh, little Lord Snooty won't like that,' said Jane. 'He'll have to mix with the riff-raff.'

'It'll knock the rough edges off him, might even do him some good.'

'It might,' Jane agreed.

chapter thirty-five

I started secondary school in September. There was a primary school adjacent and my brother transferred here so that we could travel to and from school together. We were still commuting; Monday, Wednesday and Friday nights we were in Cannon Hill Lane; the other nights of the week we were in Deodar Road. At some point my mother told me she had decided to seek a divorce and that she would ask for full custody. This was set in train but she explained these things took time and that was why nothing had happened yet.

On 25 October 1965, my father received notice from his solicitors of my mother's divorce application. One Wednesday, about three weeks later, I found my father waiting in the hall when I got in from school with my brother.

'Get in to my study,' he ordered us.

I followed my brother into the study. I noticed a pot of sealing wax bubbling on the stove.

'Sit down,' my father said.

We both sat down on the sofa.

'It's crunch time. It's make-your-mind-up time,' he said. 'Do you want to live with me, or do you want to live with your mother in Putney? You must decide, right now, and you must write your answer down.'

He told my brother to leave the room. Then he handed me a Biro, a piece of Basildon Bond writing paper, and a record sleeve (with a record inside it) to rest the paper on. It was Shostakovich's Symphony No. 7, the 'Leningrad', one of his favourite records.

'Now, you write down who you want to live with, do you understand? And remember, what you say now is binding. This is when you decide on the shape of the rest of your life. Do you want to lead a good life or do you want to throw it down the drain? And you won't leave here until I have an answer. Do you understand me?'

He went out of the study and closed the door behind him.

I looked at the record sleeve. Written across the top were the words, without any capital letters, 'the czech philharmonic orchestra conducted by karel ancerl'.

What did I write?

And at the bottom, 'a new high-fidelity recording/a deluxe two-record set'.

I didn't want to write anything. But unless I wrote something, he wouldn't let me out of the room. I'd be here for ever.

I stared out the window. The leafless branches of the trees on the common were black against the grey sky. The distant pavilion was a dark brown smudge. The wind blew. The woodbine that grew outside made a small tapping sound against the glass.

I could leave myself now, I thought, and float up. But what would that achieve? Nothing. This could not be postponed. I would have to write something down.

I could lie, I thought, and say I wanted to live with my

father. I shuddered at the idea. If I wrote that down, it might come to pass and then I might never see my mother again. It was better, surely, to write the truth; yes, he'd rage, yes, he'd call me weak and corrupt, pusillanimous and venal – I could predict all that – and yes, that would be the end of us, him and me, for ever; but better that than a course of action that might take me away from my mother.

There was nothing else for it. I just had to do it. I clicked the end of the Biro and wrote:

17 November 1965

To my Dear DAD
I must admit I prefere living in Putney at the moment. But in years to come I will probly have a different atti- tude. I just don't know.
Signed your loving son Carlos xxx

I looked at what I had written and read it back to myself. He would not like it. No, it was worse than that. Once he had read this and he knew, without any doubt, what it was I wanted, even though I had said that later in my life I might think dif- ferently and I might want to be with him, something between us would be severed, and that something, once cut, could never be repaired thereafter. He would never forgive this. Never. What we had now hardly amounted to anything; but, once he read this, the possibility of him ever loving me (for which I still secretly yearned) would be ruled out, for ever.

My knees trembled and at the back of my throat I got the raw feeling I always felt before I cried. But I must not cry, I thought, I must not.

'You done in there?' he called from outside.

'Yes,' I called back.

The study door burst open and my father came in.

'Let me see,' he said.

I proffered the piece of paper. He took it brusquely. He carried it over to his desk, sat down, put on his glasses, lifted up the piece of paper I had written and clicked on the light.

'Get out of here,' he said, 'get out of here and send in that brother.'

chapter thirty-six

My mother went to court and applied for sole custody. (This was a separate action from the divorce; that was still trundling through the system and it was not finally granted until 12 May 1967.) The judge granted her application. We began to live with her full-time. Once or twice a week, at her insistence, she would send us to Cannon Hill Lane to see our father.

One afternoon, in the early summer of 1966, I came in from the nice new preparatory school to which my mother had recently sent me (it was the kind of place where the girls wore seersucker dresses and straw boaters and there was an after-school chess club – I thought it was bliss) and discovered that she had arranged for us to visit my father. I wasn't pleased. *The Avengers* was on television that night but I knew we wouldn't be back until after it was over.

I said I didn't want to go. My mother said I had to. The arrangement was made; it couldn't be broken; my father was expecting my brother and myself.

In the end, my mother could only get me to agree to go on

the understanding that if there was any change left over from the taxi money (as my father wouldn't collect us, the last part of the journey, from Wimbledon station to Cannon Hill Lane, was always made by taxi), I could split it with my brother and spend it on sweets and comics.

Our taxi arrived at the house on Cannon Hill. I paid the driver and then we got out. We waited while the taxi turned and drove away (we knew better than to let my father and Jane see how we had come in case they used it against us), then we went to the front door. I rang the bell. After a while my father appeared and looked at us gravely. I said, 'Hello,' and without saying a word he stepped back to allow us to pass inside. I could tell there was something unpleasant coming but it was too late to escape.

I went down the hall and into the kitchen. Jane sat at the breakfast counter reading the *Wimbledon Borough News*. She greeted me with unusual cheerfulness and warmth. Now I knew for certain something was looming. Whenever she was especially friendly, something unpleasant always followed. Whether this was a trick to put us at our ease or her way of distancing herself from what was imminent, I could never decide.

We talked for a few moments about my nice new preparatory school. Jane, a self-declared socialist who normally disapproved of private education, was surprisingly generous and uncritical this afternoon.

While we spoke I heard my father coming into the kitchen. He reached for a couple of sheets of paper that were lying on top of the wireless. They were sheets of American quarto typing paper and I saw the top sheet was covered with the big black letters made by his Remington typewriter.

Out of the corner of my eye I saw my father glance at the papers. I heard him chuckle quietly at something he read; I guessed these were the notes he was going to read from when he gave us the dressing-down that I knew for certain was coming.

My stomach prickled and my thighs wobbled. The worst part of an ordeal like this was the anticipation. Once it actually started, I always felt relieved. This was not because my father's words were never as bad as I had imagined. On the contrary, they were usually worse than I imagined; he could cause pain with his words like nobody else that I knew. Nonetheless, it was always better once the ordeal started because then (knowing it couldn't go on for ever) I could tell myself that it must, at some point in the not-too-distant future, come to an end.

'Come to the study,' my father said, in his most mild and disarming way.

I went down the hallway and turned into the study. I sat on the sofa. My brother sat beside me. Jane stood in the doorway, beaming, the white face of the grandfather clock looming over her shoulder.

It was early June. The windows were open and young leaves were showing on the trees outside. Children were playing cricket with their father on the level ground just in front. They were using orange boxes for wickets.

'Shall we look at the facts?' said my father smoothly. 'You were living half with your father and half with your mother.'

He glanced at the papers leaning against the typewriter.

'"You left your father completely to live with your mother on your own choice, although you were already living four days a week with her."'

He was in profile; I saw his forehead, his nose, large and flat like my own, and his strong chin. His shirtsleeves were rolled up and the T-shirt sleeves underneath ran down his forearms like cladding on a pipe.

'"You abandoned your father completely although he had never been even unkind to you. You went to live entirely with your mother because you said it was 'nicer' there. You had a television in your bedroom on which you could watch any rubbish you wanted, any time you wanted, and you were free to do more or less what you liked."'

I heard the whack of a tennis ball being hit by a cricket bat.

"'That is now over six months ago, isn't it?'"

The little boy who had hit the ball now began to run.

"'During that whole six months you have never once, not once, written a letter to your father. You have never phoned him purely to ask how he was, i.e. if he was lonely, if he was sick, if he'd like you to call and help him clean up the house, though there is a telephone in your mother's hall.

"'You have *never* asked to come and spend extra time with him. You have *never* asked if there was anything you could do for him. Your attitude has a sort of calculated contempt to it . . .'"

The little boy was back to the stumps where he started. A girl bowled, the ties of her dress streaming behind.

"'It is obvious to me now that you come to visit me for an hour or two once or twice every week solely because your mother tells you to.'"

Bat and ball connected again.

"'You have forgotten, obviously, that for eleven years of our lives I have tucked you in at night, and cared for you with love and attention.'"

The tennis ball flew high. The boy dropped his cricket bat, made as if to run, then stopped.

"'Your visits of an hour or two simply remind me afresh each time of waste and desolation, as well as depressing me for days so I cannot work.'"

The father of the cricket-playing children ran swiftly across the grass.

"'I am trying to regain my peace and write as I used to.'"

Shouts of 'Howzat'.

"'You come here with ill-grace and the result is depression and pain for me.'"

Cheers and hurrahs from the girl who bowled.

"'You have no apparent feelings in the matter; and it appears to me you would save yourselves an extra hour or two a week in which to watch television by not coming to see me for the next couple of months, or even longer. You would also relieve me from that weekly reminder of the kind of cold, cruel and unfeeling children I once founded my life on.'"

The girl went to the stump swinging the bat, her shirt streaming behind her.

"'On your weekly call you are so careful never to speak of anything of your life in Putney and the only reason for that can be that you are under orders by your mother. Your weekly hour or two here, with your blank non-communicating faces, and your lack of all normal feelings in the matter, and the destructive effect it still has on me, makes me think your visits are not simply pointless but dangerous.'"

The girl took her place.

"'Your conduct towards me has been outrageous, as your mother's conduct was outrageous. There is no reason why I should suffer it. And as you see no reason why you should see me, let me put an end to it.'"

The boy bowled. Bat connected with ball and trickled across the grass. The girl began to run. She was in bare feet.

"'I can only hope that as you grow you may come by some humanity but I really have no hope of that; the conditions in which you live are against it, as is, apparently, your heredity.'"

'Good, Anne, that's one run,' the voice of the father drifted in from outside.

"'You may well be drawn to ask in years to come,'" said my father, "'why you have no father. I hope your mother will be able to give you an answer.'"

He folded the paper he'd read from. He was finished.

We went back to the kitchen. We had strong brown tea, tomatoes and brown bread. Jane talked non-stop. Around eight o'clock, my father said he would drive us to Wimbledon station. I heard him reverse the car out of the garage. He sounded the horn. We went out and got into the roomy leathery rear of CDF 22.

At Wimbledon station we said goodbye to him and got out. He drove CDF 22 around the turning circle and drove away.

A few minutes later I was back on the platform at which I had arrived earlier. The indicator board said a District Line train would soon be along. A British Rail express hurtled through, after which, in the unusual silence, I saw a swift skimming nimbly along under the station roof.

chapter thirty-seven

I walked along the street with my mother. We were in the West End of London. There were big houses with stucco façades and black railings around the basement wells. There were also big red-brick blocks of flats. A man waved from the window of one of these and called to us.

A few minutes later we were in his flat. He was introduced as Jack Clayton, the film director. He was making a film, he explained, called *Our Mother's House*; a mother dies and the children, fearing they will be separated once the authorities learn their mother is dead, go on living together as if nothing has happened. He was looking for someone, he said, to play the oldest son. That's why he called us up. He'd seen me in the street and thought I might do. Maybe. Would my mother let me audition?

A few days later I was back. Jack Clayton gave me my lines and told me I was to light a fire. There were twigs and news-papers lying on the hearth, ready for me.

I knelt down and started. The words were simple. So was

fire-making. I twisted the paper, threw on the twigs and hey presto. I had lit the fire in Cannon Hill Lane so often I didn't have to think.

A few days later Jack Clayton telephoned my mother. I had got the part. No one at my prep school believed me when I told them.

About a month later, very early one morning, I was taken by car to the studios and then brought on to the stage. The set was a bedroom in an old house. The walls were painted on canvas flats; the furniture was old and rickety. There were film lights shining everywhere. The air was hot. A woman introduced herself.

'I'm your tutor,' she said. 'Is there anything you especially want to do?'

The children at my new school had all done Latin for years in preparation for the Common Entrance exam. I hadn't and now I saw I had an opportunity here to catch up.

'Latin,' I said.

I was taken to wardrobe and put in costume – an old jersey and horrible corduroy shorts. I was brought back to the set. There an actress was lying in the brass bed which previously was empty. This was my mother, I was told, and she was dead. In the scene I had to look at her, then open the door and say to my sister, 'Our mother's dead.'

A woman put drops in my eyes and streaked glycerin for tears on my cheeks.

I went to my starting mark. The actress on the bed winked at me. She didn't seem at all dead. On the contrary, she seemed very much alive and well. I wouldn't be able to look at her and think she was dead. I knew that. So I decided to imagine it was my own mother who was dead in the bed and not her. After a few seconds I felt a trembling in my stomach. This was exactly the kind of feeling I knew I'd get if this was really happening.

A man called out, 'Mark it.'

The clapperboard was tapped.

I looked at the corpse. That's my mother, I thought again. My stomach fluttered. I walked over to the door, opened it. 'Our mother's dead,' I said to the girl outside.

I repeated the action a few more times; then I went to the classroom and spent the day with the tutor.

The days that followed were all the same as this first one. At some point I'd have to say something over and over again or look out a window; that was the work part of the day; for the rest of the time, I was with my teacher. I had her undivided attention; she taught only me. It was paradise.

It was a Sunday evening, a couple of weeks later. For supper we had lamb chops, peas and mint jelly. This was what we always had on a Sunday evening. Afterwards, I went to my bedroom to get ready for bed. I had to be back on set the following morning.

The telephone rang and I heard my mother pick up the receiver in the hall. She was on the phone for a long time. Then I heard her put down the phone and start to cry.

She came into the bedroom. I was sitting on the bottom bunk and I stood up. I knew what she was going to say even before she got the words out. My father had contacted the producers, she said. He had said they had not got his permission to employ me; he had threatened legal action. The producers had no alternative. They had re-cast the part. The following morning I would not be going back to the studio, my mother said. I would be going back to school instead.

Later that night, I lay on the bottom bunk. The curtains weren't fully closed and the yellow light from the streetlamp outside lit up the ceiling.

I was not surprised. How could I be? When I wrote the

note saying I preferred to be with my mother, hadn't I known it would cut something that could not, afterwards, ever be repaired? This was simply the consequence of my action. There was no point in complaining.

On the plus side, at least I was living with my mother. Imagine, I thought, if I was living with my father, even for part of the week, and this was going on? It didn't bear thinking about.

At the same time as thinking this, I also felt an ache, somewhere between the solar plexus and the spine.

This feeling always came when I was sad or disappointed. However, perhaps this time, I thought, because I knew exactly what was making me feel as I did, it would soon go away.

But it didn't. Understanding didn't appear to help. I realised I would simply have to put up with it. After a while the pain would fade. It always did in the end.

I went on staring at the ceiling, and by the light of the streetlamp I made myself count the bumps.

chapter thirty-eight

We stood in a corner of the farmyard at Wern Watkin. We were myself, my brother, and our friend Roc. The sheep were driven in through a gate on the other side of the yard. When they were all through, the gate was closed.

The sheep clustered in the corner furthest from us. Their wool was white if you didn't look closely, but grey when you did. Their coats were dirty where they brushed the ground and had bits of twig and fern caught up in them. The animals were nervous. An hour earlier, they were free on the hills; now they were trapped in the yard with us. Droppings poured endlessly out of their backsides. These were round and black, and glistened like olives.

Roc was a bit younger than me and a bit older than my brother. He lived in Deodar Road too. That's how we knew him. His parents were the author Nell Dunn and the playwright Jeremy Sandford and they owned this small Welsh hill farm outside Crickhowell in south Wales. We were staying there, as we had many times before, and today we were going to do some real farm work. We were going to help with the sheep. I was excited.

On the far side of the yard, the shepherd opened a small door at the side of a shed and told us to drive the sheep in.

I waved my arms and ran forward calling, 'Go-on, go-in,' the words elided to form a single guttural exclamation. As I had observed, this was how men who moved animals always spoke when they were working.

The sheep surged for the doorway and began to squeeze into the shed like commuters trying to force their way on to an overcrowded train. It was strangely thrilling that a little arm waving and shouting could produce a reaction like this.

When the animals were all in, the shed door was closed. I looked across the empty dung-strewn yard at the stone farmhouse with its grey slate roof. Inside, the house smelt of cider and condensed milk but out here the smell was wet peat, wet stone and sheep.

The shepherd came and gave me a large pair of clippers. These comprised two handles that looked like the legs of a pair of tongs, and two large ugly blades kept apart by a spring.

I followed him into the shed. It was unexpectedly warm and the mutton smell was far stronger than in the yard.

The shepherd grabbed a ewe, turned her over and pinned her between his knees. She kicked a few times, then went quiet. The hair on her belly was short with dark nipples rising through it. They looked like a line of thimbles.

The shepherd took the ewe's right leg and, with a few sweeps of his clippers, cleaned away the filth on the end to reveal the hoof below. It comprised of two hairy knuckles, with a lump of horn, like a knobbly piece of fudge, growing out of each.

The shepherd explained that first I had to check all round the foot. If I saw anything strawberry red, that was foot rot, and I was to call him. Then I had to trim the nails. He pinched the edge of a nail between the blades of his clippers and squeezed. A filthy piece fluttered away. The new exposed nail face was white and grey like salt and pepper, except where pin-pricks of blood began to leak through. Finally, the shepherd explained, when I'd done a sheep, front and rear, I was to put her in the yard.

The moment to start had arrived. I grabbed hold of the sheep the shepherd was holding. The fleece felt oily, dense and wiry.

The man released the ewe and I began to manoeuvre her between my knees. She struggled. I feared I would not be strong enough to hold her. But I got her between my knees and pressed until I felt her ribs. She scrabbled and shuddered and then fell still. I took a hoof, closed the clippers over the nail, and cut. A piece of nail fluttered down. I was on my way. I could do this . . .

When all the sheep had been checked for foot rot and the job was done, Roc's father, Jeremy, said he'd take us riding as a reward. We saddled the ponies and rode off. At first we went through fields. Then we reached heathland. The ground con-sisted of a series of rising hillocks that were, in turn, part of Llangattock mountain. Some of the little hillocks were extraordinarily steep. As my pony dashed up one bracken-covered incline after another, its muscles straining, its breathing loud and forced, I felt as if I was riding an enormous piece of rope which a giant was snapping and cracking.

Eventually, we reached the Dramway, a grassy road that ran along the side of Llangattock mountain. Years earlier there was a narrow-gauge railway line here, used to carry slate from an old mine, now abandoned.

We cantered along. It was a good flat ride. After a while we came to a tall slender rock, very very high, which stood on a mound to the side of the Dramway. Peaky Stone (or the Lonely Shepherd as it was also known) had the features of a face if

you looked closely enough. It was like one of the stone heads
on Easter Island, which I had seen on television.

We were very high here and the clouds were low. Wreaths of
cloud mist floated and swirled just out of reach. There was a
smell of wet earth and bracken, of leather and saddle soap, of
cud and saliva. The ponies had snatched mouthfuls of grass on
the way up and were still chewing.

We turned to go home. We were all in high spirits.

When we got back to Wern Watkin and the ground was
level, we started to race. I chased my brother and Roc across a
field. I stood in the stirrups and urged my pony on. They were
in front; they opened a gate, intending to go through and
escape. I came up behind, intending to overtake.

As I came through, a gust of wind caught the gate and it
closed behind me. The bars smacked against the back legs of
my pony. The pony whinnied and slithered. The terrified
animal tried to escape the gate, but rather than going forwards
and into the field beyond, it went sideways.

I saw the gatepost coming towards me, although in fact I
was the one who was going towards it. I saw the large nail
sticking out of it. It was a six-inch nail with a round head like
a grey unblinking eye. When the gate was closed, the string
that kept it shut was tied to this nail. I had tied and untied
string from around this nail many times myself.

The head of the nail somehow struck the side of the knee
that was against the saddle. I vaguely wondered if the skin
would tear and the knee bone would shatter? I was also
vaguely aware of my brother and Roc astride their ponies, a
few feet away, half-turned in their saddles, looking back
towards me, appalled.

I lifted my leg away from the nail and, at the same time, I
began to tumble backwards. The pony went forwards. I went
on moving backwards. Next thing, the pony was racing across
the field and I was dragging along behind, my left foot caught

in the stirrup. I felt the left back foot of the pony pounding the ground beside my head. I felt the long wet grass swish past. I saw the animal's sweating flank above me and the low grey sky beyond. I felt no pain. I had no fear. I believe I was just slightly above the ground and sliding on air. I was certain I would not collide with anything.

Finally, my foot came out of the stirrup. Suddenly, I was still and so was the sky. I heard the hoof beats of my brother's and Roc's ponies as they raced up. Then I saw them. From where I lay it was the faces of the ponies that I saw best, the mushroom-grey mouths, soft and creased, the bridle bits encased in spittle that was stiff and had body like beaten egg white on the end of a whisk.

Nell came out of the farmhouse, lifted me up and hugged me. She told me that the thing to do now was to get straight back on again. That way I would not be frightened the next time I went to ride.

My pony had gone to God knows where, so Jeremy offered me his pony. It was white and fierce and frisky. I was nervous but I got up in the saddle and I cantered unenthusiastically around the field a couple of times. Before the fall, when I chased on my pony through the fields, I was excited. Now I felt neither fear nor pain, just boredom and irritation. I just wanted to go inside the house and sleep.

That night I began to wheeze horribly. I was in the bottom tier of a wooden bunk, my brother and Roc above. I recited the words I always said but they had no effect. The attack raged all night. It was only in the morning that I finally got to sleep.

When I woke up much later, I noticed my knee felt sore and very heavy. I wriggled out of my sleeping bag and pulled up the leg of my pyjamas. My knee had swollen up like a balloon, and the flesh was black and white, quite like the colour of a badger, with a livid yellow eye in the centre where the nail hit.

I plumped up my pillows and lay back. The exertion of

looking at my knee was enough to set off a new attack. I'd be wheezing again soon, I realised.

I began the magic words. 'I must not be ill. I will not be ill . . .'

As I chanted, I stared through the window, at the other end of the dusty room, at dark green grass and a grey, louring sky outside. It was pointless. Within a few minutes, every tube felt as if it was being pulled and stretched like an elastic band by a pair of rough, strong hands.

Why weren't the words working? I was puzzled. Usually, when I got in quick with them, I could stop an attack worsening. Why not this morning?

The wheezing intensified to a hacking roar. I felt hot and feeble and slightly dizzy.

Minutes passed. I thought of nothing except air. Then, out of the blue, I wondered, Why do I have these attacks?

Something to do with my father, I replied to myself. Yes.

My mother and father were divorcing. We'd live with her. I wouldn't have to see him again. Not if I didn't want to. My mother wasn't happy with this. She wanted my brother and me to keep up contact. Wanted. But she couldn't force me. No. If I didn't want to, I could just say no, couldn't I? I never had to go and see him ever again. Never. Not unless I chose. Never. And if I chose not to go, well, I just didn't go, did I? It was as simple as that. And if I didn't see him any more, then there'd be no more attacks. They'd be finished. Done with. Gone. For ever . . .

Slowly, those staccato thoughts lengthened into sentences that were syntactically complete. Simultaneously, the sensation of rough hands stretching the tubes in my chest began to recede. The tubes began to unclench and open. Suddenly, the air was washing through me freely and I was breathing normally again. I swallowed one huge delicious draught after another.

That was the last full-blown asthma attack I ever had.

chapter thirty-nine

I n *Such, Such Were the Joys*, George Orwell describes his preparatory school as an expensive, snobbish, nasty, philistine Hell. In Lindsay Anderson's *If*, a fictional public school is depicted in much the same light.

However, not every private school was like this. One of these was Bedales. Here were no stuffy masters in black gowns. No uniforms. No prefects. No beating. No quaint rituals. No gruesome initiation rites. No Anglican ethos. No tyranny.

It was co-educational. All creeds and colours were welcome. It was child-centred. It had a reputation for tolerance and gentleness. But it was disciplined too (accounts of Bedalians smoking pot or having sex with their teachers did not appear in the *News of the World*) and, finally, it was academic. Most pupils went on to higher education and quite a few to Oxbridge.

In 1968 my brother sat the entrance exam. He stayed in the school for three nights and two days. There were IQ, English and mathematics tests; the rest of the time he played while the teachers observed him and the other applicants to see how they would fit in to the school. Traditionally, these tests were in early January, but my brother is certain he went in the summer. (It was an extra test week, perhaps?) He remembers the evening light flooding his dormitory, and the incessant talk of the other boys that kept him awake. If he was tired it didn't appear to matter; the school offered him a place.

My mother then asked the school if they would take me as a pupil though I hadn't undergone the admission process. After some simple mathematics and English tests, and an interview with the headmaster, the school said they would take me as well as my brother.

My mother was happy. I received the news blankly. How could they admit me? I wondered. I had neither sat the entrance tests nor undertaken the entrance procedure? It was my brother who had gone down, stayed in a dormitory, and done what was required.

Bedales had agreed to take me, I decided, only because that was the way to get him. He was the one they really wanted. I'd got in on his coat-tails rather than on my own merits. Much as I hated to admit this, perhaps there was something in what my father and Jane had always said. I was wanting, run-of-the-mill, middling, and that was what this proved. Obviously.

I knew this was wrong even as I thought it. I knew I must not believe what my father and Jane said. I knew they said these things because they didn't like me. I knew this intellectually. Yet no matter how hard I tried to persuade myself not to believe, I still couldn't stop myself. My father and Jane were right and that was proved by the way I'd got in to Bedales. Naturally, I kept these feelings to myself.

I started boarding at Bedales in September 1968.

chapter forty

It was March or April 1969. I was fourteen and a half years old. I was home in Deodar Road for the Easter holidays. I was still occasionally in touch with my father. I acquiesced with my mother's wish that contact be maintained and magnanimously he still allowed us to visit, despite what he had said to the contrary. Thus, one afternoon, I went over to Cannon Hill Lane; for some reason I went alone. It was Jane who opened the door.

'Oh, it's Lord Snooty,' she called down the hall.

My father sat at the breakfast counter in the kitchen. 'Tell him we're not having any snobs today,' he called. 'No snobs here today. Snobs come back tomorrow.'

He said this as if I was bound to hugely enjoy his jokey allusion to my new status as a public school boy. I said nothing. I had only just arrived and I already wished I hadn't come.

'But, Ernie,' Jane shouted back, 'surely you wouldn't turn him away now? He's come all the way from Putney by public transport. He's had to mix with the *hoi polloi*; it must have been awful for him.' She'd forgotten I did the last leg by taxi.

I disengaged and rose out of myself. It was a while since I had done this but I hadn't lost the knack. My father said something; I didn't hear what. Once I was out of myself, words didn't touch me and this, in turn, deprived them of the pleasure of knowing they had affected me. This was my victory.

I saw Jane was smiling. I rejoined myself.

'Your father's on good form today,' she said, and winked. She was trying to trick me. She wanted me to think she would be my friend, my ally. She had tried to do this before. Of course, this was out of the question. In the end, no matter how much she pretended we might or could be friends, she could never be my friend. She was his friend. In the end, she would always take my father's side, always.

'In you come, ducks,' she said, in her mock George Formby accent.

I went in. The hall smelt of anthracite and lanolin. I heard Jane close the door. I touched the glass-like top of the hideous Burmese table, then went to the grandfather clock with its creamy face and booming tick.

I had the feeling, suddenly, that no time at all had elapsed since my last visit. It was if I had stepped out the front door, then turned around and immediately stepped back in again. Everything was exactly the same.

Jane made tea and we sat in the kitchen together. I sat at the breakfast counter with my father; Jane sat in her chair by the stove.

'How's the snob school?' my father asked.

I said it was fine, and I liked it. I said it was a friendly, progressive, co-educational school and not at all like your traditional public school. For instance, I said, we called teachers by their first names.

My father nodded. 'Oh really,' he said.

I knew he wasn't interested. He was interested only in what he was about to say. His argument was steaming towards me like a battleship. I could see the smoke over the horizon and any moment now the attack would start. First he'd blast Bedales. Next, he'd say I was a spoilt child, a snob. Then he'd turn his guns against my mother. Finally, he would say I was just like her and what a disappointment it was to him that I had turned out so badly. These were his themes and I didn't imagine he had changed them, any more than the house had changed since my last visit. But there was one change; it was me; I could predict what was coming and that, in turn, made me think I probably wouldn't have to float off like I had when I arrived. I was getting bigger, older, more able for him, for them.

'Most people in this world get what they deserve,' he said. He spoke precisely.

'And in a way there is a kind of justice that you should become a victim of the English public school system.'

Here we go, I thought. I knew he would have prepared what he said in his head and most likely have rehearsed it with Jane as well.

'With your peasant origins, your school will turn you into a phony upper-class snob.'

He spoke quietly and gently although his words were nasty.

'Your grandmother in Clare boasted by having her house stuffed with vulgar objects,' he said.

By appearing polite, even though his meaning was hostile, he hoped to make me uncertain as to whether this was a row or a conversation. He used this trick with adults as well.

'And in turn,' he continued, 'your mother boasts by her idiot flamboyance and by sending you to a public school to acquire an upper-class accent among strangers and institutional food.'

He had another reason for his tone too – self-defence. I knew that if I challenged him, he would turn and wonder aloud, in all innocence, Why are you angry, Carlo, I'm being reasonable. I'm trying to tell you something that might help you in life. You're the one who's being unreasonable . . .

'You may remember,' he continued, 'that I warned you that when you became a nuisance she'd pack you off to boarding school.'

I didn't remember him saying this but there was no point saying so. He would just say he had and that typically I had forgotten this disagreeable truth. I looked at the fob lying in its usual place on top of the wireless.

'The natural people for children to be with are their parents – and the most natural and valuable human being for a son to be with is his father.'

I looked through the hatch into the dining room with its shiny black and white floor tiles.

'Your mother's gift to you was *not* to start you off in life with your father's abilities but with a fake accent.'

I wondered, vaguely, how long before he finished.

'And serve you bloody well right. Your conduct has proved that you have inherited the O'Brien false-heartedness and mean-mindedness.'

'Tea?' said Jane, suddenly, as if we were having a perfectly normal conversation. She sprang from her chair and took the teapot from the stove.

'I never say no to tea,' said my father. 'Never.'

He held out his cup. Jane poured dark brown tea into it.

'You have been denied the considerable resources of a man such as I am,' said my father, 'as you will discover when you come to have to fight to earn a living.'

'Oh, stop worrying the boy,' said Jane jovially. 'He's got O levels and A levels to worry about and then he'll have a private income from his mother to live on for the rest of his life. He'll sponge, not work, so be quiet.'

She turned to me.

'More tea? Now don't you pay any attention to what he's saying; your father's just a big bear with a sore head who loves you really.'

The end was in sight. She always made mollifying comments just before the end. This allowed the conversation to continue as if nothing had been said.

I held out my cup and she began to fill it. The kitchen smells of Bemax and olive oil mingled with that of tannin. This was a performance yet they fondly imagined that I believed it was spontaneous. They had to be stupid, I thought, to imagine I would not spot how contrived this was. My father had prepared what he wanted to say. Now Jane was doing her bit.

'The only thing that I really regret in my life is the day I met your mother,' my father continued.

Oh yes, the end was coming. He always ended with my mother. No surprises there. I felt bored, really, really bored.

'That was the worst thing that ever happened to me.'

He picked up the black-handled knife and grasped the brown loaf on the bread board.

'But perhaps I should be a little thankful. You'd have gone on living here but for her, and I'd have lavished on you the normal human affection of father to son, only later to discover I was saddled with an unfeeling, soulless zombie who was only interested in what he could get – his mother all over again – so really, I should be thankful she took you off my hands.'

He sawed at the loaf. A slice toppled sideways. He lifted the slab on the flat of his knife and put it on my plate.

'Try Jane's gooseberry jam. Not bad, you know.'

He pointed at the jar of dark green jelly with the label, in Jane's neat hand, 'C.H.L. Gooseberry, 1968.'

Later that evening, back in Putney, I sat in my bedroom. I no longer slept on the ground floor but at the top of the house. The bedroom walls followed the slope of the roof outside. Pale evening sunshine shone through the window and made a bright long oblong on the wall opposite.

I thought about my visit to Cannon Hill Lane. I was out-growing my father and Jane. I had not yet completely outgrown them, of course. Not yet. But I would. One day I would. I felt certain.

Yet I still didn't want to go back, ever, even though the effect they had on me was diminishing. Why would I want to listen to my father telling me how vile my mother was, how awful I was, and how awful my ghastly snob school was? Why? There was no reason I could imagine.

But even as I thought all this, I knew that I would go back; I would accede to my mother's request that I go. That's the only reason, I told myself, that I went and would continue to go.

Beneath this, however, there was another, deeper truth of which I was aware but which I did not think about; I'd go because I could never allow myself to abandon the connection for ever. Despite everything that had happened, I was still determined to cling on, on the off chance that my father's attitude towards me would change. I also knew perfectly well, of course, that this was hopeless and that he would never change. But still . . .

I stared at the white oblong. As the sun sank outside, it trembled and faded.

I yearned for attachment while knowing it was pointless. I dreamt of a future for us, even though I knew there would be none and it was stupid to hope there would be. It flew in the face of all the evidence. And yet . . .

I was like a compass needle near the north pole; I could never settle on one direction or one line of thought and stick to it; instead, I whizzed uselessly round and round, unable to find true north.

chapter forty-one

Ernest Gébler in November 1968 with
his American Academy Award, won for
England for *Call Me Daddy*, the TV
adaptation of *Shall I Eat You Now?*

I n literary terms my father was fairly successful during the
late 1960s (although it infuriated him that he was not as
successful as my mother). He wrote a number of television
plays of which the most successful was *Call Me Daddy*. He
won an American Academy Award for this play in 1968. He

turned the television play into a book. It was published in Britain as *Shall I Eat You Now?* Various film moguls (his term) expressed an interest in the book. Ben Arbeid took an option; my father wrote the screenplay from which a film called *Hoffman* was subsequently made. It starred Peter Sellers and Sinead Cusack and was directed by Alvin Rakoff. According to his diaries my father was paid twenty-one thousand pounds for the screenplay, which was a lot of money in 1969.

In April 1970, the year after *Hoffman*, my father abruptly sold Cannon Hill Lane and went to live in Dublin with Jane. In May, at an auction, he bought Cnoc Aluin in Coliemore Road, Dalkey. This was the old house-cum-fortress with the thick walls that was his final house. I remember nothing about the sale of Cannon Hill Lane or his return to Ireland. I don't think he told me about it. I think he and Jane just upped sticks and left and I only found out later.

Around the same time my mother sold her house in Putney and we moved too.

The new house was in Chelsea. There was a square in front filled with old trees and enclosed with London railings painted shiny black. Encouraged by my teacher, I delved into the local history. In the nineteenth century our lovely square was the home of a gallows, I discovered, and among those hanged on it was a house-breaker who had robbed one of the houses near to ours. It was hard to conceive that little more than a hundred years later, tall old trees and flowerbeds obliterated all evidence of what had been. My interest in history had its roots in early childhood when I spent hours in my father's study, thumbing through his books on the settlement of America. Early experience, of course, shapes later interests, but it was to be quite a while before I got the hang of that.

chapter forty-two

Bedales offered parents (and children) an assessment by an educational psychologist. This was an extra; parents paid for it. The test was conducted as pupils entered the sixth form and I decided to take it. I was curious to know about myself. That's what I told myself, anyway. The truth was that I had never sloughed off what I was told by my father and, to a lesser extent, Jane. What I hoped was that the test would say I wasn't stupid.

A week or so after sitting the test, the psychologist summoned me to his office in the school administration block. He said he wanted to do further tests.

He gave me a set of cards with words on them. I had to combine these into longer words. He also showed me geometrical drawings and asked me questions about them.

When I finished he said he wished to have a chat. I wondered if he had some good news for me. Perhaps he had discovered I was especially talented in some way I had never known. But I knew this was an absurd fantasy. I'd hoped to challenge my father's opinion with these tests but now, I guessed, they were going to confirm what my father had always said.

The psychologist spoke about the word test I had just finished. It showed an unusually large vocabulary, he said.

I waited.

I was interested in writing and in literature, was I?

I said I was.

He wasn't surprised, he said. He thought I was probably creative, although he couldn't be absolutely certain. This wasn't an exact science.

On the other hand, my mother was quite a well-known writer, wasn't she?

Yes, I agreed.

And my father? he asked. What did he do?

My father was a writer as well, I explained.

Oh, two writers in the family. Then there was an even higher likelihood, he thought, that like them I might end up a writer. Yes, a very good chance. And if not a novelist, then a journalist. Yes, a journalist. Yes, that's probably what I'd end up as – a journalist.

My sense of foreboding grew sharper. It was the way he distinguished between novelist and journalist, placing the former over the latter, and then saying the latter was for me that did it.

You want to go university? he asked.

I told him that yes, I did.

And you want to read English? he asked.

I said that yes, that was the plan.

He cleared his throat. Thus far, we had made small-talk; now came the difficult bit. His cough told me this.

How could I have expected anything but bad to come of this? I wondered. I really must be a fool. If my father and Jane were eavesdropping on this conversation, they'd be roaring with laughter by now.

The psychologist began to speak in a quiet, reasonable English voice. What he said sounded prepared. Look, he said, judging by the results of the tests, it was unlikely I'd get into an English university, and even if I did, I'd find an English university pretty tough-going. English universities were pretty tough, academically speaking, and he didn't think I'd cut it.

However, I was Irish. Did I have an Irish passport? he asked.

Yes, I said.

He beamed. In which case, why not apply to Trinity College, Dublin? I was bound to get in, well, what with my mother being who she was.

I said nothing.

The standards weren't as high in Ireland, he continued, so I would also be bound to get my degree.

He began to wax eloquent about Trinity and Dublin and Ireland. What a wonderful place, what a wonderful city, what wonderful people.

And he knew what he was talking about. Oh yes, indeed. And how did he know? Well, he said, because he too was a Trinity, Dublin man.

I must have looked surprised.

Don't look so surprised, he said. He himself wasn't the brain of Britain either. That's why he'd gone over there; if you weren't the brightest, it was the best place to go. Sadly, Trinity wasn't taking Brits like him any more but I was Irish; I had an Irish passport; it was too good an opportunity to pass up. I *had* to go. Would I promise him that I would at least apply?

I said yes, quietly.

He smiled. He looked relieved. He hadn't wanted to have this conversation. Later, I gathered from talking to the other children who were tested that he didn't talk to anyone else like he had talked to me. As far as he was concerned, when I think back now, this was the best advice he had to give me.

When the time came I got an application form from Trinity. The paper was a lovely old blue and the phrasing of the questions struck me as quaint and Victorian. I filled it in and sent it back. Trinity would be my fallback, if all else failed. I applied to various British universities through UCCA. I applied to Clare College in Cambridge as well. It was my preferred choice.

chapter forty-three

In the spring term 1972, I was approached by a younger boy; in the school library he had found a book published in 1930 called *Destiny*, written by someone called Otto Nückel, a German wood-cut artist, which he thought would make a Super-8mm film. *Destiny* was a novel in pictures which told its story with gaunt but startling wood-cuts; and what a dismal story:

At the turn of the twentieth century, somewhere in Mittel-Europe, a young girl is seduced by a salesman, gets pregnant, gives birth. Having drowned her infant she decides to kill herself but is 'saved' by an elderly tailor whom she later marries out of gratitude. Big mistake. Another salesman seduces her (clearly, she has a thing about salesmen) and she runs off with him. The jilted tailor kills himself; the new lover is murdered in a brawl. And this is only the first quarter of the woeful tale.

I saw *Destiny* – a novel completely devoid, other than the chapter headings, of words – would make a perfect silent film. I loved the illustrations; they were moody, full of detail, and powerfully evoked a dark, industrial nightmare Germany.

And finally, I was attracted to the author's fatalism, his sense – as the German proverb puts it – that 'What is born a drum is beaten until death', because this was the opposite of my father's belief that socialism could engineer a just society. Of course I would be happy to help, I said. I wrote the script and helped to direct.

The finished epic, complete with subtitles and music, was over an hour long. I showed it to Humphrey Burton, then editor of the ITV arts programme, *Aquarius*. He was making a profile of my mother and he commissioned an insert from me, on Super-8, for the programme. I shot and edited the material in the summer of 1972; then I went back to school to prepare for the Cambridge exam.

By coincidence, it was just after the transmission of this edition of *Aquarius* that I went to Cambridge for my interview. The don asking the questions had seen the programme.

What do you think you'll do if you come up to Clare? he asked.

I said I would try to make the best possible use of my time. I would read a lot because I knew I would never have the chance to read as much again. My housemaster at Bedales had emphatically told me to say this and I was glad to have got this in so soon.

Yes, yes, said the don, but surely I would spend all my time with the Cambridge Film Society?

I wanted to say that actually I hadn't thought to enquire if there even was a film society. Of course, now he mentioned it, it was obvious there would be one, but the truth was I hadn't thought about it until now.

I don't know, I said, feebly.

Really, he said. He sounded genuinely puzzled. Given my interest in film, surely it was obvious, I'd be with the Film Society all the time?

I don't know, I said. Then, I said, lamely, I suppose I'd join.

Come, come, continued the don. Surely I'd spend all my
time with the Film Society and do absolutely no work. Like
John Schlesinger, he added.

I wondered if Schlesinger was an old boy and, if he was,
whether I was supposed to know this. I never asked.

The letter came a few days later; I hadn't made Clare.

However, the University of York had said yes, there was a
place for me, and so had Trinity College in Dublin. I re-read
the prospectus I had received from each university. The
English degree at York was a three-year course, while the
course at Trinity lasted four years. At York I could study
Soviet cinema and the modern novel. At Trinity I would kick
off with a full-on year of Norse, Beowulf and Old English.
There was no contest. It had to be with-it York rather than
fuddy-duddy Trinity.

I wrote to York and said I would be taking my place and to
Trinity to say I would not. I believed I was choosing moder-
nity over convention. This was nonsense. My choice had
nothing to do with what the university offered and everything to do with the Eleven-Plus, Jane, my father, and what
the educational psychologist had said. An English university
had standards, he said, that I would not be able to match, thus
confirming (though he didn't know it) what my father had
always said: I was dim. However, if I went to York and succeeded, not only would that overturn the psychologist's
opinion, it would also overturn my father's opinion. That's
why I chose York. I wanted to prove to my father that I wasn't
stupid, even though, since he had gone back to live in Dalkey,
we had had no contact.

chapter forty-four

The kitchen of my mother's house in Chelsea was on the first floor, at the back. Tonight, it was lit with candles. People were standing round the room drinking, talking and smoking. It was December 1972, and this was a party for the cast of *A Pagan Place*. My mother adapted the play from her novel of the same name. It was running at the Royal Court in Sloane Square.

On the other side of the room a woman leant against the refrigerator talking to someone. I hadn't taken in her name but I knew she played Petronella in the play.

The woman was in her fifties, I guessed. She had a nice-looking face. Earlier in the evening I had noticed her glancing at me. Now, I noticed she was looking at me again.

A few minutes later, the woman was standing by herself. She glanced across at me again. I went over and said, 'Hello.'

She said, 'You look just like your father. Did you know that?'

'No, I didn't.'

'He was very important to me, once,' she said. Her tone wasn't mawkish or plangent but cheerful, even chirpy.

'You knew him?'

'Oh yes,' and with that she started speaking about his awkward humour, his finickiness (particularly regarding food), his powers of concentration, his love of music and combustion engines, and his talent for making and mending.

Everything she said was true; these were qualities I recognised. However, I also knew these were the virtues that my father allowed the world to see; he kept his other, darker inclinations well hidden.

I wondered how to reply. Most people didn't believe me when I described my father; they thought I exaggerated, and that my mother had warped my perception of him. I saw no reason why *this* woman would be any different. If I said what I felt I was certain we'd disagree, and life was too short for that. Just smile and nod, I thought, and whatever you do, say nothing.

The woman asked me some questions about my father. Where was he? How was he? And so on. My replies were polite but bland. Then she went off to get a drink and I slipped away. I avoided her for the rest of the evening. After she left I asked someone who she was; Sally Travers, I was told.

I knew the name of course, remembering it from childhood; I'd heard it listening at doors, eavesdropping on adult conversations.

Sally Travers was a niece of Micheál MacLiammóir, actor and founder (with Hilton Edwards) of the Dublin Gate Theatre. In 1935, her mother – who was MacLiammóir's sister – died, and Sally Travers was brought to Dublin; she wanted to act; she worked in her uncle's theatre.

In the late thirties, in between projecting films and reading Marx, my father also worked at the Gate Theatre, from time to time, as an assistant stage manager and as a sound-effects man. MacLiammóir took a shine to him, not reciprocated I understood, and he took a shine to Sally Travers.

When the war ended, she went to London to act. Meantime,

in the Royal Dublin Society library *The Story of the Pilgrim Fathers* landed at my father's feet and convinced him he must write a book about the voyage of the *Mayflower* to the New World. The only place with the books he needed was the reading room of the British Museum in London; he followed Sally across. They lived together in Palace Gardens Terrace (directly across from Linden Gardens where Adolf roomed when he was in London; my father approved of the symmetry). For two years my father worked on *The Plymouth Adventure* while Sally Travers appeared on the London stage; she supported him financially. Shortly before publication of *The Plymouth Adventure*, my father and Sally separated; their split was not amicable.

I never saw Sally Travers again after the meeting in my mother's kitchen but when I cleared Cnoc Aluin years later, I found dozens of photographs of her, dating from when she lived with my father: Sally in the park; Sally under the sun lamp; Sally on the sofa. My father had spoken of the late forties in London only as the period when he wrote his best-selling, money-making book; now, seeing these photographs, I saw something I had never known before: he was happy then. My father happy! Extraordinary – I would not have believed it if I hadn't seen the pictures that proved it.

Of course when I found these photographs I was reminded of my meeting with Sally. What, I wondered, if I had been less guarded? She would have told me a lot more, surely. I had let an opportunity to augment my meagre store of knowledge regarding my father slip through my fingers. For instance, they lived not far from Kensington Gardens; I might have discovered if they walked up and down Broad Walk together? This spot was to become very important to me when I became a student, years after meeting her, and it would have tickled me to discover that when I was pottering around, I was literally following in my father's footsteps. I had a liking for symmetry as much as he did.

chapter forty-five

Once again I was in my mother's kitchen, this time it was an evening in the summer before I went up to York university. The marble table was laid with plates, cutlery and crystal glasses. The candles were lit. A small dinner party was underway and the guest was a healthy American woman. I sat beside her. She was born in the 1920s. It was now 1973. She was nearly fifty but she looked younger. Vitamins and good dentistry, I presumed, were the foundations of her rude health. She was fashionable in a way that reminded me of the smart women in the advertisements for Virginia Slim cigarettes that appeared in American women's magazines at the time. This woman was Leatrice, an American and my father's first wife, and she had come to see the second wife, my mother.

I asked Leatrice some general questions about her life. She explained she was happily married now to Mr Fountain and they had several children. This led, as I had intended, to John Karl, my half-brother. He was now called John Bobby, she explained, and his surname was Fountain, the same as her husband and herself.

Judging the moment had arrived, I popped my question:

'I'd love to get in touch with my half-brother,' I said, art-lessly. 'What would you think about that? Would that be all right?'

Oh no, Leatrice said, without a second's hesitation. She didn't think that would be a good idea at all.

I wondered why?

Well, you see, continued Leatrice, she had left Ireland and my father and gone back to America and married Mr Fountain when John was still a baby. Naturally, John soon forgot about the time he lived in Lake Park with his real father and came to believe – as she had intended – that Mr Fountain was his father. And John still believed Mr Fountain was his father and she certainly wasn't about to start telling him otherwise now.

If I got in touch with John, she went on, well, then he would realise that what she had brought him up to believe was not true. His father wasn't the man he thought he was; his surname wasn't the name he thought it was; and he wasn't who he thought he was. And surely, she concluded, I wouldn't want to be the cause of a boy discovering his mother had lied to him all along, now would I?

Put like that, no, I certainly wouldn't.

Leatrice's directness was strangely winning.

'All right,' I said, and we left it at that.

chapter forty-six

In August 1973, my mother, my brother and I stayed in Dublin for a couple of days; we were on our way to County Clare to see my grandparents. My mother suggested we telephone my father. I thought this was a good idea. I wanted to tell my father that I was about to start at York University. It was also nearly my birthday and perhaps (though this was such an absurd wish I still hate admitting it even now) he might have something for me. Some money, maybe. Something. That's what I hoped.

So, on the morning of 18 August – it was a Saturday – my brother and I looked up my father's name in the Irish telephone directory. My brother said he would speak to my father. I thought this was a good idea because of my old belief that my father marginally preferred him to me.

I watched my brother as he picked up the phone and dialled the number of the hotel switchboard. The switchboard answered. He gave the number. He waited. Then I saw by the look on my brother's face that my father had answered the phone.

My brother said, 'We're in Dublin on our way to County Clare and we thought we could come and see you.'

He said this quietly and reasonably.

Next I could tell by my brother's face, and the fact he wasn't speaking, that the phone had been hung up at the other end. Then he put down the receiver. He told me what had happened. I was right. My father had said he didn't want to see us and hung up.

I said I would ring. I took the receiver. I dialled the switchboard. I gave the number again. I heard the ringing tone. I waited a long time and then finally the phone was picked up.

'This is Carlo,' I said.

'I do not wish . . .' my father said.

I knew, at once, what I must do; I must stop him continuing.

'This is ridiculous,' I said. 'You are just carrying on a quarrel you had with Edna . . .'

I used her name because I thought it would offend him less than the word mother.

'I do not like you or your brother,' he said coldly. 'Life is too precious to waste with people one dislikes.'

'You're not being fair.'

'Gombeens looking up their relations to see what they are going to leave them, that's what you and your brother are. I understand you. I shall leave you nothing but a moment's feeling of contempt.'

He put the phone down. I did not ring back.

chapter forty-seven

Two months after this exchange, I started at York University. This was October 1973. York was a new university. It was built on a swamp between the village of Heslington and the Retreat, a large Victorian mental hospital. The campus was divided into colleges on the Oxbridge model with numerous lakes separating the buildings. My college was built in the late sixties; it comprised big brutal cubes, all coated with a fine fawn-coloured grit. When the sun shone, provided you squinted and screened out the square modern windows and the brightly-coloured doors, it was almost possible to believe the structure, like an old Oxford college, was made of sandstone.

Unfortunately, when it rained, the fawn-coloured grit went from sub-Cotswold gold to dark khaki. That was York, really. It tried to be Oxbridge. On a sunny day, it almost convinced. But the truth was, it wasn't. It was a new, artificially created, totally non-organic institution ordered up by civil servants from a catalogue.

What I remember most of my first term were the marathon games of strip poker in the kitchen of my hall of residence. Night after night I would sit in my room, listening to the squealing of undergraduates as they shed their inhibitions. Those who lost everything had to jog around the halls of residence in the buff. This was a greatly feared penalty yet those who had made the circuit were revered. Like tribesmen, after an initiation ceremony, they had the status of elders in the poker circle. None of the participants in these rites, I gathered, had ever been away from home before. Sniffily, I assumed their behaviour arose from the fact that, for the first time in their lives, they were free from parental control. It goes without saying, I was a bit of a prig.

It was then discovered by the poker players that one of the more successful contestants, a grammar-school girl who had never had to jog around the block, owed her extraordinary good luck less to her skill than to a pack of cards she kept hidden in her pocket. If she didn't like the cards she was dealt, she simply replaced them with cards from her secret pack. Such was the hysteria during the games, no one had noticed.

Until now that is – and now the girl's co-players knew, they were appalled; they determined to teach her a lesson.

They cornered her in a college kitchen one night, took off all her clothes, carried her, kicking and squealing, outside; then they took her to the lake and handcuffed her to a steel Second World War landing barge moored at the side (used for dredging the lake). The keys of the handcuffs were thrown into the water. The college porter was then advised that there was a naked girl handcuffed to the barge. Ha, ha, ha, another merry student jape. The porter whistled up the fire brigade. The red engine arrived, siren roaring, lights flashing. Undergraduates piled out of the bar to see what was happening.

The next night, I noticed, the grammar-school girl was back in the kitchen waiting to play yet another game of strip poker. Among the other players were some of the crowd who had attached her to the barge.

'How could you play with these people?' I asked her a few days later.

I didn't admire the girl for cheating but I thought what her tormentors had done was far out of proportion to her crime.

'Oh, they were just having a laugh,' she said, blithely. 'It was good fun.'

She would never cheat again, she added. And to prove the point she indicated the smock she was wearing; it had no pockets.

One afternoon, early on during this same term, I sat in one of the small college libraries. It was a long room with metal shelves. Through the window I could see a grey stretch of water dotted with Canadian geese, native ducks, and other species I didn't recognise.

I had come to the library to write one of my first under-graduate essays. The subject was Christopher Marlowe's *Hero and Leander*. I had chosen this text because it was both short and tragic. I was writing quickly and the lined A4 paper was gradually filling up. As I wrote, I watched my fountain pen, with some pleasure, as it moved along the lines, and the words as they formed at the end of the nib. My handwriting was joined up, spiky and rightward-sloping.

I wasn't a naturally fluent writer, I was made one. This was the work of my history teacher at Bedales. This extraordi-nary woman had made me write two or three essays a week during my second A level year. Once the essay title was set, the essay had to be written straightaway, either during her class or immediately afterwards, in the library. Only half an hour was allowed. All essays, she insisted, must have the same simple structure: introduction, argument, conclusion.

All paragraphs had to contain at least one fact. Sub-clauses and waffle were not permitted. Simple sentences only.

It was like working for a newspaper. The teacher, like an editor, would demand copy; I, the hack, would then have to produce copy quickly, no arguments or excuses accepted. My work was not always good but, I discovered, providing her rules were obeyed, it would always be readable, at least. I also learnt from the experience that there was no such thing as the perfect essay. Anything and everything I wrote was just a draft, an attempt; what really counted was not getting it perfect – it could never be perfect – but getting something out of my head and down on paper.

The upshot of all of this was that I came to see the blank page not as something to fear but as something to fill. This was my history teacher's gift to me. She made the act of writing unselfconscious and painless.

I also discovered something else from her programme. The place that the words came from, like any muscle in the body, got stronger with training. Indeed, it grew so strong that after a while I realised it must be exercised every day, otherwise I would feel sluggish. I not only found it a pleasure to write, I began to need to write . . .

I stopped to read back what I had written. The library smelt of fish batter and hot chocolate. Having finished reading I stared out at the pewter-coloured lake with its ruff of tawny reeds around the edge. I knew what I wanted to say next: now what I required was a sequence of words that would encapsulate and carry this. The trick was not to force the issue. The trick was to wait. In a moment or two the words would coalesce around the idea like iron filings around a magnet. Then I would have the words to say what I wanted and I would write them down. These words, in turn, would lead me on to the next idea.

In the distance I noticed a grey goose scramble up a muddy

bank and waddle along one of the concrete walkways that
connected the colleges. A figure appeared, heading in the
opposite direction. He had a head of big fluffy hair, like Jon
Pertwee, the current *Dr Who*, and like the Doctor, he looked
a bit like a light bulb. Man and bird passed each other and
went on their way.

I heard the click of the electronic wall clock. I glanced
round and saw the time. I looked out the window again. It
was taking longer than usual for my mind to throw up the
words I needed but I had no doubt that any moment now,
they would come. That's what always happened and the
process never ceased to amaze me. I'd never known a time
when the words hadn't come, eventually. But, my God, this
was taking an incredibly long time . . .

I looked back at the page. Maybe if I reread my last sentence, it would jog my mind into action. So I reread the
sentence. It didn't make sense. Worse still, I now realised, I
had absolutely no sense, any more, of the idea that had been
so clear to me just a few moments before. None whatsoever.
Both my grasp of what I'd written and what I wanted to say
next were gone.

But how could that be? I wondered. How could I be coast-
ing along one minute and absolutely stalled the next? This
couldn't be possible. This seizure must be temporary, surely?
During adolescence I was often woken up at night by terrible
cramps in my legs. Well, that's what this was, I reasoned. This
was the psychological equivalent of growing pains. That's
what; and like those cramps, which were horribly painful for
a minute or two and then vanished, this would pass too. It
was simply a matter of waiting.

The minutes ticked by. I looked at the clock again. I saw
forty-five minutes had passed since I last looked. Appalling.
What had I been doing between then and now?

I turned to the back of the A4 writing pad. I would write a

simple word, I thought. 'Cat', for instance. That way I would kick-start the system back to life.

I gripped the pen. I tried to picture the word 'cat'. Nothing. Though I knew the sign that represented this animal was somewhere inside my head, I could not retrieve it.

It began to grow dark outside. The machine that had produced my words to order was completely closed down. It was as if someone had reached inside my head and snapped all the wires. Everything was gone; not just what to say but worse, far far worse, how to say it.

I went back to my room in the hall of residence. There was nothing else for it, I realised; I would have to teach myself to write again. And how would I do that? Very simply, I would have to take a text and copy it. That way I would relearn how to form the shapes of the letters and later, if I was lucky, I would relearn how to get thoughts and ideas out of my head and down on to paper.

I began to copy out *Hero and Leander*. To begin with, I went slowly, ploddingly. I was like a child again, and the inky shapes that I made were ugly, ungainly and even illegible. But gradually, as hour succeeded hour, and day succeeded day, my sense of the meaning carried by each word-shape gradually came back to me. I could think 'cat' and then I could write 'cat'.

Ten days on from the seizure in the library, I found I could write again with the same easy glibness as before. But with an important difference. My handwriting had completely changed. My letters were no longer joined up, they were also small and rounded rather than spiky. (I was now writing, though it was to be years before I realised, like my father.)

But although I had regained what was lost (and even gained; I thought my new handwriting style was more mature), I was still perturbed. Why had this happened? What caused this aphasia?

One night, as I lay in my bed thinking these things over, the wails and hurrahs of the poker players drifting from the kitchen down the hall, I remembered something I hadn't thought about for years . . .

I was six or seven years old. I was living in Cannon Hill Lane. My brother hadn't started school yet, and I made the journey to and from Hillcross Primary by myself.

It was a hot summer's day. I trudged along Monkleigh Road, heading for home. I felt the sun beating down on the top of my head. The street was quiet. There were no cars purring along; nor could I hear, as I usually would, the sound of a radio in a kitchen, or the blades of a lawnmower turning in a back garden. The only sound was the clasps of my sandals jingling, and the only moving thing was the man at the house on the corner doing something to his front door.

I stopped and looked over the hedge. At first I thought the man was painting; then I saw his door was covered with faintly trembling twigs. He was sweeping these into a dustpan, then tipping the twigs into the cardboard box beside him.

After a few moments, the man turned and pointed at the broken glass below the bay window. A huge bell jar, he explained, full of his stick insects, had fallen off the window ledge, and smashed. The stick insects had got free, and now they were crawling all over his front door.

He resumed sweeping. I watched. I felt quiet, then pleasantly tranced; I got exactly the same feeling when my mother read to me . . .

The door of the hall of residence just below my bedroom banged shut. (I was on the first floor.) I heard shouting from the kitchen where the poker game was in progress. Glancing out my window, I glimpsed the grammar-school girl's white body as she jogged around the corner. Her rehabilitation, I guessed, was now complete . . .

I lay down again. I was back in Monkleigh Road. I could smell the melting tar and I heard the faint scraping noise made by the bristles of the brush . . .

Over the days that followed, at odd times and in odd places, on a bus or sitting in a lecture theatre or queuing in the cafeteria, the memory of Monkleigh Road that lunchtime would return with incredible vividness.

I began to wonder why, out of everything I might remember, it was this? Perhaps, I thought, the stopper had accidentally been pulled out of the memory phial filled with the essence of that moment; hence the memories had flooded out and were washing through me still?

Which was fine and dandy except I didn't want to believe anything in the mind was accidental. So, in the end, I came up with this explanation: if I stuck to writing just critical essays, I thought, the aphasia would return and my brain would seize up. On the other hand, if I gave in to my desperate but unfocused yearning to write, of which I was aware but which I did not acknowledge, I would enjoy the mesmerisation I'd known in Monkleigh Road and that I also got when my mother read to me as a child. Writing something proper would make me happy. I was caught between a carrot and a stick, I reasoned, the purpose of both of which was to make me into a writer.

Of course, there was no logical connection between the psychological experience of losing language and my fully admitting to myself I wanted to write. It was simply that the latter was able to flood my mind in the shape of a dreamy intuition because the bulwarks by which I had kept it out of sight and out of mind were down, for whatever reason.

However, I did have one proper idea in the middle of all this: when I next went to Dublin, I would try to see my father.

I had not had contact with him since he moved to Cnoc Aluin. Why did I want to see him now? The answer was that I now had something I did not have before, a sense of where

I wanted to go. I had started the process of becoming the writer I believed I was always meant to be when I admitted to myself it was what I wanted to do. The reason I wanted to see him, of course, though I wasn't admitting this, was that I wanted his approval. I wanted him to pat me on the back and exclaim, 'So you've discovered you want to be a writer. Well done, I'm proud of you.'

(And if he didn't, well, I'd still be all right, I reckoned; having fully and finally admitted I wanted to write, I had acquired the equivalent, psychologically, of a suit of armour.)

When I went home for the Christmas holidays, I told my mother I was going to try to see my father again. The way I put it to her was like this: he was the child, so now it was up to me to be the adult. She approved, as I expected she would. It was essential, she said, to maintain contact. Healthy as well.

PART TWO

chapter forty-eight

Sitting in the bedroom of my hotel in Dublin, I gave the number of Cnoc Aluin to the operator. The last time I had phoned it was from this same hotel (though not the same room – that would be far too neat). I was anxious my father would again say no, he wouldn't see me. My stomach felt tight. Then I reminded myself that if my father said no, well, that was his lookout. I was making the effort or, as I would have described it then, I was the one who was being adult.

Knowing I occupied the high ground, I felt protected.

'Yes,' said the voice at the other end. I had my words ready but the one to whom I intended to say them hadn't answered; it was Jane who had picked up the phone. I was flummoxed.

'This is Carlo,' I said, finally.

'Yes, I know who it is,' she said testily. 'I haven't forgotten who *you* are, you know.'

Ah, of course, I thought, so that's it; the last time I called I was a venal child with an eye on my inheritance. I (along with my brother) was that particular Irish *bête noire*, the self-serving child eager to fleece the luckless parent for his own gain. Since then, my father had further refined his status as the victim of his children. He was now old, alone, and abandoned, and I was one of his callous sons, fickle, feckless and indifferent to his fate. And this sense was all there in Jane's simple sentence, 'I haven't forgotten who *you* are, you know,' with its implication that I was the one who had forgotten him.

'I was thinking of coming out,' I said, 'to see . . .'

The next word I planned to say was 'Ernie' but my tongue refused to move. Oh dear. Here I was, trying to make contact and I was about to make a gaffe. If she guessed I couldn't say the word, what sort of a message would that send? I mightn't get to see him at all.

But then, miraculously, the brain engaged and the larynx obliged. 'Ernie,' I said. 'I was thinking of coming out to see Ernie,' I said again. 'And you,' I added, quickly.

'I see.'

I settled into silence. I had spoken. Would she now reply? It was a staring match, conducted down the telephone line. In the end, Jane blinked first.

'You'll have to talk to him yourself,' she said, finally, 'but it's not looking good. Walk this afternoon . . . guests this evening . . . tradesman tomorrow morning . . . theatre tomorrow evening . . .' she continued, as if reading out of a diary.

I heard shouting in the background. Jane broke off from speaking to me and shouted, 'It's Carlo, your . . .' She baulked for a moment. 'Son,' she managed finally.

'Let me speak to him.'

I heard my father's approaching footfalls. There was a fumbling noise as he took the handset and then I heard, 'Ernest Gébler speaking, who is that?'

The voice was thin and sounded feminine.

Was he like that the last time we spoke? I couldn't remember. That last time we spoke on the telephone was so fraught

I had observed nothing. Maybe his voice had wavered then but I just hadn't noticed.

But I noticed now. Oh yes. He's mortal, I thought. His body's running down. He's going to die.

I can't say it had never occurred to me that someone in the family might die; but this was the first time I knew for certain someone would and that it would be him.

Funnily enough, I didn't then think, Thank God I rang before he died. I didn't believe I was the negligent one who had let the relationship go to the dogs. He must take responsibility for that, I thought.

'This is your son, Carlo,' I said.

'Hello, Carlo. What do you want?'

'To come and see you.'

'I don't see any reason why you shouldn't.' I wondered if he remembered the last conversation at all.

Then I heard my father calling to Jane, 'He wants to come.'

'I know,' Jane shouted back.

'When should that be? When can we have him?' My father came back on the phone. 'Will you have Sash?' he asked.

'Yes.'

'He'll have Sash,' my father shouted to Jane.

'Not today and tomorrow we've got the theatre,' Jane shouted.

'Not the evenings, no,' my father shouted back. 'If they came in the day though, we could go for a walk.'

A walk! So what was new chez Gébler?

More shouting from Jane, this time about the mythical tradesman.

My father came back on the line. 'Come tomorrow,' he said. He told me the time to come and the time to leave, as well. 'So we can get on with *our* lives,' he said, sharply. We would walk, he said, weather permitting; tea afterwards, with all produce from the garden guaranteed DDT-free.

I said goodbye and put down the phone.

The next day the sun was shining. The tall red-brick Georgian terraces of central Dublin seemed to soak up the light and hold it like a sponge holds water.

My brother and I caught a green and cream Dublin bus. We sat on the top deck beside a sign forbidding expectoration. The penalty was a hefty fine.

We got out at Dalkey. We walked past the convent gates and up Coliemore Road. The street was silent, sepulchral. There were big houses, small houses, gardens with shrubs. The sea sounded faintly in the distance. Out of the stillness came a woman on a bicycle with a loose chain that clanged. Tied over her front and rear mudguards were plastic fan-shaped covers intended to stop water splattering her legs. I hadn't seen these devices since childhood, since Morden. This sleepy backwater would be my father's last home, I guessed, and seeing the bicyclist, I understood this was absolutely the right place for him to be.

We came to a gateway at an angle to the pavement. There were stone piers bearing the words Cnoc Aluin. I peered up the short, sharp drive. I saw a building with steps and a white front door with a Georgian fanlight above.

We walked up the steep drive, climbed the steps to the front door and knocked. Behind us lay Dalkey Sound, with Dalkey Island moored in the middle, long, low and rounded like a submarine; Dublin Bay lay beyond, with its pewter-coloured waters.

The door opened back. I saw Jane, with her black arching eyebrows and her wide Cheshire cat smile. She wore ski-pants and flat shoes and a tight jersey. Thirty years earlier, in a Soho coffee bar, she would not have looked out of place. She was thinner than I remembered and her bones stuck out through her clothes; she had aged, I thought. Perhaps, as with my father, it had been happening over the years only I had never noticed.

Carlo Gébler (far left) with Ernest, Sasha and Jane, Cnoc Aluin, Dublin 1977

'Come in,' she said.

I stepped into the hall. It smelt of lanolin and coal dust, mixed with the chalky smell of geraniums. The carved Burmese table stood by the wall, in exactly the same place it had stood in Morden, and its dark smooth top reminded me, as always, of a still brown pond.

The booming chimes of the grandfather clock drifted from

the back sitting room. The sound was instantly familiar though I hadn't heard it for years.

A few moments later we were ushered into this room and there it was – the coffin-shaped clock, with its heavy brass pendulum, its creamy clock face, and its black spidery arms trembling from the chimes. It was as if the stage set of Cannon Hill Lane had been rolled up, taken across the Irish Sea, and re-erected. Odder still, it felt surprisingly good to be reconnected with these objects.

We went for a walk on Killiney Hill, climbing to the obelisk at the top. We had tea then in the gloomy basement kitchen (home-made yogurt, Jane's brown bread, small sweet toma-toes from the greenhouse). Our conversation was banal, cautious, distant. However, beneath the crust of superficial civility, Jane and my father were suspicious and watchful. Though nothing was said, or even hinted, they thought my brother and I had come to get something out of them. I could see them looking at us and thinking, What are they up to? But we weren't up to anything, we were just being friendly and I derived a perverse pleasure from the certainty that they would never be able to understand, let alone accept this.

chapter forty-nine

I left the University of York in 1976 and went on to the National Film School at Beaconsfield to train as a director. One Saturday afternoon in the spring of the following year, 1977, I found myself in Kensington High Street. It was thronged with shoppers and there was that Saturday-afternoon-in-London feel in the air, that sense that the best night of the week was only a few hours away.

I climbed Church Street and turned into Vicarage Gate (the street at the end of Palace Gardens Terrace, as it happens). It was quiet and the bustle of the high street was a distant hum. There was a dilapidated terrace on my left. I found a scuffed door and rang the bell. I heard someone cough inside. The door opened.

I found myself looking at a man in a black suit and a white shirt, a living André Kertész photograph. He was part of the Irish family who looked after this boarding house. They lived in the basement. Nashat, the friend I had come to visit, called them the Troglodytes. He was at the film school, in the year above me.

I stepped into the hall. It was lit by a feeble twenty-five watt bulb. There were hundreds of letters piled on the table, old, dog-eared and stained. When letters arrived for departed tenants, the Troglodytes simply piled them here and over the years they had formed a paper stalagmite. It was a perfect image, Nashat said, for the loneliness of modern city life, these dead letters calcinating in the gloomy hall.

I climbed the stairs. There was a smell of Dettol, linoleum polish and (most mysteriously) sauerkraut. I knocked on Nashat's door. He appeared after a few seconds wearing only a towel. Nashat's body was brown and small. Around his neck he wore a chain with a tablet etched with a quotation from the Koran.

Nashat was on his way to the shower. Later he was going to the Concorde club, and a boy had to look his best, he said. He went off to the communal bathroom. I went in to his quarters, as he sometimes called them.

His room was eight by ten. There was a bed, a hand-basin, a buckled plywood wardrobe, and a small set of rickety shelves. On the bottom shelf Nashat kept his beautifully maintained Super-8mm equipment, boxed as when he bought it, while his well-cared-for books were on the shelves above. There included works by Freud and a life of Vincente Minnelli. Although Nashat was wealthy (before Colonel Nasser his family owned 10 per cent of Egypt, he used to boast), a stranger would assume he was a Third World student who treated his belongings with such reverence because they were all he had.

Nashat and I had opposite tastes. Cyd Charisse and Gene Kelly were his icons, Minnelli his favourite director. I was an Ingmar Bergman double-feature man. Yet he was one of my closest friends. He showed me how much meaning could be wrapped up in a sugary coating, and how much nourishment there was in Fred Astaire and Ginger Rogers dancing together. What also bound us was an interest in childhood, and the relationships we had had with our parents, and those they had had with us. We talked endlessly about these subjects not because we felt nostalgic for what was gone, but because we wanted to remember, as far as it was possible, what our child-hoods were really *really* like.

The counterpane on Nashat's bed was stretched as tight as a drum skin; I couldn't bring myself to sit on it and crease it. I stood at the window, opened a can of his beer and lit one of his Marlboros; the smoke was sweet and hot.

Nashat returned, his hair slicked back, his face scrubbed.

'Sit down,' he said.

'I don't want to rumple your bed.'

'Do what your Jewish mother says. Sit down.'

I ignored him. While he dressed I looked at the green, sticky leaves of the elm that grew in the street, just in front of the window. I could hear traffic and human clamour and the clatter of shoe on pavement – the soundtrack of every Saturday afternoon.

Nashat sat down; now I could sit. As I did so I saw he had *Time Out* on his lap.

He was excited, he explained. It was Hitchcock's *Vertigo*, the master's masterpiece. After years in limbo, the film was back. What's more, it was a new print. Nashat pointed at the *Time Out* listing circled in Biro.

Had I seen it? he asked.

No, I said. Then I told him about the Sunday afternoon party in Mitcham, and the grown-ups talking about this *Vertigo*, made by this Hitchcock fellow, and then another film, also made by him, *The Man Who Knew Too Much* beginning on the big televi-sion, and my becoming so excited I vomited in the sink . . .

Did this happen, Nashat wondered, when I was living in Morden after my mother had gone?

Yes, I said, and from there it was back to fathers and what he called the whole Freudian caboodle.

We talked for hours until Nashat suddenly noticed the time and sprang to his feet. He had to hit the Concorde in ten minutes.

Then he looked at me.

Your father didn't care for queers, did he? said Nashat.

No, I said.

Why not come to the club then? he said. If any of the old man's thoughts or attitudes still lingered, the sight of fags having fun would soon see them off.

The Concorde was dark and smoky. Without exception everyone that evening addressed me as Straight, as in (Barman), 'Hello, Straight. Carlsberg did you say?' and (Accountant, offering spliff), 'Hey! Straight! Have a puff a this,' and (three lorry drivers on a jolly), 'Oi! Straight, what d'you make of all these poofters?'

I thought the Concorde was an over-priced dump. After an hour I made my excuses and left.

chapter fifty

Sunday morning, a week or two later, Nashat and I went for a walk in Kensington Gardens, as we often did. We were on the Broad Walk heading north, the Round Pond to our right.

Nashat was hung over. The night before he had been at the Concorde.

'How was it?'

'You know . . . the usual.'

'You mean awful?'

'Well, a little less than wonderful.'

I wondered why he went? Drinks were twice the normal price and the clientele was miserable. Nashat agreed, but what else could a boy do? He was looking for love, he said. And it was possible that one Saturday night in the Concorde the love of his life would appear. They would exchange glances across the dance floor and then walk out into the London night to start their life together.

The Concorde, I said, was a place men went to find other men to have sex with.

Yes, said Nashat, I was quite right, but also no. He might get lucky.

Might! I was incredulous.

But didn't I understand? he said. He couldn't give up the dream; there'd be no reason to live otherwise. He'd lose his bulwark against depression; or the Black Lagoon as he called it. It was a thick, syrupy goo and if you tumbled in, the goo stuck and then you sank, and if you were unlucky, you drowned. This was a sequence I knew intimately since I had fallen into my own lagoon a few times. Here was another point of contact, perhaps the deepest and most significant.

Now Hitchcock, he continued, seguing effortlessly from his own life to the cinema, he was no stranger to melancholy either. He had his bulwarks – wife, work, and his gallows humour – but he never defeated the blues. He couldn't hide them either. Depression showed on one's work like finger-prints on a gun.

And how did one tell Hitchcock was a depressive? he continued. Simple. His idealised female heroines of whom the supreme example was Kim Novak in *Vertigo*. Had I met up with him, he continued, as arranged, I would have seen this brilliant film and so I would know what he was talking about. It was a shame I hadn't (and I can't now remember why I didn't meet him).

Vertigo was a masterpiece, he continued; it was also sur-prisingly painful, even Bergmanesque. The sequences where red-haired, working-class Kim Novak lets James Stewart make her over, turning her back into the bottle-blond, middle-class madwoman he was in love with, these were some of the most painful in cinema history, he said.

As I listened I remembered what Nashat had told me about his childhood. When he was born his mother was desperately disappointed; she had wanted a girl. When he contracted polio a few years later, she opted to care for him herself; she took him into the women-only end of the palace where the family lived and, giving him a girl's name, dressing him as a girl and treating him as girl, she made him into the girl she'd always wanted and she kept him that way for over a year until he got better. In short, she made him over. No wonder he responded to *Vertigo* in the way he had.

I stopped walking as something struck me. If Nashat saw the world as he did because of his mother, then of course I must see the world as I did because of my father. He made me over like Nashat's mother made him, or fifty per cent of me anyway.

It was a horrible thought.

I looked down the Broad Walk. A girl in a corduroy bib-dress ran towards me, a Saudi matron, her dark eyes staring through the slit in her yashmak, following behind.

I'll not pursue this, I decided.

Nashat and I walked on.

chapter fifty-one

In the summer of 1978, I went to Connemara, in the west of Ireland, to make my film school graduation film; it was an adaptation of Anton Chekhov's great account of peasant cruelty and cupidity, *In the Ravine*.

For one shot we needed the exterior of a Victorian church but the only one we could find that would do was the Chapel of Rest in the Galway corporation cemetery.

The day came to film. We put the camera on a gantry and wheeled it along the paths between the graves in search of our shot. Somehow, I stumbled on something and when I looked I saw this was the grave of William Joyce, the Brooklyn-born, Galway-reared, English fascist known as Lord Haw-Haw, who broadcast for the Reichsrundfunk during the war, was tried for treason in 1945, found guilty and hanged.

Back in London, I started reading up on William Joyce, and that, in turn, led me on to the seedy world of treachery among the Allies. I was particularly struck by the story of Stoker Rose, a Royal Navy sailor and POW who spied for the Germans. After I left the film school, I made a film based on the Rose case called *Rating Notman* but this didn't exhaust my interest in either the period or betrayal.

I moved on to Francis Stuart, the Irish writer who, in 1939, after the declaration of war, hurried to Berlin where he had the offer of a university job. Later, he translated William Joyce's broadcasts from German to English, and later still, broadcast talks of his own for the Reichsrundfunk to Ireland. Stuart was arrested in the French zone at the end of the war but subsequently released without charge. As the citizen of a neutral country, the Irish Free State, his broadcasts did not constitute a war crime. Yet Stuart's behaviour appalled many; artists were supposed to side with the victims not the victimisers.

Stuart, I thought, was a find; his life story was fascinating, his novels were wonderful (whatever one thought of his morals) and he was almost untouched by television. Of course he was also the sort of writer my father would have hated (which he did), which was another very good reason to like him.

I decided to make a film about Stuart. What I didn't know, when I began the project, was that it would take five years.

I left the film school in 1979. I worked occasionally as a director of documentary films. I began to write. I managed to get two or three stories published in *The Literary Review*. Then I started a story about a boy and his grandfather at a race meeting in Ireland (roughly based on my own memories of childhood holidays in County Clare). Only when I had finished did I realise that I had actually written the first chapter of a novel. I submitted this to a publisher, got a commission and began to write *The Eleventh Summer*. On those days when the words flowed, I got that faintly tranced feeling of pleasure I enjoyed so much. At last, I thought, I really was going in the right direction.

During the same period, I began to visit Dublin regularly, to talk to Francis Stuart. One lunchtime, during one of these research trips, I found myself in a miserable pub in Booterstown with Tibor, the producer. That afternoon, we were not working; we were going to visit my father, instead. I was looking forward to it – his mad opinions on diet and literature couldn't fail to interest Tibor – but at the same time I was anxious. What if my mad, strange father outraged my Eastern European colleague? Just to be on the safe side, I decided on some copper-fastening.

'Can I just remind you about something,' I said.

Tibor took a sip of Guinness and filched a crisp from the packet on the table.

'Go on.'

'Umh . . . he might go into a long rant. For instance, Joseph Stalin, greatest figure of the twentieth century, thank God for the Nazi-Soviet non-aggression pact, et cetera. I think I've told you that before.'

Tibor nodded. 'What about the Poles?' he enquired. 'What does your father say about them?'

'Not much. So they were invaded by the Soviets in 1939. Tough. They were liberated at the end of the war, weren't they?'

'Not many Poles see it that way,' said Tibor.

We drove to Cnoc Aluin, parked, and climbed the steps. I lifted the knocker and banged it twice. The door opened almost at once and there was my father. Had he been waiting for us?

'Come in,' he said. He was now incredibly thin and his voice was even more etiolated and feminine than ever. In fact, the change was so extreme that though I knew this sixty-nine-year-old man was my father, I couldn't stop myself thinking this was really a rather bad Xerox copy of him and the real man was somewhere else.

Then I noticed he was wearing a black knitted waistcoat with green piping, which I remembered him wearing in Cannon Hill Lane. Oh yes, it was him all right.

We trooped to the back room and sat down. My father looked at Tibor. 'Where are you from?' he asked.

'Budapest via Cheltenham,' said Tibor. Both his parents were Jews, he explained, who as children had sat out the war in Palestine; they had only returned to Hungary after the defeat of Germany. His father subsequently became Hungarian military attaché in France. When Tibor was twelve, his father defected with his family and settled in Cheltenham.

I heard my father clear his throat. 'You know what?' he asked.

Tibor shook his head. He didn't. But I did. It's what I'd warned of in the pub; the Stalin rant was coming.

'You young men, you don't remember the thirties, but I can tell you, no one was prepared to stand up to fascism except Joseph Stalin. Without him we'd all be under the Nazi jackboot.'

I sighed; initially this would be a hoot, witnessing Tibor's reactions as my predictions came true, but then it would become boring when my father degenerated into his predictable monologue.

In 1938, he said, Stalin found himself in a hopeless position. The Soviet Union had been so busy defending herself against Whites and anti-communists, she hadn't industrialised. She was incapable of defending herself. She was ripe for conquest by fascism.

So what did Stalin do? he asked rhetorically. The non-aggression pact of 1939 with Germany, he continued, that's what Stalin did, and it was a stroke of genius. The Germans thought they'd duped Joe; what they didn't know was that, actually, he was hoodwinking them. He was buying Russia two years in which to rearm. He used the time well. He upped steel and coal production; he put his factories behind the Ural mountains out of range of the Luftwaffe; he rebuilt the Red Army.

Because of this, my father continued, when the Germans invaded in 1941, they met a Red Army with teeth. The German Army was halted at Stalingrad and later sent scuttling back across the Oder. Hitler's Wehrmacht was said to be the greatest army in the world; the war showed it wasn't; the Red Army was.

'What about the Poles?' I queried. I couldn't let Tibor think I was a pusillanimous son who took this sort of nonsense lying down.

Bloody Poles, my father exploded. If Stalin hadn't gone and invaded in 1939 and thereby bought himself two years' grace, there'd have been no Red Army to liberate Poland. He saved the Polish people. But had they ever said thank you? Oh no. Whinge, whinge, whine, whine. But that's Catholics for you.

'Instead of Jesus Christ,' he continued, 'it ought to be Joseph Stalin on the wall of every house in Ireland with a perpetual light burning underneath. Ireland'd be under the yoke of Hitler, like the rest of Europe, but for Stalin. Of course, Holy Catholic Ireland could never bring herself to honour a communist, oh no . . .'

There was silence. I heard Jane washing dishes in the kitchen downstairs. My father stared into space. Tibor glanced at me. I think he almost suspected we had colluded, my father and I, so close were his words to what I'd predicted in the pub. But we hadn't. I just knew my father so well: once my father knew Tibor was Hungarian, his Stalin speech was as inevitable as day following night.

I could pass myself off as him, I thought. Well, of course I could; I did know him. However, I also knew that the best writers of parody could only do their work once the original subject was thoroughly internalised and made their own, made indistinguishable from their own personality. In which case, I wondered, was it perhaps less that I knew him well than that I was him? It was a question that had arisen before, and once again I put it aside, unconsidered.

chapter fifty-two

At the start of the 1980s I acquired a flat in Little Venice. It was on the top floor of a Victorian house, two very large white rooms; my landlords were the Church Commission. One summer's day when the windows were thrown open and in the communal gardens, three floors down, sprinklers turned with a soft hiss, Anna came to visit.

'I have a girlfriend you'd just love,' said Anna, moving the ice in her glass. 'Trouble is, she's getting married.'

Anna was German, and her intonation was, yes, a little like Marlene Dietrich.

I can't remember why she came out with this remark, but it was not a taunt, simply a statement. She knew me; she knew Tyga; she knew we would fit hand in glove; but Tyga was marrying someone else, *tant pis*, so that was that.

Dissolve to six months later. Anna was giving a party in a large flat in South Kensington. I remember a vast room and pine floorboards. A girl was dancing with abandon. She was a stripper having a night off, someone explained to me. A middle-aged female hippie, dressed in a buckskin suit and a

Davy Crockett hat and carrying a shaman's wand, moved on to the floor and started to dance with the girl. The guests watched, waiting for something to happen. For a minute or two it was interesting. After twenty minutes, less so. I decided to leave. As I went to get my coat, I glimpsed a woman with black hair and coal-black eyes; she was wearing a green skirt that rustled as she moved. We were not introduced but I guessed, from Anna's description, that this was Tyga, and I saw right away that what Anna had said was right.

I did not see Tyga again until the following year. London was cold and gloomy. I invited Anna to come over with her boyfriend to play Scrabble. They were invited for eight.

At six, Anna was on the phone.

Did I remember Tyga, the one she had told me about?

Of course I did.

Then Anna told me the story.

Tyga had fallen pregnant and, in January, just a month earlier, she had married the father. Anna had been to the wedding. Tyga's husband was an artist, a much older man, divorced, and he had a child by his first wife. Tyga had lived with him for years and they had always intended to marry.

Then, continued Anna, six days after the wedding, Tyga's husband suffered a massive heart attack and died shortly afterwards.

Tyga, twenty-four, a widow, pregnant and grief-stricken, was now staying with Anna and her boyfriend – for understandable reasons Tyga didn't want to go back to the flat where she had lived for six years with her husband of six days – and Anna's question was, could they bring her? I was adamant: they had to bring her. Four was a much better number than three for Scrabble.

At eight the bell rang and I pressed the buzzer. I heard footsteps on the stairs and my own front door opening. I turned and saw Tyga for the second time; same dark skin, same coal-black eyes, but her expression was one of heightened anxiety. She looked to me like someone who thought some terrible creature was lurking, waiting to pounce on her.

We started the Scrabble game, playing on the floor. Tyga was opposite me. We may even have partnered one another. I can't remember. All that sticks in my memory is that every so often she went to the bathroom and returned after a moment or two having applied a new coat of lipstick.

We started to see one another, socially. Then it was St Patrick's night and she came round to see me. The Irish are in luck tonight, I thought. We went to bed. Her stomach was a small hard round, about half the size of a football.

We began an affair but it didn't last long. One Sunday morning, Tyga came bearing a white box filled with eclairs from the local patisserie. A propitiatory offering. She told me she was not ready for a relationship so soon after her husband's death. She told me this was to be expected; after all, she was carrying his baby. She told me that our relationship was too complicated and too fraught. I did not like what I heard because I was in love. We parted badly.

September came and the first leaves were burnt in the communal garden below the flat. One evening, Nashat and I were sitting at my glass-topped table, talking and doing lines of coke and drinking wine, when the telephone went. It was Anna with the news that Tyga had just given birth to a perfect little girl.

Nashat had met Tyga of course, and he had also heard me talk about her a great deal. News of the birth stirred him deeply. He pulled a ring off his finger; it was a gold ring with a large red stone set in the middle. He declared that we must now go to the hospital, he and I, immediately, and present the newborn infant with this gift. I demurred. It was a terrifying thought: the two of us waltzing around Queen Charlotte's Hospital in the middle of the night, coked up to the eyeballs, and locating both the newborn baby and the exhausted mother, and then presenting our gift. I said something about it being too late.

But Nashat was adamant. He said we had to go. He said it was our duty to go. He supported his case with quotations from the Koran and references to ancient Islamic tradition. I said I was too drunk to drive. He said we would go by taxi. I think then I told him the truth. Or he guessed it. I was in love with Tyga, I said, and given the stimulants in my system, I would probably end up looking stupid. Nashat made me take the ring anyway, made me wrap it in tissue paper and put it away in a drawer.

When I went to see Tyga the next day, I handed over the gift, as I had promised Nashat I would. Then I went and peeped at the new, small, blond baby lying in a Moses basket, wrapped in a blanket. The name of the child was India. And what did I feel? Well, nothing really. Not at that moment. All I saw was a baby. I knew about the baby's unhappy circumstances; I knew it didn't have a father; but I had no sense whatsoever (despite what I felt for the mother) that this newborn child was someone for whom I could become responsible, that this newborn child was someone to whom I could be a father. Oh no. To be a father. What a horrible idea. There was nothing to recommend the position. Nothing. If experience had taught me anything it was that fathering and misery went together like bacon and eggs. It was a state to be avoided. At all costs. Never to be entered into. That way led the Black Lagoon.

So, there I was, attracted to the mother but with no feelings for the baby she had just delivered. It was just a baby, a small thing that cried, ate and slept, nothing more. Nor did I find the sight of new life thrilling, and I certainly did not understand the mother's desire for her pride and joy to be celebrated.

My not understanding this particular need came to the fore
the next week when I went to see Tyga at her flat and she suggested a walk. The three of us. I thought it would be a great
opportunity for us to talk. The two of us. About our relationship. Us.

We walked down the Goldhawk Road and turned into
Ravenscourt Park. Of course, I'd got it completely wrong.
The mother didn't want to talk, not about us; what she
wanted was to show off her child; and what she also wanted
from me was a hint, at the very least, of fatherly or masculine
pride; after all, she had just brought a new life into the world.
If I'd stopped to think, perhaps it would have been obvious
that now, so soon after India's birth, and with her husband
dead, this is what Tyga, a widowed mother, would crave. If
her husband had been around, he'd have let everyone know
he was with a new child, his child, and how proud he was.
But I didn't stop to think. I just walked and I talked; Tyga
grew silent, which I interpreted as grumpiness, and India
slept sweetly under her covers.

Despite this disastrous excursion to the park, and despite
other similar experiences, when we were together but wanting completely different things from each other, our
friendship, our attachment to one another, never quite died.
We never did anything terrible enough to kill it off.

Consequently, over the years that followed, during which
we each had other relationships, we would always see one
another a couple of times a year. Our meetings were never
amorous but always cordial, and on each occasion I would
find India a little older, a little bigger. While she lay in her
Moses basket and gurgled, or later, while she played with
her tea set or her dolls, her mother and I would talk. Neither
of us said much – that is to say neither of us said anything of
any importance – but when we parted there was always a
shared sense that under the crust of the conversation, deep

and powerful feelings were moving around and waiting to get out.

Some time in the middle of the 1980s our relations became amorous again. After a while we decided to live together. One morning Tyga appeared outside my flat in her rusting Fiesta. She was wearing a bright African skirt. I carried her boxes of plates, saucepans and kitchen utensils up to the flat. But she was not moving in completely. We had agreed on a trial period. She was keeping her flat in Shepherd's Bush. There was her daughter to think of. What if she gave up her flat and our relationship collapsed? I agreed. Absolutely.

India was nearly five when her mother came to live with me. I didn't know anything about children. Nor had I, until I met Tyga, ever (at least consciously) imagined that my life was going to involve children. I can be more categorical. I had always assumed that the life I was going to lead would never, under any circumstances, involve children. My plans were quite other; I was going to be a writer and occasionally a director of films. I was going to travel. Relationships, yes; marriage possibly; but offspring, no. Never.

Because of this certainty, I was very careful and emphatic, in the beginning, regarding my status with the child. I was not father or stepfather; I was the mother's boyfriend; I was Carlo, and India called me Carlo. This went on for several months, Carlo this, Carlo that.

Then, one afternoon, when I was at my desk, Tyga crept up, a silencing finger across her lips. 'Shush!' she said, and led me to the corridor which connected the two huge rooms that comprised the flat, at one end of which there was a full-length mirror. India was standing in front of the mirror in her tartan dress, her fine blond hair in a ponytail that snaked down her back. A Norman Rockwell painting if ever I saw one.

India was saying something to the mirror. For a second or two I couldn't quite hear what it was, so fast were the words

tripping off her tongue. Then my ears adjusted. She was con-
ducting an imaginary conversation, sometimes calling me
Carlo, sometimes calling me Dad. As her stream of talk continued, she said Carlo less and less, and Dad more and more.
Then her focus became just the word – Dad – and she tried
saying it in her happy voice, her sad voice, her loud voice, her
commanding voice, her princess voice, her wizard voice, her
robot voice, and so on. This rehearsal lasted for several minutes, throughout which India was quite unaware we were
watching.

Tyga and I slipped away. What did I do? I wondered. It
didn't seem I had any alternative, I said, but to follow India's
lead. That evening, I heard Tyga suggesting to India, as she
put her to bed, that she was free to call me whatever she
wanted, Dad, Carlo, whatever, and the next morning it was
Dad when she woke me up, and it has been ever since.

My position, I know, was special. Most stepchildren have a
living mother or father to whom they can return, or at least
refer. India had no such figure. She knew about her father,
Mike, of course, knew he was her biological father, and that I
was her other father; however, there was no living person she
could talk about or go and see; that original father was gone.
This made the life we started living together much easier than
I know has been the experience of other step-parents. There
was no figure of whom I could be jealous, no figure she
could use to taunt me. There was just us and we had to get on
with it.

I did not love India when she appeared in my life, not for
herself, I mean. She came into my life because I loved her
mother. Then I loved her because I thought I ought to (which
was not love) and then because I wanted the mother to love
me (which was self-interest). What happened over the course
of several years in the company of each other was that slowly,
and without either of us always knowing it was happening,

we began to grow into each other. Shared experience between the step-parent and the stepchild is what forges love. It won't necessarily be all good (the experiences, I mean, the love, of course, is always good); also, most of the experiences are minor, domestic and they make poor copy. But there are, as I look back, certain key moments in this process that are big and have narrative weight. On the road which I travelled with India these – for me – are some of the milestones.

The first occurred one summer's afternoon about the same time as she started to call me Dad. India was peering out the window into the communal garden. The boisterous screeches of children and the lower tones of supervising mothers drifted up from below. It was Lawrence's party; he was one of our neighbour's children. India knew the boy vaguely. He was a couple of years older than her. He had let her play with him a few times when there were no older children around, and in her mind that made them friends.

India ran out of the room. I heard her clattering around in her bedroom. She came back wearing her best dress, her best shoes and her best Alice band. I knew what was coming, felt sick already about it, and then her words confirmed the worst. Would I take her down to the garden to her friend Lawrence's party? she asked. All the other children were out there, all the other children she knew and played with were in the communal garden.

I explained quietly that although what she said was true and she did know Lawrence and several of the guests as well, unfortunately, she was not invited, possibly because he was a boy and he was a bit older and he just wanted boys of his age.

She shook her head. It was a children's party. She was a child. Ergo, the party was where she belonged.

I told her I couldn't take her down.

She insisted. Would I please take her down?

I explained to India that it would embarrass Lawrence's

mother if I appeared with her. As I explained this, I could see the expression on her face slowly changing from gleeful anticipation to sorrowful acceptance.

I suggested a walk, the park, the shops, I can't remember. India fetched a big chair, dragged it to the window, got up on it. No, she insisted, she was going to watch the party. She didn't move for the rest of the afternoon.

That was my first lesson in fatherhood. Hurt was inevitable and there was nothing I was going to be able to do. Fatherhood was not only bath-time and ice cream and stories, it was also failure. And as I recognised this, I was filled with a hubristic ambition. Never again would the child suffer. At least not at my hands. What I had to learn next was that not only was it impossible to protect her, but that I also would be a cause of hurt (including the heartache that comes with exclusion). I was not and never would be perfect.

At that time the documentary film I was making about Francis Stuart was still on-going. Or perhaps waiting to get on-going would be more accurate.

Because the subject was 'difficult' the funding of the film was erratic. Over the previous three or four years, work on the film had started, stopped, restarted, and then stopped again countless times. We were on and then off with the regularity of a metronome.

Then, during the first winter Tyga and I were together, Francis Stuart came to London. I decided to give a dinner. I liked him. Also I wanted to keep him committed to the film. This was a big occasion; twenty people, starched tablecloths, a four-course meal.

The guests were assembled. They stood or sat around the big room in my flat drinking and talking. Suddenly, I saw a little face at the door scrutinising the room. What was India doing? I wondered. I thought she was in bed. She was supposed to be in bed. Mummy had had a long talk with her earlier about the importance of being a good girl on this important evening.

I called India in but she disappeared. I heard her feet in the hall as she ran off. Then, a few moments later, she reappeared, dragging her small scaled-down bedroom chair, the one that matched her small bedroom table.

She dragged the chair across the floor, manœuvred it into the small space beside the guest of honour, and sat down. That was the moment when I saw that what she wanted, more than anything, was the assurance of a guaranteed place in every situation, and that my first task as a stepfather was to always make her feel included and never to leave her out.

Another memory; the event was small, yet the significance remains massive. One Sunday, we went to the flat below ours for drinks. When it was time to leave, the host, Ivan, followed us along his hall towards the door. Suddenly, there was a loud crash overhead. The ceiling shook and the light bulb dangling from the ceiling rose went pop. Three sets of adult eyes swivelled upwards. The crash was India of course. Her room was directly above Ivan's hallway. She was seven years old now. A keen and ambitious gymnast, India had taken to jumping and tumbling, somersaulting and cartwheeling in her bedroom, just like she did in the Little Tots gym class at the Kensington Sports Centre.

As we apologised, Ivan opened the hall cupboard. From floor to ceiling it was filled with boxes of light bulbs. As Ivan removed the broken bulb and put in a new one, he mentioned that he did this as many as half a dozen times a week if India was being particularly athletic. We were embarrassed but our host was blithe. She was a child, of course she was going to break light bulbs. Would I have my daughter any other way? he asked.

Of course not, I said, and then it struck me that he'd used the word daughter without saying step, and that pulled me up. Ivan knew about India's circumstances and yet, I realised, as far as he was concerned I was her father. That was the moment I recognised that part of this mysterious bonding process had nothing to do with oneself and everything to do with others and the way they would push you together. The ending of *Gregory's Girl* (when John Gordon Sinclair's mates sort out his love life) might be saccharine but it was also true.

Also, I had always felt I would lose my squeamishness to fathering without my volition; I would go to sleep as myself, as someone who did not think fathering and children were for him, and I would wake not thinking that any more. But apparently it didn't quite work like that.

What happened was that others made assumptions, just like Ivan had, and these had an effect. Or they had an effect on me. I hadn't changed internally (not that I was aware); I was just expected to be fatherly and, as a result, I found I was. I suppose this is the up side of peer pressure.

Or perhaps I'd always wanted what I was getting, only I had never known it.

Anyway, I ran straight upstairs after Ivan showed me his stash of light bulbs and gave India a hug, although she hadn't a clue what this was about.

chapter fifty-three

After living together for a while, we decided, Tyga and I, that we would have another child. A sibling for India. A proof both to her and to ourselves that we were committed to being a family, an expanding family. A proof of our love. And Tyga wanted more children. She always had.

Jack was born in the flat on a sweltering June night, with all the windows thrown open. India was in her room. The midwife went and told her she had a brother. She bounced on her bunk with joy and proclaimed with Freudian gusto that now she had someone to marry; Jack would be her future husband.

Over the weeks that followed, while Tyga lay in our bed, suckling the infant and receiving a stream of visitors, I went into shock. A ready-made fully-formed five-year-old had been my first experience of fatherhood. She talked, she walked, she even brushed her own hair. But now, here was a small, helpless ball for whose care I was responsible. For ever.

It vaguely occurred to me that I hadn't ever felt anything like that for India. She had never been a small helpless ball for whom I knew I was responsible. With Jack's birth, I saw that I needed to be more India's father than I was. I'll rephrase that. I saw I hadn't yet taken on board – or 'internalised' – a sense of absolute custodial responsibility for her. In India's case that word 'step' was still there before the word father (despite all the hugs and all the shared experiences), and not until that word was completely erased would I be, for her, what it was immediately obvious I was going to be to my son – the unconditionally loving (though far from perfect) parent, or, to paraphrase the child psychiatrist Bruno Bettelheim, the good enough father.

When she got out of bed Tyga decided we would go and see my father. His first grandson had just sprung into the world. We had a duty to bring the child over to Ireland and show him to his grandfather. I wasn't certain what reaction we would receive. It would not be warm, perhaps. But Tyga was adamant. Even if nothing happened, *we* would have done the right thing.

And so it was, sometime in early August, I nosed the car up the drive of Cnoc Aluin, and parked. We tumbled out and climbed the front steps. I was about to grasp the knocker when I noticed a small note attached with a rusting thumb-tack (hoarded, presumably, for years): 'Door open. Push hard.' We were, it seemed, expected.

We pushed open the door and stepped in to the hall. George Gershwin's 'Rhapsody in Blue' drifted from the room at the end of the corridor.

My father appeared holding a velvet cylinder. It was filled with distilled water and it was for cleaning fluff balls and dust spots off records. He had one in Cannon Hill Lane which I wasn't allowed to touch as a boy. Perhaps this was the same one. It was quite possible.

He clocked each of us in turn, then gazed at India and smiled. Only she seemed to delight him.

We ambled into the back room filled with Gershwin's music. The volume was lowered. Introductions were effected, hands were shaken. My father and Tyga had never met before. I couldn't even be certain if I'd mentioned her on one of my awkward visits.

Tyga placed herself in front of my father. The moment had arrived.

'This is your grandson,' said Tyga.

My father looked shifty, alarmed. He didn't move or reach out. The seconds ticked by – my father frozen, Tyga waiting – and I knew, as they ticked past, that she was wondering, why? Why didn't he react? Of course, I had told her about him beforehand. (In fact, I'd bored her for years with details of my childhood.) I had told her not to expect anything and she had nodded and said she understood. But no amount of forewarning could prepare her for the utter non-reaction of a grandfather to his first-born grandchild.

Yet now she had to accept it because it was happening. She was standing holding the baby out to him and he was ignoring it.

The moment seemed to last for a long time. In reality, it was probably only a second or two.

As I watched and waited I wondered why I had come? Tyga was hurt. This was a disaster. I should have stuck to the routine I knew. I should have just popped in to see my father by myself, told him he had a grandson, and left after an hour.

I was expecting Tyga to back away, thus ending this excruciating moment. However, to my surprise, she pushed the little bundle against my father's chest instead.

Involuntarily, his arms rose like the two prongs on a forklift truck.

'That's Jack,' explained Tyga, and she stepped back, leaving my father holding him. She said one or two other things. My father stared down, wrinkling his brow. Was it disgust or annoyance or indifference that he felt? I couldn't tell.

There were a few further moments of silence, during which nothing was said, and then he reached forward and tumbled the baby back into his mother's arms, exactly mirroring what Tyga had done a few moments earlier. The moment was over. The introduction of grandfather and grandson had passed without comment. Tyga would be disappointed but, well, I had warned her, hadn't I?

My father gazed again at India. Who was this lovely little girl? he asked. India, overcome with shyness, backed away towards the window. The questions continued. Where did she come from? What was her name? Again I wished I hadn't come. It wasn't that I didn't want him to pay attention to India. I did. She was his granddaughter. Not just technically. I was trying to be her father like I was Jack's father. But I also wanted him to pay attention to the baby.

My cousin, Isolde, appeared from the basement. (She was the daughter of my father's sister Louise and a man called Breen, neither of whom I remember ever meeting.) Isolde lived in Dalkey, I gathered, and called round to Cnoc Aluin most days to see her uncle.

There was another round of introductions. Then Isolde, whom I had met only briefly once or twice before, began to gush and enthuse. Lovely new baby. What was he called? How much did he weigh? How was the birth? And so on.

The fact this virtual stranger (even if related) could ask these perfectly normal questions pointed up my father's inability to manage them at all. But then he wasn't like other people, I reminded myself; so what the hell was I getting upset about? He was the way he was. There was no point expecting him to be otherwise. That was futile. A mug's game. I should have learnt that lesson by now. But apparently I hadn't.Isolde said goodbye and left and an instant later, just like in a play, another set of footsteps sounded and Jane appeared from the kitchen below.

She smiled and said hello. Everyone was kissed and welcomed effusively. This didn't make sense. Jane never went over the top like this; it wasn't her way.

But perhaps, I thought, she had stood at the bottom of the basement stairs earlier and listened; heard Tyga plop the baby into my father's arms; heard Tyga's words; then registered my father's deafening silence that followed. Jane was compensating for him. Now I felt even more irritated.

'I need to have a pee,' I announced. This was a lie.

There was a cloakroom at the end of the room with a notice pinned to the door that I had read on my way in. This warned the lavatory floorboards were rotten.

I raced towards the door.

'Don't go in,' I heard my father.

I would ignore him. I was going to open the door as if I hadn't heard, step forward and put my foot through the bloody floor and out the ceiling underneath. That would teach him. And purge my fury.

As I grasped the handle I heard Tyga saying, 'Don't go in there.'

She said this very reasonably. She also signalled, with her tone, that though she understood why I was about to do this, she didn't think it was wise. After all, what would it achieve? Nothing. Just a big hole. And did I really want that to be what this visit was remembered for?

I faltered. Tyga was right. This was no time for accidentally-on-purpose acts of vandalism. 'Oh, sorry,' I said. I pointed at the notice as if I'd only just spotted it. 'I see. You can't go in.'

'I can hear the kettle boiling,' said Jane, 'shall we go down?'

En masse, we descended the rickety stairs, the faint smell of gas rising from below to meet us.

chapter fifty-four

The kitchen was a long dark room with a low ceiling. There was a cluttered table with a reading lamp.

Jane sat down on a form and began to shell peas. I noticed a 1930s map of Dublin tacked to the side of stairs. Its colouring was a lovely *mélange* of green and yellow, red and blue.

In addition to its aesthetic appeal, the map looked interesting because it had pins stuck into it and blocks of text obviously referring to the pins, in my father's hand, were all round the margins. I went to inspect; my father followed me over.

The first thing I noticed was a pin at Broome bridge; near here my father had written, 'This is where Behan swam with his urchin friends.' There was another pin beside Finglas quarry. In the text my father explained this was where he trained for the Liffey swim.

'Was that where you used to empty your lungs, sink down to the bottom, and then climb up the rock face like an underwater mountaineer?' I asked.

I had never forgotten his accounts of doing this.

My father ignored my question and tapped the map. 'For the autobiography, I'm writing,' he said.

'Oh.'

'For the autobiography, I'm writing,' he repeated.

It sounded like a warning. Beware, autobiography coming. You won't like it. Of course, I might have been wrong. He may simply have been communicating information, but I didn't think so. Years of antagonism had taught me that he never simply stated facts; whatever he said it was with the intention of hurting.

I wandered over to the stove where there appeared to be two different meals in preparation.

'Ah, spotted the two dinners,' Jane called.

'Yes,' I said.

'And now I suppose, being the nosy sort of fellow you are, you'll want to know why?'

'Yes,' I said.

'Well, I shall tell you,' she continued, with an exaggerated smile on her face. 'One meal is for dear sweetly beloved, totally non-eccentric Ernie, while the other is for the rest of us poor ordinary mortals.'

Perhaps mine was a sheep's heart? I made a face.

'Don't do that,' Jane said, tartly. 'Let me explain. You see, your father's convinced, no, he knows this to be a fact: Dublin tap water is poisoned.'

'What with?' I wondered, obtusely.

'Let's see,' she said. 'With lead from the old pipes put in by the Victorians in the nineteenth century, with strontium-90 from Sellafield, and with muck and filth from the city's sewers. All Dublin water is recycled and the city sewerage works, it's a well-known fact according to him, are incompetent.'

'So, every month, dear sweetly beloved Ernie boils up several gallons of tap water, puts it through a worm and produces distilled water for his personal use. This is his drinking water and this is the water that his vegetables are cooked in. The small saucepan filled with potatoes on the right – d'you see it? – that's full of distilled water.

'Now I suppose you want to know what's simmering in the little casserole dish at the back?'

'Yes.'

'Venison.'

'Lovely.'

'You can stop that right now. That is not for you, that is for his lordship. He does not eat commercially produced pork, beef or lamb.'

'Why?'

'Because it's a well-known fact that all Irish farmers are crazy and irresponsible and money-mad, and feed their animals steroids and antibiotics to up their yield. The only animal in Ireland that isn't fed these chemical poisons is the noble deer, so the noble deer is all that he eats.'

Our meal was on the left-hand side of the stove; lamb from a butcher in Dalkey and vegetables boiled in Dublin tap water.

'Your father's dietary habits have become more bizarre with each passing year,' Jane continued. Then she winked at me. It's ridiculous, of course it is, her gesture said, but indulge him.

My father was still gazing at the map. Now he turned towards me, as if he had suddenly become aware that he was the subject of conversation.

'Yes, my darling Ernie, what is it?' Jane cried across to him.

'I'm going to have you know,' said my father, in his joshing voice, 'I'm going to cure my allegories . . .'

'You mean your allergies,' Jane interrupted.

'My allergies,' said my father, and laughed, 'and my hay fever, and my sore eyes, and my anchylosis spondylitis and I will do it with diet. You know, ninety per cent of all illness is an allergic reaction to what you take in to your body . . .'

'Yes, dear, of course, dear, three bags full, dear. Everyone else will drink Dublin tap water and die but you, who won't, you will live for ever. Won't you, chuck?

'And you're going to win the Nobel. Twice. Once for medicine, once for literature. No one here doubts it. You're a genius.'

She sounded like a wife from an old Hollywood film, the kind who has to give endless encouragement and succour to a slightly useless husband. But beneath the patter something else lurked. Why was she trying so hard?

Beside the stove was a small shelf with a shaving mirror, several toothbrushes, toothpicks, tubes of toothpaste and files in a cup like arrows in a quiver. Ah, the dental corner, I thought.

He was always obsessed with his teeth. He brushed them several times every day when we lived in Cannon Hill Lane, varying the brush according to what he had eaten (soft bristles after carbohydrates, harder bristles after meat). And many a mealtime, he would harangue us on the dangers of white refined sugar; it was, he used to say, after tobacco, the next best killer designed by consumer capitalism. He frequently visited a dentist in those days (as did we) but if he thought the bite on one of his own teeth was wrong, rather than wait until his next dental appointment he would fix it himself. He used his shaving mirror (the very one I saw now) and he did the work at the sink. If I was in the kitchen I would stare at the mirror, mesmerised by the larger-than-life reflection of his tonsils, his throat, the top of his oesophagus, the wet flesh purple and puce, and the little file going backwards and forwards over the troublesome molar . . .

'Tyga, Carlo, India, Ernie, me,' I heard Jane saying from her bench. 'Ernie, be a dear, go and get another chair,' she continued, in an enhanced Yorkshire accent. 'We're one short.'

'I will,' I said.

'No, he can. You're the guest and he's still good for *some* things.'

'Chair – Ernie,' she said emphatically, 'go – get – a – chair . . . for you to sit on . . .'

'Ah, yes,' said my father, eventually. He disappeared up the stairs. Then we heard his footfalls through the ceiling.

'Does he still fix his teeth?'

'It's more that he plays with them, really.'

'And how is he? I mean, how is he really?'

'He's all right,' she said. She shot a line of peas out of a pod. 'By the way,' she continued, 'I should explain. I'm doing a week's worth of peas. You won't have to eat them all.' She laughed quietly at this idea.

'Do you do all your cooking at the weekend so you're free in the week?' I asked.

'Something like that,' she said, in an odd voice.

'Ernie really is getting a bit forgetful, isn't he?' I said.

'Forgetful, oh yes,' Jane agreed, 'just a tad. But who isn't? It's the curse of age. But you're too young to understand. You're still a spring chicken.'

She smiled again.

'All in good time, though. First there'll be the little aches, the little creaks. That'll be the body running down. Then there'll be the little lapses of concentration, and of recall. That'll be the brain going. This'll happen about the age of fifty, or there-abouts; after which, no matter how hard you try, and by God Ernie's tried, you can't reverse it. Goodness no. It's irreversible.'

Once you passed fifty, she continued, you were like a piece of knitting that gradually comes undone. Thread after thread comes free and you end your days, she said, as a soft confused jumble of tangles and knots.

'So enjoy your life while you're young,' she ended.

This was the only philosophical opinion she expressed during all the years I knew her.

'Where is that man?' she exclaimed.

We looked up. There was complete silence above.

'He's quite prone to wander off,' she said. 'He could go upstairs to find a book and not come back for three days.'

'He wanders regularly, does he?' I asked.

'Well, yes,' she said, 'but there's nothing you need worry about.'

'No.'

'He doesn't wander out of the house and step out into the traffic. He doesn't turn on the gas and forget to light it. He doesn't forget to eat. He's just a bit forgetful, now and then, about chores, like fetching a chair.'

'Oh.'

'How old is he now?' she wondered.

We both calculated quickly.

'Seventy-three,' she said.

'Seventy-three,' I said.

'He's had a good innings,' she said, 'and at his age, a little wear and tear is inevitable.'

A muffled sound came from above. A footfall? I wasn't quite certain.

'Would you go up and see? He's probably up there thinking, What have I come up here for? I can't remember . . .'

I climbed the linoleum-covered stairs. As I came to the top, I saw my father standing in the middle of the big square room. He stood side on to me, his hands in front of him, like a painted figure in an ancient Egyptian tomb.

'Where's the chair?' I asked, cheerfully.

He didn't hear. Or appear to hear. He was looking at something.

I climbed the last step and went across to him. He was

looking at the floorboards. His expression was rapt, concentrated and diffuse, all at once.

'Where's the chair?' I asked.

He didn't hear me.

I squeezed his arm. He shook his head like a man waking; then he smiled and whispered, gently, 'The chair, yes, the chair. That was why I came upstairs, wasn't it? I came up the stairs, you see, and then, when I got upstairs, I couldn't remember why. What I'd come for. It went clean out of my mind. So I stood here and tried to remember and then . . .'

He waved his hands several times indicating, I presumed, that then he got lost in his thoughts and forgot what he had come for.

'Chair,' I said.

He pointed at the dining table ringed with chairs. I took one. He turned and began to go down and I followed. I stared at the back of his head. The skin on his cranium was wrinkled and rumpled like a carpet coming loose.

He was showing his age physically as well as psychologically. Suddenly, I felt an unexpected tug of sympathy for Jane (whom I had never been able to think of as my stepmother and whom I had never much liked). I didn't know how old she was but it was my impression that she was – what? – twenty years younger than my father? Maybe more. She was certainly middle-aged, while he was certainly old; she had years to run; his life was nearly done. It occurred to me that perhaps that explained why she was so edgy and over-emphatic, almost hysterical. It was because she knew he was going to die.

'What kept you?' Jane called out cheerfully, when we appeared. She was speaking to my father, not me.

My father shrugged. He'd forgotten even that he'd forgotten. So that was short-term memory loss for you.

Old age, terrible in theory, much worse in practice.

chapter fifty-five

We sat down at the kitchen table, and while the meals bubbled on the stove, we drank tea and ate Jane's home-made brown bread spread with her home-made black-currant jam. After the first pot of tea was finished, Jane made a second by adding new leaves to the old. The tea that flowed from the spout of the teapot was the colour of mahogany.

'I can never get enough tea,' my father said, 'never, never . . .'

We talked about his legendary tea-drinking and, as we talked, my father kept looking at India. His expression was a mixture of concern and curiosity. Suddenly, he broke off from what he was saying and asked her if she was all right?

India said yes.

He smiled.

Was she sure she was sure? he asked.

Yes, said India. She nodded and affirmed again that she was happy. The exchange pleased him.

We went on talking again but he kept on looking at India.

He couldn't stop himself. It was a compulsion. I knew he'd always wished he'd had a daughter. Now I couldn't help wondering if perhaps he saw the daughter he never had sitting across the table from him.

'Would you like to draw?' my father suggested to India.

When I was a child and he said such a sentence, it was freighted with rebuke. It meant: why don't you do something useful instead of mooning about?

This afternoon, on the contrary, it was as if he saying: India, I see you sitting with nothing to do while we adults natter away. Why don't you draw? At least it'll pass the time.

India nodded. Yes, she'd like to draw. He smiled again. He handed her a pencil and a scrap of paper. (Not the wrapper from *Time* magazine, alas.) He told her to draw what she wanted and that he would keep her drawing; it would remind him of her. He said this in his nice voice.

When we lived together in Cannon Hill Lane, his anger, his resentment and his infinite disappointment gushed out of him in a ceaseless torrent. This was especially the case during the years after my mother left; he could never fathom why I preferred her to him and my preference infuriated him. On the other hand, his capacity for affection and warmth he mostly hid. I got a glimpse of it only very occasionally; for instance when he spoke of Adolf after he died. But such glimpses were rare and he released his true feelings like drops from an eye dropper: drop, drop, drop, out they came, these infinitesimally small blobs of real tenderness.

Now, however, all these years later, all was utterly changed. Now there was no more caution, or parsimony or exactitude with the expression of feeling. He liked India. He liked her a lot more than his grandson. She interested him. She pleased him. And he was happy we should all know. Absolutely delighted.

Here was another sign of age and rather a good one, I thought. In this respect age had improved him; it had made him almost benign.

I enjoyed this idea for a second or two. Then, as India began to draw, his expression changed. He looked around. He looked like he'd suddenly remembered something incredibly disagreeable.

Have you ever met the woman Edna? he called across to Tyga.

His dark brown nearly black eyes were magnified by the lenses of his glasses. The nice voice was gone. The nice expression was gone. The man of a few seconds earlier was gone. The man I now saw looked grumpy, very focused and demented. Here was the father I had always known. He had reverted to type.

Yes, Tyga said, she had met my mother. Several times. She said this cautiously. She knew something tricky and probably quite unpleasant was coming.

So, you have met Edna then, my father mused, malevolently rolling my mother's Christian name around his mouth.

He always used her name and avoided, as far as grammar allowed, any reference to the fact that she was the mother of myself and my brother. It was a way of denying her place and contribution to the family. It was a way of minimising (if not obliterating) the fact that she and he had two children together.

So, you met Edna, he said again, like an interrogator.

Yes, said Tyga, many times.

And did you like her?

Yes, said Tyga.

Very charming, Edna, said my father, and very plausible, meaning, of course, precisely the reverse.

Tyga said nothing.

Was Tyga aware, my father continued, that it was he who had written Edna's first two books and not her?

Again, Tyga said nothing.

Oh yes, my father continued. It was he who'd written them. Didn't she know that? *The Country Girls* and *Girl with Green Eyes*, he continued. The two successful books.

Tyga had the baby on her breast. She swapped the baby from left to right. I knew she couldn't be surprised by this. She knew he said things like this, I had warned her. These remarks were one of the unending themes of my late childhood and early adolescence. She may even have read an article in which he made this claim. Since his return to Ireland, he always said he wrote my mother's first two books in any interviews he gave to newspapers.

Did Tyga not know about this? he continued. Tyga said nothing. In which case, he said, he would explain. Edna wanted to publish and he wanted children; so, they did a deal. A book for a child. He wrote the books. She gave him the children he wanted.

And how did it work in practice? he then asked rhetorically. Simple. She wrote. He rewrote. She re-rewrote in order to make his work look like hers. Then she published and got famous.

While he spoke I recalled my mother, during our first miserable winter in Cannon Hill Lane, talking to herself under her breath as she hammered away at her typewriter. That was when she was writing *The Country Girls*. Later, I remembered spotting her through the filthy window of the hut at the bottom of the garden. This was when she was writing *Girl with Green Eyes*. I had witnessed my mother writing the books herself, and yet despite that, he could come up with this. It was incredible.

Suddenly, my father stopped. This too was familiar. He had his act down to a fine T. There was a moment of silence.

Why did he do it? he asked. Why did he write her good books? Did it do him any good?

No, of course it didn't! he replied to himself.

He must have been a fool, he said. Of course he was. Because having kept his part of the deal, what did Edna go and do? Get a taste for the London high life, that was what she went and did. Then, exactly like Leatrice who stole his first son, Edna upped and deserted him, in the middle of the night, taking his children with her. It was so cruel but then, that was Edna. Couldn't think of anyone but herself. A monomaniac if ever there was one.

While he delivered the what-my-ex-wife-did-to-me part of his monologue, I swirled the slops in the bottom of my tea cup. I'd had to live with these lies all my life. Now I was what – how old was I? almost thirty-three. I'd be thirty-three any minute now, 21 August (not that my father would notice, he always ignored birthdays), anyway, nearly thirty-three and I was still having to listen to his bilge.

It was unconscionable. It was not for this that I had come all the way to Dublin. I wanted to tell him that I had not one single happy memory from the times we had lived together. Not one. Then I wanted to storm out, dragging my family with me.

For a moment I savoured the scene: stamping up the stairs, slamming the front door, driving away furiously . . .

There came a pause, at last, in my father's flow of words. Did I really want to get up and go? I wondered. Here it was, my perfect opportunity, but could I? Could I really do it?

The trouble was, I told myself, he wouldn't understand this gesture. He was a mad, selfish monomaniac whose mind was turning to mush. He would either dismiss my action as melodrama or, worse, fail to notice I had even gone. Either way, it would be futile, wouldn't it?

But what about the value to my psychic health of such an

action? There must come a day, must there not, when the
son stands up to his father. Was this that day? Perhaps.

But then, I wondered, what would I actually feel, driving
away? Tyga beside me in the front passenger seat, asking why
I had got us up and made us leave? Through Tyga's eyes I
imagined I would look childish, spoilt and immature.

The fact was, we weren't here for me, were we? Not at all.
We were here, well, for Tyga to show off the baby, not that my
father had shown much interest. And we were here for India.
That hadn't been our purpose in coming but that's how it had
turned out. He was being nice to India. So I couldn't leave,
could I? No, of course not. Not with him being nice to the
child who had no grandfather, biological or adoptive, other
than him. I couldn't leave now, could I?

It's interesting what you're saying, I now heard Tyga say to
my father. She spoke in her diplomatic I-don't-want-to-cause-
a-row-I'm-just-making-my-point voice. What about Edna's
other books? Tyga asked. She'd written those since he and
Edna had parted company. They'd been well received. They'd
sold well. Given that Edna wrote these, surely, it followed,
Tyga continued quietly and logically, that she wrote the first
two books herself, as well.

My father scowled and waved his hand, dismissing what
she had said. What was Tyga talking about? Had she read the
later books? Only the first two books were any good, because
he wrote them; the others were patently not.

Not at all, said Tyga. She didn't agree with him. She talked
book sales and popularity. My father rebutted what she said.
She counter-attacked. Their dialogue seemed to go on for
ever. I now wanted to shout at him, Shut the fuck up. But I
didn't. I said nothing. I just sat there, like someone at a tennis
match watching the ball go tick, tock, tick, tock, backwards
and forwards across the net.

Then, without warning, the discussion stopped. Perhaps

my father was exhausted by Tyga's polite but tenacious rebuttal of his argument. Anyway, the kitchen was suddenly quiet. I heard the vegetables boiling on the stove.

'You know,' said my father suddenly, 'I really loved Edna.'

He said this as if the words were underlined, as if what he was really saying was, She was the one.

I tried to judge the truth of this. One part of me thought, no, this was meaningless nonsense. His mind was like a circular saw after the motor was turned off; this was just a puff of sawdust thrown up by the whirring blade.

But another part of me thought, yes, it's possible. It's more than possible. In the end I decided he meant it, not that my feelings towards my father were altered one jot by this.

The rest of the visit passed off without incident. We ate, we talked about I can't remember what and then we said goodbye, climbed into the car and drove away.

A few minutes into the journey, I asked Tyga what she thought of my father. She said she found him quirky and quite interesting. He was a strange but not unpleasant eccentric. It was weird that she saw him so differently to me.

'So you enjoyed yourself.'

'Oh yes. What about you. Did you?'

I felt too tired to explain that I felt worn out and that, on balance, notwithstanding his friendliness towards India, I thought it was a complete waste of time to have gone.

chapter fifty-six

Now that we had Jack as well as India, we decided to move. We sold the flat and bought ourselves a terrace house at the top of Ladbroke Grove. The house was built in 1922 on the site of the old St Quintin Park. It was built of brick and painted white. It had a bay window, a metal gate and a bumpy path leading to the front door. As you went through the front door there were two rooms on the right and stairs straight ahead. Upstairs there was a boxroom over the front door and stairs, a big front bedroom and a smaller back bedroom. At the back of the house was a London back garden, full of grey-black London earth.

Proportion-wise, design-wise, age-wise, geometry-wise, in fact every-wise, the new house completely replicated Cannon Hill Lane. And funnily enough, I liked it; I loved it. I felt much more at home than I'd ever felt in the flat. This taught me something. The things that shape you, become you. I might have liked to think of myself as suited to a stucco mansion near Regent's Park, or a large house like Lake Park in the Wicklow mountains, but actually, the truth was, I didn't belong in houses like these. What I fitted were bog-standard three-bedroom suburban houses. I grew up in one, and now that I was back in one I felt as if I had come home.

I always used to think I was going to outgrow the past. Then I realised I could never outgrow it: as I grew older I came to understand that with the passing of time I just became more and more what I was always destined to become. I was the past and it was me.

chapter fifty-seven

I t was a Monday early in May 1989. I was in my study overlooking my suburban garden. The telephone rang. It was a
friend from Dublin.

'Are you sitting down?' she asked. My father's died, I
thought, that's why she's rung. But he hadn't. It was Jane who
had died. She died cutting the grass in front of Cnoc Aluin. It
was my father who had found her.

I put down the phone. My very first thought was that
surely, with my stepmother dead, my father would now have
to leave Cnoc Aluin to my brother, Sasha, and myself, which
would surely mean that he did love us after all. I hated having
this thought but I couldn't stop myself.

I dialled Cnoc Aluin.

'Hello, yes, this is 859195,' I heard him saying in his high-
pitched voice.

'This is Carlo.'

'Who . . . oh yes, I know who you are.'

He didn't sound testy; he sounded genuinely pleased.

'You heard my bad news?' he said.

'That's right.'

'It's so sudden, you know. One moment the person's perfectly fine and the next moment – wham! That's it, they're dead . . .

'They look the same. She looked exactly as if she was alive – only she wasn't. She'd stopped working. For no reason at all, the vessels in the brain had ruptured and she'd suffered a massive haemorrhage. But her face was white and composed; no sign of what had gone on inside her skull.

'I couldn't make sense of it. It's not like an accident, someone being mangled in a car. You can't accept that but you can understand it. But these ruptures, no one knows why the brain just has this explosion. I can only think it was a decision. She'd had enough, so the system closed down . . .

'This is a very neighbourly place . . . as soon as the man next door heard, he was straight round though I'd hardly spoken to him in years . . .

'The whole funeral's being looked after by other people . . . I'm not going. It may help other people to see someone being put in the ground in a box but it won't help me. I can do without that . . .

'I was very close to her. It was the only relationship I had with a woman, you know, that didn't turn out to be a failure. At first there was passion but after a few years that sloped off and this other thing developed. Companionship . . . I would have done anything she asked and she, apparently, would have done anything I asked . . . It was a great thing; we get too isolated, we writers . . .

'Anyway, she's gone. There it is. I've got this pain in my middle and there's no way out of it. It's like I have to walk sixteen miles along the track to the next station because there's no train . . . Maybe I should have had a couple of whiskies but what good would they have done? You have to live through pain and no palliatives can do any good . . .

'Only time will heal. It'll wear thinner and thinner and pare away and pare away, until finally it's gone. It'll take as long as it takes.

'In the meantime, I go on trying to be normal. Eat a little bit of food. Walk down to the sea and look at it. I'm going to try and get down to some proofreading . . .'

He went on like this for an hour. Finally, I couldn't listen any more.

'I have to say goodbye,' I said. 'Do you have my number?'

'Let me get a pencil and paper,' he said. He went away, came back and said, 'OK, who are you?'

'Carlo.'

'You see, I can't remember details any more. And the connection between names and faces, I've lost it.'

'Gébler,' I said.

'Oh yes,' he replied, his voice a mixture of comprehension and wonder, 'I've got that.'

I gave him my number. We said goodbye. I put the handset back on the cradle.

I looked out the window. This was the first time he'd ever told me what he felt.

At the back of my garden there was a bedding nursery where a workman was busy loading big terracotta pots on to the back of a flatbed lorry. Every time he dropped a pot down, there was a boom like a drumbeat.

chapter fifty-eight

A couple of months later (when Jack was two and India was nearly nine) we left London and went to Ireland, to Northern Ireland, to Enniskillen to be precise. I was to write a book. It was to be a Troubles book but, unlike most other Troubles books, I was going to eschew the cities and towns of Northern Ireland, and the paramilitaries; instead I was going to write about conflict in the countryside from the point of view of those who were afflicted by it. I thought it would take six months, at most a year, to write this book.

At first we lived in the nursery at the top of an old Plantation house. Then Tyga discovered that if we bought a house, the mortgage would be half what we paid in rent. So we bought an old school set amongst drumlins. Eighteen months after it should have been completed, I finished the book I had come to write. We then decided to stay.

India, meanwhile, had been at a local primary school; she had acquired a Fermanagh accent and developed a loathing for the country. Her fantasy was that we would live in a modern house on one of the satellite estates around

Enniskillen. Jack went to the Salvation Army playgroup and grew into a lusty infant.

As she grew older, India was inevitably developing her own personality, and acquiring aspirations not only different from those of myself and her mother, but often in direct conflict with them. As this was starting to happen, Tyga and I decided to have another child (perhaps unconsciously to compensate for losing India). In June 1990, Tyga gave birth to a boy whom we called Finn, and soon after his arrival quite unexpected anxieties regarding our mortality suddenly began to affect us.

What would happen, we wondered, if we both died? I had a brother and a mother to whom our sons could go, but India was still a Rudston-Thomason (this was Tyga's married name). We had no contact with India's father's biological family but who was to say, in the event of our deaths, that India wouldn't be sent to them? It seemed there were tales in the paper every day of heavy-handed social workers splitting siblings and half-siblings between their respective blood relatives. I decided to adopt and make India a Gébler. However, on enquiring, I discovered the law required I marry the mother first.

So be it; we would marry. Invitations were issued; the banns were published in the *Impartial Reporter*, the local paper. In August, we exchanged vows in the Register Office; the newborn, Finn, was firmly clamped to his mother's breast.

Next, the business of the adoption was set in hand. I was assessed by numerous social workers. My GP submitted a report on my mental and physical health. The RUC reported that I did not have a criminal record.

At last the great day came, the day the adoption would become legal, 13 February 1992. As a family we presented ourselves at the courthouse in Enniskillen. The clerk told us that the final interview with the judge, the one that would make the adoption legal, would not take place in the court but in the judge's chambers. A domestic setting, after all, said the clerk with a smile, was more appropriate, given this was not a criminal matter. Absolutely right, mate.

We followed the official down the steps, then found ourselves in the bowels of the building, walking along a corridor, cells to the right and left, and all packed with manacled paramilitary prisoners (both varieties) who were shouting abuse and banging their handcuffs on the bars. These twenty or thirty men were in the courthouse because of the things Northern Ireland is famous for; they were there to answer charges for conspiracy to cause explosions, causing explosions, murder, attempted murder, kidnapping, extortion and membership of an illegal organisation. Like us all, India was fascinated, silent and a little unnerved as she moved through the mêlée.

The judge, when we reached the chambers finally, was a quiet man sitting behind a large desk. He introduced himself, then explained he needed to ask India a few questions. Did she understand what was happening today? he asked. She shook her head. 'No,' she said.

Tyga and I were astonished. We had been preparing for this moment for over a year. India had also had numerous solo interviews with social workers who had gone over this ground. She had understood. She knew what was happening. God damn it, she'd agreed to this.

The judge smiled kindly and then explained that I was to become her legal father. Then I understood a little more about India; she enjoyed having it all explained again because she enjoyed the attention.

It was also true, however, as she explained afterwards in *Scoops Ice-Cream Parlour*, where we took the children for celebratory knickerbocker glories, that with the commotion of the remand prisoners in the holding cells, she had felt confused too. So there were two different reasons for her not answering the judge, but neither of them signified unconscious dissent.

The following Monday morning she changed her surname on the school roll, and she changed the name on her exercise books when she came home in the evening, and I think, with that, the word step was finally, finally erased and I became simply Dad, or Father.

chapter fifty-nine

The Irish Sea glistened and glittered; this summer afternoon it could pass as the Mediterranean. I was sitting in
the bay window of the Killiney home with my father. When
he arrived here he was incontinent, confused and distressed.
Now he could haltingly dress, walk, eat and talk. This was a
miracle the nurses said; Alzheimer patients weren't suppose to
recover.

We were drinking tea out of thick white cups and nibbling
Nice biscuits.

'Very nice boots,' said my father, suddenly, staring at my
feet. The boots were all leather, six eyelets, black.

'I got them in Blackman's near Brick Lane,' I said.

I bought all my shoes there when I lived in London during
the 80s. It was Jewish-run, ultra-Spartan; nothing but benches
with shoehorns attached by string and silent male assistants
who never talked their shoes up. I admired the anti-retail
ethos that was so at odds with the times, when it was almost
government policy to improve the quality of service in British
shops.

'Yes, very proletarian,' my father continued. Along with everything else his sarcasm had come back too.

'Do you remember your childhood?' I asked.

'Yes,' he said slowly.

'What did you like doing?'

'Making things.' Long pause. 'I made . . . little dustpan and brush, broom, little car, train engine. No money for toys. Had to make 'em, you see.'

'What with?'

'Wood, paper, paste, string. I was always making things.'

He had exhorted me to make toys as a boy, and now I wondered if he did this because he thought or hoped that if I had the same sort of start as he had, I'd grow up to be like him – handy, practical, useful.

I had certainly made things as a child – I had too – and as an adult I could still make things were I so inclined. The trouble was, I hated doing anything with my hands, I hated tools, and paintbrushes and sandpaper and anything associated with manual labour. They were part of what I wanted to bury.

Some of the other things he'd tried to inculcate into me when I was a child I had also withdrawn from. Anything that smacked of left-wing doctrine, for instance, I had absolutely no time for now.

His biggest failure was my mother. He wanted me to turn against her, he wanted me to decline to love her. I'd done precisely the reverse.

His programme was a failure. Or was it? Once I discovered Blackman's sold the best hand-sewn, all-leather English shoes for less than anyone else, I bought all my shoes there. Not only would my father have approved, but I could see him traipsing off to Blackman's every six months, just as I had. That was very like the way he was in his prime. A great deal of him had in fact rubbed off on me.

'Bread, too,' he announced suddenly. 'I made things with bread.' He mimed the action of moulding.

I knew prisoners did this. Had Adolf brought the skill home from internment camp and shown his five-year-old son? It was possible but it was a question I decided not to pursue. Early memories, being the most fragile of all, were surely the first to vanish, I thought. I changed tack.

'Do you remember you were a writer?'

This was a subject I felt certain he would recall.

'Yes.'

'Do you remember what you wrote?'

'No, I can't quite put a name to them, but I know I wrote books.'

I listed them. He nodded. Then the cloud lifted. *Hoffman* was his best, he said. It was simultaneously funny *and* serious. He stopped. I waited. There was a long silence. Then he said, abruptly, 'Always loved looking at leaves.'

'Leaves?'

'Blowing in the wind. Used to stare for hours. Loved them.'

This was new to me. I'd neither heard him say this nor seen him staring. As for our walks on windy days, well, he restricted his comments on those occasions to instructions: 'Stop dawdling . . . Don't trail your scarf . . . Mind that dog's mess.'

'Every one of us . . . locked inside his skull . . . a prisoner,' he continued. 'We're in here, can't get out.' He touched his forehead. 'That's what I tried to write.'

I had never had such a complete explanation of his core beliefs and surely, now he'd started, there'd be more. I waited but nothing more came.

'We're all locked up in our heads?' I said, hoping to prompt him.

He looked at me, his eyes unfocused and slightly fearful. He could not remember what he'd just said. I decided to ask about what I was certain he hadn't forgotten.

'Do you remember your wives?'

'Yes, Edna.'

'What about the others?'

He shook his head. A nurse manœuvred a man past us. She wore white tights like a pantomime fairy. My father glared.

'What's the matter?' I asked.

He said nothing.

'Do you know where we are?'

'Oh yes,' he said brightly.

'Where are we then?'

'The – British – embassy.' He paused between each word. When I was a child he called this his 'imbecile voice': it was for stupid people.

'Why are you here then?'

'In honour of my writing.'

Why would the British honour you? I wondered, unless of course, he now thought of himself as British. There was a thought.

A patient with a Zimmer frame went by, the rubber caps on the leg-ends squealing as they rubbed along the floor.

'These people will be going at five o'clock; that's when they close the passport office. Have it all to myself then. Lovely. No more people cluttering the place up.'

He nibbled a biscuit. Sugar crystals stuck to his lips.

'That branch, it's rotten.' He waved outside. 'Must lop it off.'

He'd tie his ladder to the tree, he explained, so he wouldn't fall, and use a rough saw; then he'd daub tar on the stump to keep out parasites and the awful Irish rain.

He gazed into the distance. The curving coast was a charcoal line, the Wicklow hills were a deep purple (like the blue remembered hills of Housman), and the galleon-like clouds were white with grey dust sprinkled over them.

Was he moved by what he saw? Hadn't he always loved

Ireland's eastern lip, first seen when he returned from vile
Wolverhampton?

Or perhaps, I thought, he was mourning Lake Park, his lost
house hidden in the distant hills? When I was a boy he said
selling it was the worst thing he had ever done. It was all
Edna's fault of course. She made him do it. I didn't believe
this. No wife made him do anything. He did it himself then
regretted it afterwards and blamed her.

'Mysterious clouds,' he said suddenly. 'Mysterious clouds.'

'Tell me about Adolf?'

'Who?'

'Your father.'

'Don't know him,' he said, firmly.

I went on greedily asking questions but all I got now was
gibberish. The lucid interval was over. I'd had my lot.
Mysterious clouds were as good as it got.

chapter sixty

We had just finished the tape of *The Secret Garden*, read by Glenda Jackson in her stern and scolding manner, when I saw the gateway to the Killiney home.

I indicated right. The clicker came on. It sounded very loud in the after-story quiet of the car.

'Nearly there?' Finn asked. He was three-and-a-half now; Jack was five-and-a-half; both wore baseball caps. India sat dreamily gazing through the window. She was nearly a teenager.

'Not nearly, we *are* there,' said Tyga.

I accelerated up the steep drive. Old trees rose from the banks on either side, their bare branches meeting above us.

We emerged into the car park; the home was in front of us, and the formal garden – arranged as a series of terraces – lay to our right, dropping towards the distant glassy sea.

Everyone clambered out. It was cold. The sun was hidden by a veil of cloud. The smell of burning leaves hung in the air.

Suddenly, I was back in the garden in Garville Avenue, on a winter's morning when I was three or four years old. My father, in his signature corduroys, was digging a flowerbed. I watched a ribbed, fleshy earthworm curl over the broken earth and wriggle into a gap . . .

Everyone milled round the car boot; Roses chocolates, Whites lemonade, bags of grapes, apples and mandarins were dug out; baseball hats were straightened and beads of chewing gum rolled up in tissue paper for disposal; best behaviour was promised; and finally, the Gébler family stepped into the overheated vestibule.

Ivy, a fixture, was sitting just inside in a fawn suit and polished shoes, handbag on her lap, fuchsia-coloured lipstick coating her thin lips.

She smiled; we said hello.

'Who you looking for?' she asked.

'Ernest Gébler.'

'Oh, Ernest,' she said, as if reciting a lover's name.

She pointed a crooked finger. We stepped into the big sitting room. The floor was parquet. There was a fake fire and the plastic coals glowed dimly in the grate.

My father sat motionless in the bay window. His spot. His face was scrubbed, his hair combed flat. He wore a jersey and a shirt buttoned up to the neck. No tie.

'Hello,' the children cooed.

Two women on a sofa smiled in the hopeful way of the old when the young bound up. My father went on staring into the distance, utterly absorbed either by what he was thinking or what he was seeing. Or perhaps his head was empty. That was the trouble with Alzheimer's. You never knew.

Chairs were pulled up; we sat; he looked round, his expression suspicious. A child handed over the Roses. My father began to examine the box. It was broad at the top and narrow at the bottom like a coffin. Suddenly, his eyes lit up as he recognised what he had.

He began to pick at the seal with a ragged nail. We waited. He must be allowed to try even if he couldn't manage it.

'Let me,' said Tyga, after a decent interval. She opened the flaps. My father tipped the box, scattering dozens of chocolates across the table top. He selected a sweet, unwrapped it, put it in his mouth. He chewed with his mouth open, and I saw little strings of chocolate-coloured saliva stretching between his even, yellowing teeth.

This sweet wasn't even swallowed and he was reaching for a second. He had the paper off in an instant and then the dark brown cube was popped in his mouth.

As he began to chew, he took a third sweet and put that in; then a fourth, and a fifth followed swiftly.

My children stared; here was a sight to warm young hearts; smiling and laughing – not at but with him – three pairs of hands grabbed sweets; they were courtiers following the example of the King.

I took a sweet myself. The pile was shrinking. Squares of Cellophane and foil were everywhere. My father stuffed another chocolate into his already chocolate-crowded mouth. It was – what? his seventh? his tenth? It was extraordinary; the sweet-hater had become the sweet-lover.

We opened the lemonade. His went in a beaker and he guzzled away happily as he chewed. He was jolly; the children were jolly.

'Any gin in that?' he said, suddenly. These were the first words he had spoken. 'I want some gin in that.' He proffered the beaker. I could hardly believe my ears.

'There is gin in that,' I said.

'Is there?'

He knocked the beaker back and asked for a second. With lots of gin. Amazing. His entire life he was a devotee of Apollo and self-denial, but now, at the eleventh hour, he'd switched to Bacchus and self-indulgence. Alzheimer's had released his inner reveller.

Here was an unexpected up side to the disease, I thought,

levering the top off the beaker and beginning to refill it. Meanwhile, my father stared. That's my gin coming, his smiling face said.

'Gin up,' I said when I finished and my children wriggled with delight.

We broke out the fruit. Ivy appeared, handbag held like a sporran.

'How's Ernest?' she enquired. Then: 'Having a little party?'

'Have a grape,' someone said.

As Ivy reached forward, my father grabbed her wrist and smiled at her lasciviously, like Pan smiling at a snared nymph. How wonderful, I thought. No matter how many parts of his brain had dropped away (and that's how I pictured it; his brain was like an old spaceship dropping bits of itself as it hurtled into space) the core instincts remained.

Ivy went off and my father went back to slurping make-believe gin. 'Do you remember who I am?'

'Adrian.'

'No, I'm not your brother, Adrian, I'm Carlo.'

My father shook his head. No, he couldn't remember.

I asked about his childhood.

No, he didn't remember it, either.

Did he remember making things?

No.

His parents?

No.

Writing books?

No.

Did he know where he was?

No.

Did he recognise his three grandchildren?

No.

After twenty minutes of this I was exhausted. I got up and went over to the carved wooden fireplace. At moments like these I thought of my father as a handful of sand that was slipping away no matter how hard I tried to hold on to it. It was both exhausting and infuriating like nothing else I knew.

When I felt rested, I turned back. Jack and Finn were now sitting on either side of him. Jack had put his baseball hat on my father's head.

I watched as my father touched the hat, turning his head this way and that. He was puzzled, astonished. What was this on his head?

Finn took off his hat and put it on Jack's head. My father watched, first curious, then comprehending. Ah, so that was the game.

My father took off Jack's hat and put it on Finn's head. Jack took off Finn's hat and put it on his grandfather's head. This time, he put it on back to front.

My father reached up and felt the hat again. So the brim didn't have to point forwards? It was a game of so many possibilities . . .

This pastiche of a Beckett playlet filled the visit until it was time to go.

'Come on,' I said. 'There's a ferry waiting.'

We all moved off together, the children bouncing like balls, my father crawling like an injured crab.

In the hall, a nurse appeared.

'Did you have a good time then, Ernie?'

No response.

'Can he come out?' I asked.

'Yes, but I'll come too,' she said. He had to be watched, she explained. The week before he'd wandered halfway to Dalkey, for instance, walking the whole way in the middle of the road. His old obsession with road safety had also gone to pot, it seemed.

'He's a lovely man,' she went on. 'Aren't you lovely, Ernie?' She stroked his cheek. 'You're a lovely man, aren't you?'

She had little gold sleepers in her ears, and ruddy cheeks. A countrywoman. 'We do so like him,' she said.

'Does he know we're leaving?'

'Oh yes. They know a lot more than they let on.'

We trooped out and all piled into the car. Safety belts were tugged out and engaged. Then I drove off, the children calling and waving through the open windows. At the top of the drive, I stopped and looked back. My father stood with the nurse, stiffly waving goodbye with his thin right hand.

Was this really my father? It looked like him but without the qualities that were the kernel of his being (his humour, sarcasm and unrelenting hostility to my mother, his children and the world), he didn't seem like him.

I felt sad. Did I miss the old monster? No. I didn't want my childhood back and I never wanted to hear him malign my mother again. What I wanted, I realised, was for him to see how I had turned out. I hadn't turned out nearly as badly as he had predicted, had I?

I drove down the ramped drive. It was dark under the trees. At the bottom I went left for Dun Loaghaire where the ferry waited that would carry us to Britain where we were having a fortnight's holiday.

chapter sixty-one

Green buds showed on the trees around Queen's University. The lid of cloud that had hovered twenty feet above the ground throughout the winter, threatening to crush everyone in the city's streets below, was slowly rising into the sky. And our paramilitaries had generously agreed to stop killing us. Spring had come to Belfast.

I now had a job. I worked for a documentary film company. Monday to Friday I stayed in Belfast; at the weekends I went back home to Enniskillen. I had an office, a desk and a phone. One morning Tyga rang.

'I've just had a man on to me looking for you,' she said. 'I gave him your number. He'll ring you. He's got something for you.'

'What would that be?'

'I won't spoil it for you. Let him tell you.'

A few moments later my phone went again.

'My name's John Carroll,' said the etiolated voice at the other end. The accent was working-class north-side Dublin, overlaid with middle-class south-side Dublin. Very like my father's in fact.

'You don't know me, but I was the secretary of the Irish Transport and General Workers' Union, and I knew your grandfather, Adolf. When he died in California . . .'

'When was that?' I remembered the event and my father crying behind the study door – that was something I was not likely to forget – but I had no idea what year it was.

'1963.'

The year Kennedy died, I thought.

'Anyway, in his will,' continued Mr Carroll, 'Adolf left me his library of musical scores, his clarinets, his conductor's baton, his medals, and so on . . .'

It had started to rain outside and the roof slates, in every direction, were shiny blue with wet. A train clattered down-line at the end of the yard, direction Holywood.

'I'm not getting any younger,' said Mr Carroll, 'and what I wonder is, do you want these things?'

I certainly did, I said, which was true.

He was coming to Belfast the following Thursday on union business, arriving on the first train of the day from Dublin. Would I meet him? The bag was very heavy. His son would help him at the Dublin end but he'd need a hand in Belfast.

'Certainly,' I said, 'but how will I recognise you?'

'Oh, don't worry, I'll recognise you.'

'Will you? How?'

'You're a Gébler. It shines through every word. You're Adolf's line. That's as clear as the hand in front of my face. I'll know you, don't worry.'

'But Adolf had a German accent, I've an English one.'

'I'm talking about the way you construct your sentences, and the feeling that comes through your words, not the way you sound. You're a Gébler, same as him. Don't worry, I'll find you.'

And with that, he put down the phone.

chapter sixty-two

T he train from Dublin pulled into Central Station and stopped. The carriages were packed. Now we were at peace, southerners were coming up in droves. Passengers swarmed out. There were businessmen with mobile telephones, ladies in good hats, and a party of art students with sketchpads.

I squinted down the platform. Mr Carroll said he'd find me but what if he didn't? Maybe I should have my name on a card, I thought, like the chauffeurs waiting at the front of the station?

The crowds began to thin. At the other end of the platform I saw a man looking at me. He was slim, lightly built. He wore a hat and a big coat belted at the waist. He looked like Erich Honecker, the old East German leader.

The man began to move, dragging an enormous brown suitcase. He walked down the platform and came right up to me. Then he said, pointing at my face, 'You have Adolf's nose. I'd know it anywhere. You're a Gébler all right.'

It was Mr Carroll.

I humped the heavy suitcase to the front of the station. A man from the union was waiting. He drove us to Transport House, the headquarters of the Amalgamated T & G, the UK-based equivalent of the IT&GWU. I followed Mr Carroll inside. We took the lift to the boardroom.

It was a big room with a huge table. The walls were covered with union paraphernalia – pennants, banners, flags – fraternal greetings from workers around the world. Together, we lifted the suitcase on to the table. Mr Carroll undid the zip and threw back the lid.

The case was crammed with music scores, Mendelssohn and Brahms, Beethoven and Mozart, all of it stamped 'La Bohème' in a vivid, violet-coloured ink. There was some of Adolf's own music, written for Dublin revues in the 1940s and 1950s. There were a couple of records he cut, thick, heavy 78s, his conductor's baton, his two clarinets. And there were photographs.

'This is Adolf,' said Mr Carroll, taking one of the older ones, 'when he was interned in the First World War.'

The man in the photograph had a wide forehead, a small mouth and a pointed chin. He wore drainpipe trousers and striped long johns underneath. He parted his hair on the right. He looked like a young Richard Wilhelm Wagner. He looked arrogant. I'd seen this photograph as a boy. My father had a copy.

'Did you know Adolf then?' I asked.

'Not then, no, not in the First War. I wasn't even born. I met Adolf in 'thirty-nine. My father was in the union and he heard there was this musician who was training the union band. My father took me along to see him. 'Can you teach this boy to play?' he asked and the man said, 'Certainly,' in this thick German accent. That was my first introduction to Adolf and here he is looking more like he was when I knew him.'

This second photograph, taken in 1947, was mounted on

Adolf Gébler (front row, seated middle) with the Irish Transport & General Workers Union Prize Brass and Reed Band, All-Ireland Winners – Feis Cheol 1949

grey card with 'Irish Transport & General Workers Union, Prize Brass and Reed Band' along the top, and a list of the band's achievements in competition plus the information 'Conductor – Mr A. Gébler' along the bottom.

In the photograph, the band was ranked on the steps of Liberty Hall, with my grandfather at the front, a shield at his feet. He wore a heavy coat and his hat was balanced on his knees. His expression – it was utterly miserable, dejected, broken – reminded me of Freud in London, right at the end of his life, when he was dying. Richard had metamorphosed into Sigmund.

Mr Carroll began to reminisce. Adolf believed in discipline, especially at home. He deplored the opulence and conspicuous extravagance of Roman Catholic churches while the congregations lived in abject poverty. However, he scrupulously avoided any discussion of religion in Dublin. He was a Slav émigré. What did he know of the strange ways of the Irish? Physically, he was as strong as a bull. He believed cultural development was a necessary prelude to progressive social development. He believed socialism and communism were inevitable as well as laudable. His humour was dry. He was often described as caustic. He yearned for deep relationships. He was lonely and isolated. His family rarely went to hear him when he conducted or played. His language was coarse but not crude. He said bloody but not fuck. He grew more testy with age and he practised the clarinet less. He also drank more with age. That might have been unhappiness. Or loneliness. During and after the war, he was a familiar sight, cycling home from Lynch's pub in Summerhill with cider bottles clinking in a bag that hung from the handlebars. He suffered with his stomach. He consumed enormous quantities of Rennies, and the white powder of these tablets was often at the side of his mouth, like chalk.

'Did you like Adolf?' I asked.

'I was a fourteen-year-old working-class boy, and here was this educated man, who loved Strauss and Brahms, who was into workers' rights in a big way, and was never condescending. Yes, he was marvellous.'

'A good teacher?'

'The best,' said Mr Carroll emphatically. 'This is what he taught me on.'

Mr Carroll took out a clarinet. The instrument was in pieces. He deftly slotted the sections together.

'Adolf didn't believe in the Boehm system,' Mr Carroll explained. 'He preferred what was called the "Simple System" – that's the fingering system on this clarinet – which, I can tell you, is anything but simple.'

Adolf had not only taught him how to play, Mr Carroll continued, but he had also taught his protégé how to reproduce his master's sound.

'As part of my training, I'd go to Adolf's house,' explained Mr Carroll, 'to pick reeds – Adolf favoured Vandoren reeds – and then I'd cut them for him; and I'd never fail to pick the reed that was right for Adolf and I'd never fail to cut it so that it was right for him, either.'

If Adolf had an engagement that he couldn't play, he sent the pupil in his place. And why not? A casual listener couldn't tell them apart. Adolf and Mr Carroll split the fees fifty-fifty, though the pupil had to pay his teacher half-a-dollar for the hire of the clarinet, so Adolf always came out of these transactions slightly better off than his pupil.

'That doesn't sound very socialist,' I said.

Mr Carroll blew a note, firm but sad.

'How was his marriage?' I asked.

'We don't want to talk about that, do we?'

He broke the clarinet back into pieces and wrapped them in a square of silky cloth.

Sometime during the war, he said, he called to Adolf's house. He found my grandmother and her four daughters, my father's sisters, sitting round the fire. The women all wore party frocks. They were either on their way out to a dance or just in from one. Mr Carroll said something but the five women did not speak, or turn, or invite him forward. They just went on staring into the hearth, the firelight playing on their faces. As he waited, that was what he saw, girlish backs, averted faces, dancing firelight. And he waited in vain. They kept their backs towards him.

Where was my father when this was happening? I wondered.

My father was probably lurking in the house, he explained. Whenever Mr Carroll called or came for a lesson, if my father was at home, he always hid himself away.

'Later,' continued Mr Carroll, 'when we were both older, I would often bump into Ernie around Dublin; we had the same left-wing politics, we went to the same theatres and cinemas; but he always cut me and he maintained that silence until just a few years ago, until just before he got sick, in fact.'

Mr Carroll stared at me with his pale eyes. 'He's got Alzheimer's?'

'Yes,' I said.

'Ernie came to see me a few years ago when he was collecting stories about Adolf for a book.'

'That would be the autobiography,' I said. 'He never managed to write it. He got ill before he could get going. I'm relieved he didn't. I dread to think what he'd have said about my mother.'

As I spoke, I thought, my father ignored Mr Carroll for fifty years because he was jealous of the attention Adolf paid his pupil. Then, when he realised he needed the information that was locked up in Mr Carroll's head, he approached Mr Carroll, assuming he'd ignore his past behaviour. Unbelievable but typical.

'Did you talk to him?' I asked.

'A bit. He wasn't very well.'

'Did you know Adolf refused to teach my father an instrument? My father never got over it.'

Yes, said Mr Carroll, he had heard that.

'Do you think my father resented you?' After all, I said, he had been treated like the first son, whereas the real first son, Ernie, had been spurned by Adolf.

'Indeed,' agreed Mr Carroll. He referred back to the story of the women sitting round the fire with their backs turned towards him. That was why they froze him out, he explained; they resented the way Adolf treated his protégé as if he were his own son, while he ignored his own flesh and blood . . .

I didn't hear what Mr Carroll said next because I was

thinking so hard. If Adolf treated John Carroll as a son or an adopted son, I thought, and ignored my father, what would my father have felt? Usurped, of course. So was it any wonder then that my father told me endlessly that my half-brother would return, one day, and take over my position in the family. My father couldn't help himself. It was all he knew.

The thought that followed this was even more unexpected.

My childhood and my father's childhood might seem similar but they were not symmetrical. I was only ever threatened with displacement. My father actually experienced it. But then, the devil is always in the detail, isn't it?

And finally, right at the end of this sequence of thoughts, came this one: even if I didn't do anything else right in my life, I'd at least managed one thing; I'd managed a proper adoption and I hadn't squashed anyone in the process. In the light of family history, it was something of which I could feel proud.

I lugged the suitcase of Adolf's musical scores and effects back to the Belfast office. That weekend I borrowed a car and took the suitcase home. As I heaved it into the house, the children crowded round.

'Oh wow,' they cried, 'what's in there?'

I unzipped the suitcase, got out the photographs and spread them on the table.

'Oh, look,' said Jack, now eight years old, peering at the photograph of a melancholy Adolf on the steps of Liberty Hall, his prize-winning band ranged behind him. 'He looks like us.'

He was right; Adolf did; there was something about the body shape, the stance and the nose, that screamed Gébler. I don't know why I had imagined Mr Carroll wouldn't know me at Belfast Central Station; there was a family look and it was as plain as the nose in front of my face.

chapter sixty-three

I stood in the circle in H-block number 2, HMP Maze. The broken cistern in the toilet was flushing and gurgling as usual. There was a strong smell of disinfectant. A prison officer sauntered up.

'Morning,' he said. He was a middle-aged man with a white face. It isn't just the prisoners who develop the prison pallor in jail.

The officer went to the grille and unlocked it. A prisoner was on the other side. He stepped back to let me through. He wore flip-flops, Manchester United shorts and a white singlet. The blocks were overheated, so all the prisoners dressed in beach-cum-club-cum-holiday wear. I wore a suit. I now taught in the jail one day a week.

The grille banged shut behind me. The key turned. I was on the prisoners' turf now. That's how things were in HMP Maze; the prisoners ran the wings and the prison officers, for the most part, stayed off-side. It was after the Hunger Strikes that this you-don't-bother-me-and-I-won't-bother-you agreement had evolved; it seemed to work fairly well.

I went down a stub of corridor and turned on to the wing proper.

'Giles,' I shouted.

The wing stretched away, spanned by arches decorated with Orange insignia – the mason's hammer, Jacob's ladder and the all-seeing Eye. There were Union flags and lots of red, white and blue bunting. It was early July, not far from the Twelfth. On the day itself, the block's very own flute band would march up and down here.

'Giles,' I shouted again.

'Yeah.' I saw Billy's slight figure at the end of the corridor.

'I'll wait in the band room,' I shouted.

He nodded and ducked back into his cell to get his work.

A moment later I found Daniel in the kitchen, morosely washing a plate in the deep stainless-steel sink.

'Hello,' he said.

Daniel wrote complex poems that drew their inspiration from the Talmud, the Old Testament and Arthurian legend.

'Why didn't you come last week?' I asked.

He shrugged. He looked depressed.

'It'll cheer you up if you come.'

'Well you would say that, wouldn't you,' he said, bleakly.

Midday, I went to the Welfare department. It was in a Portakabin. Inside I found a woman eating an orange. She wore very thick and very beautifully applied lipstick, in the pre-war style.

We introduced ourselves. She was Helen, a survivor of German concentration camps who now lived in Belfast.

'Where are you from?' I said, predictably.

Trutnov, she told me. It was in Bohemia, not a million miles from where Adolf hailed.

'Does the name Gébler mean anything to you?' I asked. (I hate it when Americans assume Ireland is a village where everyone knows everyone, yet here I was doing just that.)

She thought about this, then said, 'Gébler, yes, maybe I heard this name.'

I left the prison with a strong sense something was going to happen.

The next day I got a parcel from the *Financial Times* containing a book for review; it was *The Cunning Man*, by the Canadian author Robertson Davies. I opened it at random and my eye fell on this: '. . . it was a bigger orchestra and a better one . . . and its long-suffering conductor . . . Gébler, called forth more music than might have been expected . . .'*

Of course Robertson Davies' choice of name was a coincidence; I don't believe he ever heard of my grandfather, let alone met him. Yet first there was the meeting in the prison with the woman who thought she remembered the Géblers and now there was this; surely it meant that something was going to happen and it involved the family. I was certain of it, anyway.

---

* *The Cunning Man*, Robertson Davies, London, 1995, page 65

chapter sixty-four

It was October 1995, four months after I met Mr Carroll. My wife rang the office and said I was to expect a very important call. 'It's your half-brother,' she said quickly. 'He's called John now, John Fountain.'

I put down the phone and it rang again immediately. I picked it up.

'Hi, I'm Linda,' said a cheerful American voice. 'I'm the girlfriend of Ernie's "early" son, John.' She was calling, she added, because John was too nervous to speak to me himself.

They were in Ireland, she continued, in Dublin in fact, and they had visited John's father, Ernie, also my father, several times in the home. Now they wanted to come and see me.

At seven the following evening, I was at the office window, looking for a shiny hire car with southern plates. Watching the passing traffic, I wondered what my half-brother would be like? It was a fruitless question. I had nothing to go on, not even the sound of his voice. All I had was my father's old threat that one day his first-born would replace me. As a child I had fretted about this but this evening I did not; I was excited. At long last I was going to met the one I had long believed I'd never meet.

I went back to my desk. I was writing a play. The dialogue I produced was wooden, awful. My thoughts kept drifting to the encounter I was about to have. I went back to the window and looked out again . . .

I shuttled between desk and window until I saw by the wall clock in the office it was eight. They were an hour late. They're not coming, I thought. Of course not, as I obviously should have guessed from the fact John had been too nervous to speak to me the day before. Linda would probably ring any moment now to say they'd broken down. Or had a double puncture. And if she didn't ring, she'd send a card. Sorry, couldn't make it, she would write. Or, Sorry, we couldn't face you. Or, Sorry, something . . .

From childhood on, pessimism was always my solution to the problem of impending disappointment. By always assuming the worst, I was able to con myself into believing that I was wise and intelligent. Well, I was, wasn't I? I anticipated and I adjusted my feelings before I was overwhelmed by events. Wasn't that a sign of wisdom and intelligence?

And as a child, once I convinced myself all was lost, I would then busy myself; in Cannon Hill Lane I would often tidy the tools on the workbench (which had the advantage of being likely to attract my father's approval). This evening, I decided to clear my desk; then I would go back to the house where I rented a room.

At half-eight, while I was putting away some papers, I was surprised to hear the buzzer. So they'd come after all, I thought.

Not for the first (or the last) time, I had convinced myself that the worst was going to happen (in this case a no-show) and then it hadn't (they had shown up). But I was an old hand at dealing with this too.

Oh well, I thought, better to have assumed the worst, than to have hoped and been disappointed. Expect the worst and you always come out the winner.

I pressed the door release. I heard the front door bang, then footsteps on the stairs, then an American voice call up, 'This is John.'

My half-brother came up the stairs. He was a dark-skinned, stocky man with brown eyes. He looked remarkably like Adolf. Linda followed. We shook hands. We started talking and didn't stop for several hours. This is the story that emerged from our conversation:

John and Linda were boyfriend and girlfriend. In January 1995 Linda's Los Angeles apartment was badly damaged by the earthquake. The building was condemned. She had nowhere to live.

Leatrice, John's mother, feeling sorry for her son's girl-friend, offered to put Linda up while her landlord repaired the building; in return for a roof, Linda agreed to help Leatrice with her filing.

Linda went east to Leatrice's house and started work. One day, she picked up a thick bundle of letters marked Ernest Gébler. He was Leatrice's fourth husband; Linda already knew this; Leatrice had never made a secret of her marriage before Mr Fountain. Everyone knew that she'd been married to this unlikely sounding Irishman, Gébler, and had lived with him in an old house in the Wicklow mountains. They had no children, she and this Irishman, and the marriage lasted only a couple of years. Then Leatrice divorced this Gébler and married John Fountain, and pretty soon they had a son, John; several more Fountain children followed. That was the story Linda knew.

Gébler, who had penned these letters, was a writer, Leatrice explained. Ah yes, of course, Gébler, thought Linda, now she knew why the name rang a bell. The film *The Plymouth*

Adventure with Spencer Tracy, always shown on American television at Thanksgiving, was based on a novel, wasn't it, by
this same Ernest Gébler.

Unfortunately, continued Leatrice, bringing Linda up to
date with the saga of Ernest Gébler, he didn't write any more
because now he was in a Dublin nursing home. He was old
and ill, Leatrice added; it was all very sad, really. Linda filed
away the letters and thought nothing more about Ernest
Gébler.

Time passed. The repairs to Linda's Los Angeles apartment
block were finished. She went home.

At this point John entered the story. At the time he was
making a living cleaning swimming pools for wealthy Los
Angeleans. One day, he cleaned the pool of J——, an old
friend of Leatrice's. Leatrice and J—— went back fifty years,
at least. While John worked, J—— began to reminisce. J——
said she remembered John, when he was a little chap, only a
year or two old, running round the swimming pool in
Virginia City, Reno.

This puzzled John. According to family lore, and as far as
he could remember, the Fountain family had only ever lived
in New York, and then in Connecticut; they had never lived in
Reno. Never.

Linda agreed. Reno was a place people went to get
divorced. Perhaps Leatrice went there to get divorced from
this man, Ernest Gébler, the fourth husband and J—— went
with her to lend support? That made sense but why was John
there? His mother had yet to marry Mr Fountain. John wasn't
even born yet, apparently. Yet J—— was adamant; she remembered John by the pool.

Linda made enquiries in Reno. Four days later she had the
Decree of Divorce, granted to the plaintiff, Leatrice Gébler,
against the defendant, Adolphus Ernest Gébler, in the Second
Judicial District Court in the State of Nevada, on 24 October

1952 at 3.30 pm. The divorce papers made no mention of a child.

Then Linda remembered *The Plymouth Adventure*. Ernest Gébler was an author; Leatrice had said it too. In which case, why didn't she look him up in the Dictionary of Authors and see if there was any further information about the divorce?

She went to the library. In the 1966 edition of the Dictionary, my father's entry described him as being married just the once, to my mother, Edna, and as having just two children, myself and my brother, Sasha. So nothing new there.

Linda, however, decided to check the later, 1981 edition. In the entry here my father was described as having been married three times; the entry also noted that by his first wife, Leatrice, he had a son, John Karl.

Next thing, Linda and John went and got my father's books, among them *A Week in the Country*. This is the story of a man filled with pain because his wife steals their son away from him. Now John and Linda were certain they had stumbled on the truth; Mr Fountain senior was not John's father; Ernest Gébler, Leatrice's fourth husband, was John's father but John had never been told this.

And now of course it was clear, Linda continued, why Reno had never been mentioned. If John had known that he once toddled around a pool while his mother was getting a divorce, he'd have worked out his father was not Mr Fountain but his mother's previous husband.

'So how did you find Ernie?' I asked. (I said Ernie because I wasn't ready for 'our father' yet.)

It was all easy-peasy, I gathered, just as the discoveries that preceded were easy-peasy. Linda contacted the Irish consulate in Los Angeles, who put her on to the Arts Council in Dublin, who of course knew exactly where to find the old author Ernest Gébler.

Next thing, she and John bought the cheapest tickets to be

found and flew to Dublin. They couldn't afford a hotel, or even a bed and breakfast, so they had brought a tent although it was October. (How my father would have admired this economy.) They found a campsite near Killiney; they went to the home several days on the trot; then they rang me; and now they were here in Belfast, and we were talking.

'Well, how do you feel,' I asked John, sounding like the worst kind of television interviewer, 'now you've discovered Ernest was your father?'

Confused and bewildered and a little angry, he explained. He said he believed that many other people, besides his mother, had known who his real father was, but that they had never bothered to tell him.

'You must think I was really dumb,' continued John, assuming that I must think he'd taken an inordinately long time to find out the truth I'd always known.

'No, you weren't dumb,' interrupted Linda. It was hardly difficult, she averred, to bamboozle a toddler into believing a stranger was his father, especially when he last saw his real father when he was only one.

Now it was John's turn to talk. He asked me what Ernie was like?

Tell the truth but keep it brief, I had decided in advance.

He was stern, I said, rather left-wing, fairly austere, not very pro-child and very pro-discipline. A Victorian father, really.

Then John wondered if my father had ever mentioned him, the 'early son'.

'Oh yes,' I said.

'What exactly did he say, do you remember?'

I explained that according to my father the real Karl, that was him, would return to the bosom of the family one day and replace me. That's what he told me, I said.

'Oh, but that's terrible,' said Linda and John together, 'but are you sure that's true?'

I was, I said. I remembered very clearly.

'Have you seen *The Jerk*?' asked John abruptly. 'It's a movie with Steve Martin. He's a white guy brought up by a black family. He's white but he thinks he's black. He's the Jerk, and that's me too. It was so obvious, all my life, I wasn't a Fountain, it was staring me in the face, yet I didn't see it.'

'No it wasn't,' said Linda, nicely.

'Yes it was. I only had to look in the mirror to see I wasn't a Fountain, but I didn't see.'

The end of the evening came. John and Linda were about to drive back to the campsite in Dublin.

'You know,' said John, as we went down the office stairs together, 'I got the farming genes and you got the writing genes. I guess that's why I clean swimming pools and you write novels.'

chapter sixty-five

A couple of months later I went to Dublin to see my father. In the hall of the home I met a fug of hot air smelling of cabbage and sweat; it was exactly the same as in the overheated blocks in HMP Maze. A stuffed animal in a case followed me with its glass eyes.

In the dispensary I found a nurse with a face like a scallop shell.

'Ernest Gébler?' I said.

'He's on the ground floor. He can't manage the stairs,' she said.

I made my way along several corridors; the carpets were brown and man-made. Every time I reached for a door handle, my fingers crackled with static.

At last I came to my father's room. Inset into the doorframe was a little half-door, with a bolt on the outside. He was wandering, I guessed.

I peered into the room beyond. It was a double. My father was now sharing. His roommate lay in his bed in the corner; he was gurgling as he stared with milky eyes at the television attached to the wall.

My father sat on the other bed. He wore grey tracksuit bottoms and a hideous patterned jumper. A nurse was with him. He had one sock off and one sock on.

'Come on, Ernie,' she said in the nice, bossy way of nurses, 'put your other sock on!'

'Hello,' I called.

My father looked up and scowled.

The nurse turned.

'Who are you?' she asked.

'His son. Carlo.'

'Ah yes, come in, I've seen you before,' she said. 'You haven't been for a bit?'

'No.'

I banged through the swing door, and she turned back to her charge.

'Come on, Ernie, sock on now. Your son's here. You can't see your son without your shoes and socks on. You've got to look your best.'

I saw my father's bare white foot with veins sticking up under the skin like string around a parcel.

'How is he?' I asked.

'Marvellous, really,' she said. She pushed his sock on.

'Does he recognise people?'

'Aye, on a good day, he knows the people he's used to.'

The nurse pulled the sock right the way up his shin, just like my own children liked to do when they first wore socks.

'What did you say your name was?' the nurse asked.

'Carlo.'

'Ernie,' the nurse shouted, 'say, "Hello, Carlo."'

He said nothing, just glared.

'Will you get him some new trainers like these?' she said. 'Size nine.'

She showed me a heavy trainer, then slipped it on to his foot.

'Any style as long as we can wash them.' She began to tie a bow. 'When he soils his shoes, it's handy if we can just throw 'em in the washing machine. Size nine.'

The lace was tied. She picked up the other trainer.

'Of course,' I said.

Until this moment, I imagined my father was having his second childhood. But now, after the throwaway remark about the soiled shoes, I realised he'd passed through childhood to an earlier stage. I was reminded of the Scott Fitzgerald story, 'The Curious Case of Benjamin Button', in which a man is born old and grows backwards. According to the iron rules of reverse atrophy, it was only a matter of time before my father reached the newborn state, at which point, like Benjamin Button, he'd pass into non-existence; he'd be dead.

'How much of the original him is left?' I asked.

'Och, he's still a gentleman. You can see he had lovely manners.'

She smiled into his furious face. 'Weren't you a real ladies' man? Weren't you a lady-killer, Ernie? Weren't the women mad for you?'

It was at this moment that I noticed four seven-inch SuperSize photographs stuck to the wall above my father's bed. They showed Linda and my half-brother with my father standing between them.

'Where did those come from?' I asked.

'John,' said the nurse.

'What are they doing on his wall? Photographs like this are for the folks back home. You don't leave them behind in the old country.'

'John put them up before he went back to America so Ernie would know he'd been,' she said

Ah. Stupid me. They were there to prove the 'early' son had come.

My next thought was even less charitable; I'd never put a photograph on the wall, I thought, for my father to see. Our relationship had been literally too awful.

How lucky then for my half-brother that he could. How lucky to be unencumbered by the past.

In fact, I thought, to have arrived just now was fortunate really. If John had found his father pre-Alzheimer's, he would have found a man who was cranky, awkward and even horrible. They might have got on but then again, they might not; nothing, where my father was concerned, was ever guaranteed. This was better. At least this way, they wouldn't fall out.

I stared at the photographs again. John looked quite old and authoritative in glossy colour. Suddenly, it struck me. I, who'd always thought of myself as the first-born (even though I'd always known that technically, I wasn't), would have to re-adjust, wouldn't I? I had become the second, the middle child I was always supposed to be.

The laces on the second trainer were tied.

'Come on, Ernie,' said the nurse. She began to lead him out. I followed. My father didn't lift his feet any more; he slid them.

Several tedious minutes later, we shuffled into the room with the bay window. The rubber soles of his trainers shrieked on the parquet.

At last we sat at our usual table, in our usual position; he faced Bray, I faced Dun Loaghaire. Tea appeared. I got a cup. He got a beaker.

'Do you know who I am?'

'No.'

'I'm Carlo.'

'Oh. Yes.'

Pause.

'I'm your son.'

'Really.'

'Do you remember Adolf?'

'Who?'

'Your father, Adolf.'

'No, he definitely wasn't my father. He's gone away.'

I continued with the questions; he batted back his bland replies. First I felt annoyed, then I felt angry, finally I was filled with an overwhelming urge to say everything I had always wanted to say but had never said. I wanted to shout, You are a monstrous egoist. You never gave me a moment's happiness.

It was ridiculous. Today, he knew less than yesterday; tomorrow, he'd know less than today.

He tipped his beaker and drank; when gurgling gave way to whistling, I knew the beaker was empty.

I levered off the top, half filled it with milk, poured in just a little tea and snapped the top back on. Looking up, I noticed my father staring oddly at me.

'Do you know I am?'

'No, I can't quite put a name to you,' he said, taking his beaker.

'Is there anything you want?'

He stared out the window. After a very long time he lifted his arm and, pointing at the flowerbeds just outside, he said, very slowly, 'Horse manure.'

chapter sixty-six

In early spring 1996, John and Linda returned to Dublin. I invited them to Enniskillen for the weekend. 'We'll get down the trunks with my father's papers,' I said on the telephone, 'and we'll disinter the past.'

They arrived at ten in the evening. I opened a bottle of champagne. We all stood around the dining table nervously drinking. I had met John and Linda only once; Tyga had never met them. Really, we were strangers to each other.

We sat down to eat. Conversation started; inevitably, there was only one subject of conversation

John began to speak about how rotten our father was to my brother and myself, and how puzzled he was that our father had never come to the US to find him. John thought that if our father had met him, it would have taken some of the heat off us. Then he wondered how our father would have treated him?

I explained how Adolf, our grandfather, ignored Ernest,

his son, and so all our father knew was how to ignore his children.

'He wasn't good to you guys, so he probably would have been rotten to me as well,' John agreed.

We began to talk about the home. Was Ernie well treated there? they wondered.

Did they have any evidence that he wasn't? I replied.

They didn't; however, in the United States, they continued, footage – recorded with hidden cameras – of nurses beating up old patients was often shown on television. For all I knew, they said, Ernie could be getting the same.

I explained I chose the home with precisely this problem in mind. Because it was always open, day and night, one could go in any time one wanted and that, I said, was the best defence against maltreatment.

John and Linda changed tack. They were worried about our father's condition. He got no exercise. No mental stimulation. No one talked to him. He was deteriorating, they said. Couldn't more be done for him?

'But he's old,' I said. 'He has Alzheimer's. That's what happens when you are old and senile; your brain goes.'

They weren't convinced; I sensed they thought me hard, cruel.

After dinner, I got a suitcase down from the loft. It was filled with all the photographs I got from Cnoc Aluin.

When I lifted back the suitcase lid, a smell drifted out, a mixture of dust, old Kodak photographic paper and the dank stone of the passageways in the basement of Cnoc Aluin.

We each took a handful of photographs and began to leaf through what he had, discarding one photograph after another like unwanted playing cards. Everything in my hand was vaguely familiar because when I'd thrown everything into the suitcase years before, I'd had a quick look to see what there was. I got through my hand very quickly.

I dived back into the suitcase. I found a Sun Alliance envelope with 'Photos – America' written on the front in my father's handwriting. This looked interesting.

I emptied it out. It *was* interesting. There were pictures of John, as a baby in Ireland and later as a child in Connecticut. There were also pictures of John's half-brothers – Christopher and Gideon. These photographs were sent by Leatrice to our father over the years that followed their divorce. (Her handwriting was on the back of the photographs.) Why send our father pictures of her children by the husband she married after she left him? Weird.

John looked to see what I was doing. One photograph caught his attention. It was a picture, taken in June 1956, of himself and his baby brother, Christopher, in America. The boys have Eisenhower haircuts and are mucking around with a watering can. On the back of the photograph, John discovered that our father had written 'Bobby = Ernie's son' and calculated John's different ages over the passing years:

1956 – 4
1966 – 14
1976 – 24
1986 – 34
1988 – 36

'You see,' said John, excitedly, 'Ernie did this because he wondered what happened to me.'

At that very moment I turned over another picture of John from the same envelope. This was a picture of John as a baby. On the back, I saw our father had written, 'Bobbie, my son by Leatrice. Said to have become a drunk in Hollywood.'

I took this photograph into the hall and called Linda out. I showed her the inscription on the back. I said we had to be careful. There were all sorts of nasty things lurking in the archive.

'Don't show it to John but don't hide it from him either,' said Linda. 'He's been lied to so much.'

I did what she said. I went back to the table and put the offending picture back in the envelope. Meanwhile, we all went on looking through the pictures. To my surprise there was a letter among the hundreds of shiny squares. It was from our father to Leatrice and it was dated 1987.

'They went on speaking all their lives,' said John, amazed, 'and she never told me.'

'Well, we don't know if he sent it,' I said. 'He may have but then again he may just have written it and forgotten to put it in the postbox.'

I read out the letter. It was a bland old man's letter. It said, I've had a good life, Leatrice, did you have a good life? It also contained the line, 'My eldest son, Carlo, works for television and has written two slight novels.'

'I see he was cruel,' said John. He went back to looking at the photograph with his age at different years written on the back . . .

John had his glasses on the next morning. He blinked often and stammered slightly as he spoke. He wanted a loving father but the figure who emerged from the photographs in the suitcase was an awkward, prickly man. Not exactly an ideal father figure.

In the afternoon, John returned again to the subject of our father's current medical condition. He talked about halting his deterioration. He thought it was even possible that our father might get a little better with the right treatment. In the US, apparently, Alzheimer patients had improved after physical therapy. Linda mentioned a job interview in Dublin. She said she had already secured permission from her ex-husband to bring their son to Ireland to live with her. Suddenly I realised John and Linda wanted to come and live in Dublin.

'It'll allow him to get to know the guy,' said Linda, indicating John and meaning our father. 'And he's got so little time left.'

So my half-brother was turning out to be the perfect son, after all.

chapter sixty-seven

One Saturday in November 1996, with my sons, Jack and Finn, I drove to Dublin. We found John waiting outside the Dart station in Killiney. He had now moved to Dublin. He lived in a caravan (one up from a tent, he said) and worked as a night porter in a hotel. Not a bad life, he said. He visited his father most days. Linda was still in California. The Dublin job hadn't worked out.

We set off for the home. As we crawled along (there was a match in Dublin that afternoon and the traffic was terrible) I felt the first prickles of anxiety. I never exactly relished coming to see my father but lately I had begun to dread my visits.

The explanation was this: at some point in my forty-second year, my theoretical understanding that one day I would pass away had turned into a fully realised understanding that one day I would die.

Most of the time I could shove this new realisation to the edge of my mind. I'd know the anxiety was there because it niggled, like a stone in the shoe, but I wasn't overwhelmed by it.

Unfortunately, when I visited my father, wherever I looked I saw the watery eyes and the sagging flesh of old people; I smelt the perspiration and lavender and eau-de-Cologne smell of old people; and I heard the hushed, cracked, whispering voices of old people. Ah yes, I couldn't help but think, I'll be that old one day and then I'll die.

Those moments were not good, but worse was the way these thoughts would linger long after I left the home. Sometimes, these thoughts stayed in my head for days, like a melody from an obnoxious piece of music that one can't shake off.

A line of cars passed, horns blaring, flags flying out of the windows. Instead of thinking of myself all the time, I thought, I would do well to remember this was for the children . . .

We pulled up, a few minutes later, in front of the home. We tumbled out of the car and went in. The stuffed animal lurked in the hall and the fuggy air hadn't changed either.

My father was dressed and waiting for us; his hair stuck up like the bristles on a toothbrush. He looked like a bald little boy.

John pulled up a chair and sat down. 'Hey! How you doing, old buddy? You want to shadow-box? You want to clown about?' he said, pummelling the air.

My father paid no attention. He looked angry but I knew he wasn't; now his circuits were burnt out this was how he looked all the time.

I sat down opposite my father and my sons sat beside me. They were apprehensive, I thought, and uncertain.

John opened his knapsack and pulled out bananas, oranges and monkey nuts. My father saw the goodies and something showed on his face, something close to delight.

John peeled the skin off a banana, delicately pulled away

the little ropey cables half-buried in the flesh, then offered the bare fruit. My father stuffed the whole thing in his mouth and swallowed it with a gulp. So, no more Mr Mastication, I thought.

John said he thought his father was thin. Were they feeding him enough in the home? he wondered.

I explained he was always thin. I knew this because I had spent my childhood with the man which John hadn't. It was true but tactless.

'Look, he's got my glasses,' said John.

John pointed to the spectacles my father was wearing. They had black frames and yes, now John mentioned it, I did not remember him wearing them before.

'His eyes were red from rubbing because he couldn't see,' John explained, 'so I gave him my glasses and the redness went straightaway.'

I noticed John had written 'Ernie' on a slip of paper and Sellotaped this to the frame, just like a conscientious mother might mark a child's gym kit.

I felt a ripple of resentment. I had my life with my father and it had an integrity. It was ours, mine; I wanted no one else in it; I especially didn't want this spectacle-dispensing stranger.

I simmered. John produced an envelope. He wrote our names on the front – 'John' and 'Carlo' (but not 'Sasha' whom he had never met). He gave the envelope to my father.

'Hey! Look at that!' said John, pointing at the envelope.

John began to talk. He described himself as the idiot son from America, while I was the clever one from Ireland. My father ignored him.

When he came in February, John explained, and he wrote 'John' out like this, it prompted his father to speak of his 'early son'. He was hoping for the same response today.

We waited. Eventually, my father haltingly pronounced our

names but it didn't sound to me as if they meant anything to him.

We took my father outside and manoeuvred him into the car. Then we all piled in and I drove off.

'Look at how he listens to the engine,' said John, admiringly.

We went to Cnoc Aluin.

'Last time I brought him here,' said John, 'he said, "Are we going in?" like he knew it was his old house.'

This afternoon, however, he appeared not to know where he was. He looked at his old house blankly, then stared down the street. We drove about Dalkey and then went up to the Vico Road where he had once liked to walk. We stopped by the blackberry bushes above the railway line.

We got out and started picking. Jack plucked a half-dozen big black fruits from the thorny briers, then laid them as carefully as if they were eggs on his grandfather's narrow palm.

My father instantly popped the lot into his mouth and chewed. Purple juice trickled from the corners of his lips. He made a face.

'Not sweet enough?' said John.

Back in the home, we shuffled into the big room with the fake fire. My father headed towards his usual place, the table in the bay. An old woman was sitting there. As we approached, she stood up and said, 'You can have this table. I want to escape from that horrible film about the *Titanic*.' From the television set in the room next door boomed the measured voice of Kenneth More, the star of *A Night to Remember*.

The woman went. We sat; we asked for tea. While we waited, I studied my father's teeth as he used to study mine. They were chipped and grey, with blackberry seeds caught here and there in the spaces. He was fortunate, in one sense, I thought, to have the illness he had; it protected him from registering his decline. At least I assumed it did; actually, I couldn't be certain.

The tea came. The visitors drank from cups, the patient slurped from a beaker. John kept smiling, and every now and again he carefully wiped the drool from his father's mouth.

Sunk in the chair opposite, I was keenly aware that John was everything I was not. Where he was light, happy and affectionate, I was guarded, careful and suspicious. Where he was loving and forgiving, I was recalcitrant and morose.

Unlike John, all I saw before me were the remnants of the man who had once controlled and restricted me, who had once endlessly criticised and denigrated me for being the imbecile offspring of my mother.

So what was new? Unwelcome thoughts had come storming in while I was on a visit to my father. Well, at least I wasn't fretting about my mortality. I should be grateful for small mercies.

Then, quite out of the blue, an appalling thought struck me. My father made me into the cussed thing I was. Of course, this was different from saying I had turned out like him. I was also my mother's product. I wasn't quite the depressed, miserable curmudgeon that he was; however, so much of me was him; for instance, my jealousy of John's uncomplicated relationship with him. This was an emotion he would have recognised.

At last the time came to leave. We all said 'Goodbye', and went and got into the car. John was coming back to Enniskillen.

We nosed down the dark tunnel of the drive and drove north through a Dublin filled with football fans and flags and blaring car horns.

For a while we were silent. We were all exhausted. My father was like a sponge; he soaked up everything one had to give and he gave nothing in return. An addled mind wrings you dry like nothing else.

After an hour, John finally broke the silence. 'You know,' he said, 'I've seen what a grump Ernie could be. Sometimes he just looks at me and I see this guy who doesn't like children and who just wants quiet.'

Darkness fell. The children went to sleep and our talk grew serious.

'You spend your whole life,' John said, 'trying to grow up quick – at least I did – and then you grow up and you wonder what the hurry was? Because then you realise you haven't figured out what you want to do.'

Did his mother know he was in Ireland and had met his father? I wondered.

No, he hadn't told her, he said.

'Why not?'

He didn't answer me. Instead, he began to talk about being separated from his father as an infant. Although he had forgotten the wrench itself (he was little more than a year old when it happened), he believed it had damaged him badly. It was the reason he had turned out the way he had, an adult who had never figured out what he wanted to do with his life, and probably never would.

We stopped talking. Beyond the windscreen stretched the bonnet, and beyond the bonnet lay a small stretch of tarmac lit by my headlamps. I saw hedgerows and bare trees on either side, while further ahead I saw nothing, only blackness.

chapter sixty-eight

A Saturday morning, January 1998. My wife lay like a beached whale on the sofa in our living room. She was heavily pregnant with our fifth child. The telephone rang.

'Hello, Nurse Corrigan here.' The caller was speaking from Killiney.

'Ernest has a chest infection,' said Nurse Corrigan. 'He's really not well.'

I had received many calls from the home over the years but none quite this emphatic. I put down the phone and my wife said, 'You must see him tomorrow. I can do without you tomorrow because tomorrow is Sunday; but I must have you on Monday when I go into surgery.'

The next morning was bright and crisp. I left the boys but took the girls with me, India, now sixteen years old, and Georgia, aged three. Georgia was excited and kept hooting as we got into the car, 'We're going to see my grandpa,' over and over again. My brother Sasha was staying the weekend, as it happened, and he came as well.

Filing into the home later that morning there was a

cabbage-water smell. The stuffed animal eyed us. So did a nurse.

'Your father's dying,' she said, bluntly. Wisps of her hair had come away from the bun on her head. She tried to gather the loose ends and stuff them back and, as she did, the bun fell apart and all her hair tumbled down.

'I'm useless with hair,' she apologised.

We went to my father's room. His roommate, the one with milky eyes, was gone. My father was asleep in his bed. He lay on his side, curled up, foetal style. He was wheezing heavily. The skin on the top of his bald head had puckered and ribbed as if the skull beneath had literally shrunk. Perhaps it had.

India looked around the room.

'What are those?' she asked. She pointed to a huge pile of fern-green incontinence nappies on a table.

'No, don't tell me,' she added quickly, both appalled and horrified. 'Look at the size of that!' she continued.

She nodded at an industrial-sized tub of Sudocrem, the antiseptic healing cream we used at home if our children had nappy rash.

'Ugh!' she exclaimed, and murmuring she was going out to the car, she fled the room.

I sat on a chair with a detachable seat and a place under-neath for a potty. My brother sat on the second, empty bed. Georgia clattered around in her shiny patent shoes and frilly socks shouting, 'Shush! Grandpa sleeping.'

My brother had a camera and Georgia said to him, 'Take my picture.'

She climbed up on to the high hospital bed, took her grandpa's crooked hand and assumed her photograph pos-ture – straight back and best smile.

The room was bathed with the light of the flash. The figure under the bedclothes slumbered on, oblivious. The child slithered down. India returned. Her disgust had subsided. I cut a lock of hair from the sleeping figure and put it in an envelope. We all said, 'Goodbye, Ernest.' I looked at the figure in the bed. I was reminded of a torch bulb, yellow and wavering, in those last moments before the battery dies. He was drifting away. This was death. There was no doubt about it. I knew I would never see him alive again.

We left and I drove straight back to the North without stopping. It was as if something of the same horror that had filled India now filled me. I had to get away.

The next morning I took the children to school, and Georgia to the child-minder. Then I went to the hospital. My wife's room smelt of acetone and she was dabbing at a toenail with a wet, red-stained piece of cotton wool. The day before she had painted her nails, 'ready for theatre' as she put it, and now she was being made to clean them off. Nail varnish was not allowed in surgery. She wore a hospital gown, white and stiff, with ties at the back. For the umpteenth time she gave her details to a nurse: name, address, telephone number, next of kin. Then, while I looked away and winced, a catheter was inserted and then a pre-med given.

At two o'clock we set off for surgery. My wife played her Walkman as we trundled along the corridors, and I could dimly hear the voice of Victoria de Los Angeles leaking from the headphones clamped to her head. The music was tinny yet sweet.

We arrived at a pair of scuffed doors with 'Theatre' written above. This was the end for me. I kissed her. Then she vanished inside for her Caesarean section. I went out to the car park.

I smoked a cigarette and stared at the reeds in the River Erne below the hospital. They were the colour of broom handles, a woody yellow, but unlike broom handles they bent when the wind blew.

I went back inside and waited at the scuffed doors. A

midwife rolled out an incubator. Our new baby lay inside, his face very red under a waxy coat of vernix.

I followed the incubator to the recovery room. The midwife weighed and measured the baby.

'I'll turn on the television,' she said, and on it went. The recovery room was instantly bathed by the flickering light of the set, just the same as if a fire had been lit. And in a way, that's what television is; it's the new form of hearth around which we crowd for comfort and succour.

On the television screen up in the corner, a very young Terry Wogan hosted an ancient episode of *Blankety Blank*, while in the room below, my new son opened his sticky lids and looked at the world for the first time.

My wife was wheeled in. She woke up. She was groggy and sore. Our four children came in. Everyone got a chance to hold the baby and have their photograph taken.

We left at seven, myself and the children. We bought pizza. We went home. As we walked into our house, holding the flat warm boxes of food, the phone started to ring. India rushed to pick it up. A would-be boyfriend, perhaps. She put the receiver to her ear. As she listened, I noticed, she stood very still, then her face appeared to get smaller and she went very white.

'Dad, it's the home in Dublin,' she said finally, 'and I don't think it's very good.'

By ten o'clock that night, I was on the phone to a Dublin undertaker and ordering my father's coffin. Plain, pine veneer, no handles please, and definitely no cross.

chapter sixty-nine

The funeral was on a Friday. We drove down from the North together, myself, my wife, the children and Euan, the baby. Everything went swimmingly until we reached Kells, halfway to Dublin, where Georgia threw up all over herself and the back of the car. Her sick was a mixture of Ribena and porridge; it was the colour of oatmeal and it smelt of sugar and blackberry.

We made Glasnevin cemetery. The watchman in the gatelodge gave us some water. We cleaned up Georgia and the car. There was still some time to go before the service; I thought I would go and search for the grave of my grandmother, Margaret Gébler. She was somewhere here. Then I saw there were thousands of graves, maybe more. I would never locate her; not in the time I had.

The undertaker's hearse appeared. I peered through a gleaming window at the coffin lying inside. It was yellow pine coated with thick varnish that glowed like luminous paint. My request for a trimmings-free coffin had been studiously ignored. The handles were made of rather nasty lacquered brass and they also shone brightly. My father would not have approved.

My mother appeared. She carried a great bunch of wild Italian Margarita daisies. My brother walked at her side. John and Linda appeared, shyly. I was the only one who'd met everyone before so I did the introductions.

John had a video camera in a bag. For a moment I thought he was going to tape the cremation. After all, he was an American, and Americans are famous for that sort of thing.

'I found this on a bus,' he explained, as he handed the camera to Jack. I realised the camera was a gift. He was giving it to the children.

'There's no minister this morning,' I said, although everyone knew this already. 'There won't be a service but there will be readings.'

I asked John what he would read. He said he wouldn't read. I pressed him. He was adamant; he wouldn't read. He declined, I sensed, not just because he was shy, but because he sensed he wasn't really one of the family. He had missed out all those years of shared experience and that could never be made up.

A few minutes later Jeananne Crowley, the actress and a lifelong friend of my father, appeared. Yes, she was definitely reading, she said. In the background I noticed there were two other people that I didn't recognise. I went and introduced myself. They were called Dacks. They had Wolverhampton accents. They were from that part of the family to whom Adolf Gébler went with his wife and children when they emigrated to the English Midlands in the 1920s.

At one o'clock sharp we all filed into the chapel. The floor was tiled and the air was chilly. Just like in an ice-rink, cold radiated from below. Everyone sat; we were a tiny handful of mourners spread across several slippery pews. I put the cassette of music that I had recorded for the end of this ceremony in the tape deck. It was a chunky machine, very 1970s.

The coffin was trundled in on a contraption with small wheels that squealed loudly (I could hear my father muttering, 'For Christ's sake, oil the bloody things!') and brought down to the front where everyone could see it. It seemed even more yellow and shiny than when it was in the hearse.

I went to the lectern and read John Clare's untitled poem which begins:

> Love lives beyond
> The tomb, the earth, which fades like dew!

My brother read a Shakespeare sonnet. My mother read 'Ecce Puer' by James Joyce (whom my father liked in his envious way):

> A child is sleeping;
> An old man gone.
> O, father forsaken,
> Forgive your son!

Then Jeananne Crowley read a long extract from a letter my father had written her. In one paragraph my father described lying in the bath and drinking a bottle of beer while reflecting, with a degree of contentment, on his life and achievements as a writer.

In the letter he made it appear that he found writing easy, yet even as a child I understood he struggled to write, as opposed to my mother who did not; his words came slowly, while her words flowed fluently. In his letter my father was up to his old tricks again: he was spinning, and as usual the subject of his spin was himself.

I had an overwhelming urge to shout, 'He's a phony. It wasn't like that; it was the opposite . . .'

I looked at the coffin on the conveyor belt, with the curtain behind. Soon the coffin would vanish into the furnace room where men were waiting beside the ovens to receive it. My father was dead yet I was still locked in battle with him.

We had only fifteen minutes booked and at one fifteen sharp I knew we would be thrown out to make way for the next party. I got back to the lectern. There was only a minute or two left. I read a couple of lines of Camus, and turned on the cassette player. The taped hissed and popped and then the music started. It was the adagio section of Shostakovich's 7th Symphony, the 'Leningrad'. I had made my recording from the record we had in Cannon Hill Lane, the one on which I wrote the note saying I preferred to live with my mother. That's when our battle really began and I could not imagine it would ever finish.

As the music thundered out of the speakers, I pressed the button. The conveyor belt jolted to life. The coffin began to lumber away from us. It passed slowly through the hole in the wall to the world on the other side, and then the curtain closed behind it.

We all went outside. It had got colder still while we had been in the chapel. The next party was waiting to go in. They were a big group and the women wore veils with their hats. We were small and looked bohemian.

I went round to the back of the crematorium and knocked on the door. A man answered. He wore overalls. I looked over his shoulder. I couldn't see the furnaces but I thought I could hear the roaring of the flames.

'Ernest Gébler's ashes?' I said.

'They won't be ready for a while. Do you want to wait?' he asked.

I demurred. He agreed to post them. I gave him my post-code. Our business was done.

chapter seventy

In the restaurant, where we all went for lunch after the cremation, I overheard my brother telling Jeananne Crowley a story.

When the film *Zulu* came out, he told her, Zulu fever swept our primary school. The film's centrepiece battle was re-enacted each break time. Naturally, no child wanted to be a Zulu; everyone wanted to be a Redcoat. But someone had to be a Zulu, otherwise there would be no game. Because of our Irish accents, he continued, he and I often found ourselves being made to play the part of the Zulus.

'So that's when I thought,' said my brother, chuckling, 'to hell with this, I want to be a Redcoat, and I made myself speak in the same accent as everyone else.'

Tyga turned, looked at me and raised her eyebrows.

'What was that look for?' I asked her later.

'You never told me the Zulu story.'

'I remember the film coming out,' I said, 'but I don't remember playing "Zulu" in the playground.' This was true. I didn't. 'I remember other things,' I said.

'Exactly,' she replied. 'Everyone remembers differently. Your memories are much darker than your brother's, which is amazing, particularly when you consider you both lived at the same time with your father and went through the same things.'

'What does that mean?'

'Nothing. I'm just saying he remembers quite different things from you. His father, who was also your father, seems a much nicer man than the one you knew. He probably was nice, or could be, but you never saw that.'

chapter seventy-one

It was nearly Christmas.

After a feverish bout of present-wrapping, I flopped down in front of the sofa, found the television zapper and hit a button. I had absolutely no idea what was on. Maybe it would be interesting. I would find out, anyway.

The screen lit up. And an instant after that I saw stars and the logo of Universal Pictures – Planet Earth hanging in space. The music was doomy, unsettling. It had the imprimatur of Bernard Herrmann all over it.

The scene cut from velvety outer space to a huge close-up of the left-hand corner of a mouth covered with very thick red lipstick. The camera panned sideways and the whole mouth was revealed, full and sensual and red. And there was no doubt, either, at least in my mind, what the mouth represented.

The camera then moved upwards. It went over the nose and up to the eyes. There was only one filmmaker who could start a film like this, I thought, the man whose name I first heard at the party in Mitcham where I was sick in the sink.

And this could be only one film: the film I had never seen.

The camera tracked in on the woman's right eye. In the depths of her black pupil something stirred. Accompanied by ominous violin chords, a shape spiralled out of the eye then resolved into the single word: *Vertigo*. I was right.

So thirty years after I had first registered the title, I finally watched the film . . .

The next day I had to go to the airport to collect my brother-in-law and his wife. Where the motorway runs along the southern side of Lough Neagh, the landscape is flat and monotonous. It is brilliant thinking-while-driving terrain.

I stared at the road as it unfurled from under the car and let my mind wander. I remembered *Vertigo* and then, suddenly, the stopper came out of the memory phial and I was back in Kensington Gardens on a cold spring morning, tramping up the Broad Walk towards the Round Pond . . .

Nashat had died in 1984. Back in Switzerland, following film school, he took his life. Despite the passage of time, I heard his bright clear voice now and I could almost believe we had spoken only a couple of days earlier. He was talking about the greatness of *Vertigo*. I heard him say that the film showed that inside Hitch, throughout his life, there was a passionate redhead trying to get out.

At this point memory segued into fantasy. Having finally seen the film, I started a conversation which in fact we never had. No, I said, I disagreed. The greatness of *Vertigo* was its structure. In the first half, James Stewart travels through the story thinking that he sees the world as it is. In the second half, James Stewart goes over the same ground and now he sees everything quite differently. For him it is just as Nietzsche put it: 'Life is lived forwards but understood backwards.' Here I stopped. The Round Pond vanished. There was something in all of this, I thought, that might help me with the book I was mulling over.

I had wanted to write about my father and our life together for a long time. Since I cleared Cnoc Aluin, the desire to do this had grown stronger and stronger. I knew the trunks of papers in my attic were filled with information I had not had before. This archive was a fantastic, never expected opportunity that had dropped into my lap only because Jane had died before my father and I was the one who had cleared out his house. If Jane had lived on after my father, I would never have got these papers.

But though I recognised I had a unique resource that could only improve the book, I hadn't got anywhere with the project. I couldn't see how to integrate what I remembered with what I would find in the archive. Until now, that was: *Vertigo*, I suddenly saw, as I hurtled across the flats at the bottom of Lough Neagh, had shown me the way to go. The story was in two acts: act one, what happened, act two, what I understood.

chapter seventy-two

I sat down and read every word of the diaries, the hundreds of bits of autobiography and the letters. Some of what I was told as a child, I discovered, was untrue. There was also a good deal that I wasn't told, that was simply left out.

Great-grandfather Gébler was never an entrepreneur and there never was a music factory. Great-grandfather was a doctor, a gynaecologist perhaps. According to Adolf, he worked in a hospital for 'getting babies'. Adolf was born in Adorf in Saxony, south Germany. Adolf was Czech perhaps in temperament and politics but he was German by birth. I never discovered whether the family were Jews or not.

My grandfather trained as a musician (that was true) and came to Ireland. He married my grandmother because he believed it would help his career. He grossly misunderstood her social position (perhaps because of his lack of English), imagining she was far higher up the social ladder than she actually was. War came soon after and that put an end to the trajectory of his career. He was interned. When he came out, four years later, he couldn't get work. This was always presented to me as a consequence of the times; after the Great War, I was told, great clarinetists, like Adolf, were surplus to requirements. The truth was that Adolf could not get work because he was boycotted by the musicians' union. Why, I don't know. The boycott was unfortunate because now he had a wife and family to support. He was not a man suited to struggle. He believed success was something to which he was entitled as a right, rather than something for which he had to work. He got work in Galway and Londonderry. He started to drink.

Ernest, my father, was Adolf's oldest son. My father's childhood broke into two halves. For the first part of my father's life, the family lived in the south-east of Ireland in Wexford and Tramore. He always looked back on this part of his life as a pre-lapsarian idyll. Money was scarce and my father was wild and unregulated. He rarely went to school and he spent his time stealing turf and potatoes. There were shortages but life was emotionally rich. In those days, Adolf was a loving father. He always took his family to the beach on Sundays and he always brought oranges for everyone.

When my father was ten the Géblers moved to Wolverhampton. Adolf did not prosper as either a musician or a teacher of music. He earned a sort of living playing music for silent films but then the talkies came and that was the end of that. So he tried business; he took the lease on a grocer's shop on a new council estate. It was the Depression. He had to give credit to his customers – no one had any money then. The shop went bankrupt.

As things went from bad to worse, Adolf grew more and more depressed. He hated himself because of his failure to support his family. At the same time he hated his family; he regarded them as a millstone around his neck that prevented him from being a successful musician.

Adolf and Margaret reacted to the catastrophes that

engulfed them quite differently: my father's mother became increasingly religious, while his father became more politically committed. It is not hard to see how this divergence could only make a bad situation worse.

Adolf became depressed, very depressed; he had always drunk, now he drank to excess. By nature, Adolf was domineering, a stickler for discipline, a bully even; with alcohol in him, this side of his nature became even more pronounced.

Adolf and Margaret began to quarrel ceaselessly. As the family's fortunes sank, the conflict increased. The Gébler household became a crucible of misery and conflict. Both parents sought to enlist the support of the children on their side during their interminable rows with each other. My father particularly hated being asked to take sides.

In 1929, when he was fifteen years old, my father started his apprenticeship as a projectionist in the Agricultural Hall cinema, Wolverhampton. He scrubbed floors and cleaned the machines three times a week. His hours were 10 am to 10.30 pm, daily; he was paid fifteen shillings a week. Among my father's papers I found a photograph of my father and another apprentice, Ray Scutt, standing in the semi-derelict cinema just before it was knocked down for rebuilding in 1932.

That was the same year that Adolf was offered the post of first clarinet with the Radio Éireann orchestra. The Géblers went back to Ireland. When I was a child my father told me that this move, when he was an adolescent, from the English Midlands back to Ireland, was the turning point of his life.

What he never told me (and I did not know until I read about it in his papers) was that Adolf insisted that my father remain behind in Wolverhampton and finish his training, while Adolf and the rest of the family went back to Ireland. Adolf thought his oldest son was stupid, he was certain he had no musical talent, and he was adamant his son would have a trade so that he could support himself and stop being a burden on the family. Although my father was eighteen when the family left, this didn't stop him feeling abandoned and slighted.

My father followed his family back to Ireland in 1935. He was twenty-one. Before very long, he declared himself to be a communist. (I have never discovered whether he joined the party; I have been told he did but I have found no proof.) He found work in a variety of Dublin fleapits and began the task of turning himself into a writer. He bought himself a typewriter; this was a hugely expensive object in the mid-1930s, the equivalent, today, of a laptop. He wrote some journalism and began his Gorkiesque novel, *He Had My Heart Scalded*. Adolf was horribly jealous. He was the artist and he didn't want another one in the family. Adolf was also puzzled and incredulous; my father was the simpleton, the artisan – how could he possibly be a writer?

One day, when he was drunk, Adolf decided to establish, irrefutably, his status as the family's one and only true artist. He went to the bedroom where my father was writing; he tried to grab the typewriter and throw it out the window into the street. There was a horrible argument between father and son. My father left the house and went to lodge in a cottage with a family called Hoey. It was a damp place on the River Tolka near Castleknock, north of the city of Dublin.

My father went on writing. Occasionally he published articles. He finished the novel. He sent it to publishers. It was rejected. He rewrote the novel. The Second World War started. Having made his point by staying away from his family a long time, my father now went home, to 3 Cabra Grove, the house Adolf had bought. My father thought about joining the RAF but didn't. While the war raged in Europe, Ireland stagnated and my father fumed. He mouldered, his novel mouldered; finally, just after the war, it was published.

A publicity photograph of Ernest
Gébler, London 1949

His mother wouldn't read it. His sister Ada thought he was
rich because he was now a published author and threatened
to expose him to the Irish state as a communist and
demanded money. The novel was savaged by Christine
Longford in the *Irish Times* (something my father never forgot
or forgave) and was promptly banned in Ireland. My father
always believed that if it hadn't been for this review, the book
wouldn't have been banned, and thereafter he hated anyone
from the Longford clan.

Arber's book, *The Story of the Pilgrim Fathers*, may well
have fallen at his feet in the library of the Royal Dublin
Society, as he told me when I was a child, but he already had

the idea to write a book on the pilgrim fathers before he went to the library. Another writer (the name of whom I never got) had suggested it and, recognising a good idea when he saw it, my father seized on it. He went to London, lived with and off the actress Sally Travers, and wrote *The Plymouth Adventure* in the Reading Room of the British Museum. He wrote it quite self-consciously for money and for the American market and he hated himself for doing it but he did it anyway. When the book was finished and accepted in the United States, he abandoned Sally Travers. It was an action that he later regretted, hugely.

The Plymouth Adventure made my father rich and successful. He may not have enjoyed writing it (it hadn't come from his heart, had it?) but surely, now he was a successful artist, his mother and father would take notice of him. It was all he wanted – their love, but particularly his father's love. But the book (just like the novel before) was never mentioned by his family. Nothing he could do, it seemed, could win him their love, or attention, or respect.

In 1951 my father married Leatrice. John was born. Then Leatrice left him. A horrible squabble followed. Leatrice insisted that when she followed my father to New York, as she had in 1950 just before they got married, she had slept with Mr Fountain and that was when John was conceived. My father insisted, on the contrary, that he made Leatrice pregnant when they were living together in Dublin; he went to New York a few weeks later and she followed him because she was pregnant. My father alleged – in language that mixed the bitter and the vindictive in equal measure – that Leatrice only slept with Mr Fountain as insurance; if he turned her down, then she could go back to Mr Fountain and say she was pregnant and thereby get him to marry her. That's what my father said in several savage letters. But as to the paternity, there was no doubt in my father's mind: John was his son. Leatrice took precisely the opposite view: John was Mr Fountain's son, conceived when she foolishly slept with Mr Fountain while she was in New York at the same time as my father was there; Leatrice was certain of that. There was the birth certificate of course – Number AD 0798/13 which registered the birth of John Karl, my half-brother, in the district of Annamoe, in the Superintendent Registrar's District of Rathdean, in the County of Wicklow, on 31 July 1951, to Adolphus Ernest and Leatrice Gébler – but despite this document the matter was never resolved and each steadfastly maintained in letters and telegrams what they believed, unaffected by the other's arguments.

In 1954 my father married my mother and had two more sons. He had hardly written anything since he finished *The Plymouth Adventure* bar a heap of angry letters to Leatrice. This hiatus continued. He produced only one novel during the 1950s (*A Week in the Country*). My mother, on the contrary, couldn't stop writing. She wrote and wrote and wrote. Her fluency began to eat into him.

We moved to London in 1958 and soon we were a family at war. My mother got published. She got famous. My father hated her success. He believed (incorrectly) that he was the one who taught her how to write and therefore that it was horribly unfair that she was praised and he was not. He also believed (incorrectly) he was the principal creator of her novels and it was therefore he who should be fêted for them and not she. He became awkward and curmudgeonly and the marriage started to go to pieces. The final break came when a cheque arrived from the film company who bought *Girl with Green Eyes*. My father demanded the cheque be endorsed to him; my mother demurred; my father made dire threats. In the end, my mother had no alternative but to sign the cheque over to him and leave.

My father's diaries covering this period, 1962 to 1968,

Carlo Gébler with his mother in Dublin, 1957. The hand-written note is by Ernest Gébler.

when I lived with him largely without my mother, retold a story I knew well but from the perspective of my father. The diaries for the period following 1968 told me a story I didn't know nearly as well as I rarely saw my father after the divorce. Here are a selection of entries, arranged chronologically, that particularly struck me:

Monday, 26 March 1962
Began correcting and rewriting here and there 'He Had my Heart Scalded'; at p. 25. A strange little book, obviously written by some tender female. Retitle it 'A Poor beginning'. Or 'Born Romancers' –? Much of it holds very well. Shall take out implausible, ill-judged

bits – such as love lozenges; will replace with *real* gin. Would Cape take it as a *new* book by a girl author?

Monday, 24 September 1962
Edna takes children while I am asleep in early morning.

Sunday, 7 July 1963
Cable from Marianna to say father died San Francisco yesterday. Mac and Stella to tea. Two charming sons. I suppose I'll feel worse tomorrow.

Friday, 27 September 1963
OBSERVE PERFECT MECHANISM WHICH YOU HAVE EVOLVED FOR PASSING TIME WHILE YET FEELING YOU ARE PURPOSEFULLY OCCUPIED:

Friday. Play ends on BBC at 10-0. Go into kitchen to make a cup of tea. Fry an egg, etc. Looked through *Time* magazine and a newspaper. Can't remember *reading* anything much. Tidy sink and polish taps. Go out and look at wheel of car where rust showing. Scrape rust and touch up with paint. Go for twenty-five minutes quick walk. Tidy up shelf of china cabinet in kitchen. Read film review in *Time*. This seems to be all I did. Yet when I come out and go towards study it is five o'clock in the morning. Go to bed. So in fact I was in or sitting in the kitchen for SEVEN HOURS. This is what my life has come to; not only today, 27 Sept. 1963, but every day. I never feel either idle or bored; yet the long day produces nothing – I do not even read a book.

Wednesday, 8 January 1964
Sometimes I get a deep pain in my chest from a sort of accumulation of injustice and loneliness.

Monday, 13 January 1964
My sons, selfish to such a degree that they won't wash up a cup after them or pick up an orange peel they drop on the floor. I have asked for the TV set to be taken out of the room they sleep in when at Putney, but it is still there.

Unceasing pain in right lower abdomen now = hasn't been absent now for a week.

Wednesday, 29 January 1964
Picked up *A Week in the Country* and opened it ⅔ way through. An hour later found I'd read through the end ¼. Extraordinary book. The argument is tight, exciting, like a running fight. I wrote this good writing. It's still very good, after six years. Where are the six books since? I should be sent to Siberia to chop wood for wasting my life. (So I'd fall in love with Siberia and trees and not write a word either. No, the only remedy is that I should be kept hungry. Paid a meal for every page . . .)

Saturday, 21 March 1964
Susan Marriot: A short, fair-haired, very attractive young woman, with a round, good-looking face . . . Heard today that she had been living with the playwright John Whiting for two years before he died. He was about 45. She killed herself shortly after his death, not wanting to live without him. It keeps coming back to mind, and not now any more, sadly – but as a sort of rekindling of hope about people. I had never been lucky enough to meet a woman of that true nature = but still, you see, they occur in the world. One must not let personal misfortune colour the *whole* world for you.

Tuesday, 14 April 1964

To Trattoria to meet Janice Inott, a girl who when she smiles one falls back in a kind of minor ecstasy. Age 27. A school teacher at Sydenham. Tall, pale, delicate. She is so beautifully well-bred that she never puts a foot wrong. From York. Working-class parents. Widely set dark blue eyes. A little plain in the face when in repose = but ah! when she talks and smiles how it comes alive and positively sparkles into beauty. And that is the way a face should be. She says she is a socialist-anarchist-humanitarian. She is warm and happy & outgoing. What a sense of utter pleasantness, communion, delight to be with this woman! What I've been missing all my life.

Thursday, 3 September 1964

Due to mistake in forwarding office in Random House, New York, a letter c/o them for Edna was sent on here. I noticed the postmark when about to readdress it = Riverside, Connecticut . . . And on opening it, yes it was from Leatrice. What a capital joke if I answer it as Edna! Tell her, as from Edna, what a double-barrelled bitch she is . . . It was a particularly petty, 'female' letter, full of nauseating niceness. She wants to find out from E what I am doing about 'Bobby'.

Monday, 21 September 1964

Received today letter forwarded from American publishers Random House to Miss Edna O'Brien, as before. It is an answer from Leatrice to my fake Edna O'Brien answer to her of the 12 Aug. Her answer a childish 'nuts'.

Tuesday, 29 September 1964

Carlos is a little 'backward', 'retarded', but it is my wish in life he will grow through that.

Saturday, 20 February 1965
The children had their mid-term holiday from school.
Sasha is 8½, Carlo 10½. When they go away to stay with
their mother in Putney, I try to prepare by saying 'It
doesn't affect me; they will leave you anyhow for their
own life in a few years.' But after they have been here a
few days, the first night they are not here (to go in and
look at their sleeping faces) I am sad and depressed, and
realise what it is . . . How can you put all that you have
put into your life aside for days?

Saturday, 7 August 1965
Wrote in Carlos' Autograph Book:

   A boy when little loves his mother –
   And, on occasions, his brother.

   A man when grown can love his brother –
   And even, on occasions, his mother.

   Man or lad, he learns from his dad
   How to stop women driving him mad.

Friday, 1 October 1965
Carlo wearing expensive teenage pointed fashionable
shoes, in which he looks silly.

Tuesday, 26 October 1965
Received divorce notice and summons to custody
court.

Monday, 3 January 1966 [From a letter to friends in
Dublin, tucked inside the 1966 diary at this date.]

. . . The rest of the facts are; the children are completely bought over. Total freedom to do what they like down there, roam the streets, pounds of chocolates in the bedroom, TV in their bedroom on all day, never lift a finger or have to tie a shoelace; taught by her to lie about every smallest thing. I the one who has to impose any sort of training for adult life . . .

So what was I fighting for? To have unwilling lumpy boys coming here to suffer out their days imprisonment? So that in a year or so they will turn Edna faces upon me and tell me they never had anything from me but neglect and cruelty? They said they wanted to live with their mother because it was nicer. Sasha, at school around the corner, for a solid fortnight while living with his mother, did not bother once to walk around the corner to see his father. Like her they have that piece missing from their mentality that has to do with faith, conscience, family affection. they are shot through with that O'Brien two-faced cunning . . . They are as far from my father and mother and family, our kind of feelings and inner life, as parrots or lizards.

So I gave them over to her until the divorce is heard . . . I'm going to write what I should have been writing for the past ten years . . . they can stay or go back to the bog in East Clare.

Tuesday, 8 February, 1966
Sash and Carlo here for a few hours. They have it cut down now to two hours a week on a week day – too busy on Saturday or Sunday with going to the pictures or their friends. Carlo developing that country Irish hail-fellow-well-met false-faced personality.

Tuesday, 22 March, 1966
Tuned striker on grandfather clock and oiled mechanism. What dogging obsession has always driven me to make every mechanical device work as near perfectly as possible? An easy absorption? Outside there are two motorcars, large cars. Both are in near perfect mechanical condition. Both have been put into and kept in that condition by me. I oil door locks, hinges, clocks – adjust, repair and oil everything. Somewhere in youth I got the obsession I could make anything mechanical work *true*.

[Twenty-two years later my father wrote another entry under the one just quoted:

1 April 1990 = and no change. Carlo & Sasha continue to live in London, never see me, nor write! One of them visited Ireland in April 1990 but didn't visit me as far as I remember.]

Tuesday, 29 November 1966
Marianne to visit from Los Angeles. Brought some family photos of Father. More and more I am sorry and sad about his ruined and wasted life.

Wednesday, 30 November 1966
Boys came to see Marianna. Carlo resentful . . . I stopped him acting in film. So what matter. I dare say they'll not come again for another six months, or a year, or ever.

Thursday, 1 December 1966
Marianne went today. Took her to Euston. A greedy stupid woman. Perhaps I should have let Ada deport her after all! From what she says Father deliberately killed

himself with alcohol in California. Her mindless anti-Semitism. Wish not see her again.

Friday, 12 May 1967
Appeared in high court this morning = divorce granted . . .

Tuesday, 16 May 1967
Doubleday write asking back $2,500 they paid as an advance on a book *The Old Man and the Girl* in 1954 or so. I had no intention of writing it. Have an appalling amateur novel of Jeremy Brooks in MS which I'll send them as something to reject. Jeremy gave it to me for that purpose.

Saturday, 24 June 1967
Carlo in expensive private hospital in Harley Street to have appendix out.

Sunday, 25 June 1967
Visit Carlo.

Tuesday, 27 June 1967
Visit Carlo.

Tuesday, 4 July 1967
Visited boys in Putney in evening. She not there. Sash still making boats out of solid wood. Carlo practically recovered. Told them they could come up any time they liked = but I think their pleasure life is kept pretty full. Still no sign of any 'feeling' in them for anything other than themselves.

Friday, 7 July 1967
Jane learnt she goes into hospital Sunday for leg.

Friday, 14 July 1967
To hospital 3.30. I think I am more apprehensive and
nervous than she is. Am very depressed. Try not to show
it. Poor darling looks not so well today.

Saturday, 15 July 1967
7th day in hospital. Jane not looking so well. Bruising on
top of leg swollen and painful.

Carlo and Sash have *not* asked to come up or come up.

Friday, 28 July 1967
Sent rewritten to-be-rejected copy of Brooks novel to
Boardman at Doubleday, USA, under title = *The Old Man
and the Girl*.

Friday, 1 September 1967
Oh help! Talk about my poor father's ironic life. That
stodgy, old, creaking amateur effort of Brooks = which I
edited because I feared the hoax would show through
too plainly = sent to Doubleday to be rejected but thus
fulfil obligation of 1962 (sic) contract for a novel to be
called *Old Man and Girl* on which they'd paid $2,500
and which $2,500 they were now asking back, has been
received by them with enthusiasm . . . Only to me, the
most dazzling writer not writing, as Jane says, could this
lunacy happen.

Tuesday, 12 September 1967
Victor Gollancz . . . want to consider it for publication.
This is becoming obscene. I can't get it back from
Doubleday – but by God it will never be published *any-
where* else.

Wednesday, 13 September 1967
Sore pain in right of abdomen for days. What a fate – not only to have a grinding pain in your stomach all your life . . . but to have two sons like that to boot . . .

Thursday, 14 September 1967
Called unexpectedly on Deodar Rd. Mother's night out. All watching last war programme on TV. They did not bother to stop watching TV when their father visited. Tossed on floor in their bedroom = two high-powered air rifles. I began to say how easy it was to get a slug in your head and be maimed or lose an eye – this received with resentment.

Sunday, 12 November 1967
Carlo and Sash for lunch and walk on Wimbledon Common. Teaching them to play table tennis.

Friday, 17 November 1967
Boys to dinner = spoke to Carlo severely about pulling himself together and stopping this ceaseless idiotic jabbering and incessant boasting and lying.

Tuesday, 12 December 1967
Sent Xmas card to . . . 'Bobby Fountain'. It might get in with the Xmas cards.

Saturday, 16 December 1967
My intelligent considerate sons announce they are being taken – on Monday – to Switzerland for the Xmas holiday. Just that. No suggestion of what *I* was doing or did *I* expect to see them to brighten life over Christmas. Idiot Irish-faced confidence tricksters.

Monday, 8 January 1968
Expected a telephone call from Putney. Silence.
Punishing me. Their visits only make me sad and emo-
tionally disturbed anyway.

Sunday, 14 January 1968
Carlo rang in his off-hand yet guilty way. Just back from
Wales. Oh yes. They'd gone to Wales on returning from
Switzerland. Told him I was working hard and would see
him next week.

Tuesday, 20 February 1968
Carlo rang – would like to come up Sunday.

Tuesday, 27 February 1968
Carlo and Sash to tea. Disgruntled they had to go home
by bus.

Friday, 22 March 1968
Have not seen Carlo or Sash for nearly a month . . .
Well, my little sneaky O'Briens, time will pay you.

Monday, 1 April 1968
Boys rang – to say they were going to Wales for three
weeks at Easter.

Thursday, 18 April 1968
Bound copy of *OLD MAN* arrived from Doubleday. Help!
Nice *dust jacket*. All I can do is keep my ashamed head
down.

Friday, 10 May 1968
The children have not been up to see me since

February – over two months. If only in fact one could feel about people only according to their merits.

Thursday, 1 October 1968
And so these two sons passed out of his life, effortlessly, as it were – as if being their father for ten years, loving them and caring for them, had left no trace in them whatsoever. No twinge to see him, no curiosity even if he is alive or dead.

Undated [This is in his 1966 diary where it doesn't belong.]
   The reason I moved from London back to Dublin was to escape the humiliating behaviour of my sons towards me. They were allowed to 'do what they liked' in Edna's. Go to bed at midnight, miss school, watch TV as much as they liked, etc., etc.

Tuesday, 1 December 1970
Once I seemed to know what I was doing in the world and where going. But now no . . . Sitting in the kitchen of this mouldering old house in dead Dalkey – working like a labourer all day building garage, mending roof – what on earth do I *think* I'm doing with my life? Too long the habit of letting this one & only existence go by default. All I know now is I want to be free of motorcars, of possessions – be free to come and go, travel, mingle with other people, write, write . . . and somehow do something for other human beings.

Undated [Written in the notes section at the end of 1971 diary.]
   End of a wasteful year – wasted on repairing this

house out of sheer habit. Wrote two plays only – and one of these a re-write – which, for me, with my manic facility, is disgraceful. More and more I feel like a man shouting in a locked room miles from anywhere.

Undated [Written in flyleaf of 1972 diary.]
17 Nov. 1965 Carlo and Sasha elected to go and live wholly with Edna. Where with their visits to me dwindled to an hour or less a week with taxi booked to call for them. So I told them to go to hell around 1969 and returned to Ireland 1970.

Saturday, 18 August 1973
11.30 Telephone: Sasha.
'We're on our way to our grandmother & we thought [we could come and see you] . . .' etc. as before.
'No.' Oh, I thought. Put phone down.
Rings again. 'This is Carlo.'
'I do not wish—'
C – 'This is ridiculous. You are just carrying on a quarrel you had with Edna—'
'I do not like you or your brother. Life is too precious to waste with people one dislikes—'
'You're not being fair—'
'Gombeens looking up their relations to see what they are going to leave them, I understand [you]. I shall leave you nothing but a moment's feeling of contempt.'
Phone down. They did not ring again. I expected them to arrive in a taxi . . . Didn't. Feeling of relief that I can at last conduct myself with these dung beetles. If only I'd done it before – the suffering we suffered! The insolence of these people. But what a joy to have been able to deal with fleas like that!

*

The other thing I learnt from the diaries was what happened to Jane. I had always understood that she and my father were married, though when this happened I never knew. They weren't. My father would not marry her; because, as he explained to her (and he writes this up in his diaries), his previous two marriages were so disastrous. This pained her greatly. In the end, exasperated by my father's refusal, she just started calling herself Mrs Gébler as if they were married.

After they had lived with one another for fifteen years Jane became extraordinarily unhappy and depressed and, in her view, mad. She believed my father was in some way responsible for her psychological state. She believed that she had to leave him and go away if she was going to get better. Without consulting my father, she removed a large amount of money from their joint bank account. She fled to England, where she had relatives and spent some time in psychiatric institutions.

When she went back to Ireland, she did not return to live with my father as his wife. She lived in a flat and went to see my father each day. She knew he was ill and frail and she believed she owed him a duty of care. It was on one of these visits, while she was mowing the lawn, that she suffered a massive brain haemorrhage and died. My father lived on, alone, for another eleven years.

chapter seventy-three

The biographical details that I got from what I read were riveting because they showed the divergence between what I was told and what was true. They were also illuminating. They offered a window into my father's soul. I looked through and I saw what I had never seen before.

Because Adolf didn't love him (or because he thought Adolf didn't love him – which amounts to the same thing), because of his awful childhood, because of the terrible fights his parents had, he was always clinically depressed. Always, from the very start of his life.

Then, because of his disastrous marriages and his lack of success as a writer, the clinical depression got denser until in the end he was swallowed up by his misery; or as I would have put, he was immersed in the Black Lagoon.

Of course, being a left-leaning, anti-psychoanalytical pragmatist, he not only ignored the fact that he was depressed, he was completely unable to recognise that he was depressed.

So it was as simple as that. He was ill. That was why he

couldn't love us, or show us love. That was why he could only be the dour, undemonstrative, distant man I knew.

When I understood that, I realised I had to stop wishing he was otherwise, as I had spent my life doing.

Because he was ill he could not be anything except what he was. It was pointless to expect otherwise.

Once I accepted this, the next idea followed quickly. If this was true and he was miserably depressed, and I genuinely believed that was true, then his life was an awful, unspeakable mess of ceaseless pain.

Once this occurred to me I began to feel sorry for him. I began to pity him. If his life was as horrible as I believed it was, I couldn't be angry or resentful any more. I had to stop being angry.

As this new and utterly revisionist view took root, I saw with my old friend, that part of myself that is outside and above events and that monitors what is happening, that of course this might all be nonsense. I saw that I might have arrived at this opinion only in order to cheer myself up. But did that matter? I asked myself. No it didn't, not a bit. Whether or not it was all true, or only partly true, the effect was marvellous. My new take on the past had initiated a miracle.

These thoughts made a little hole in my head and out of the hole all the toxins that had accumulated over forty-four years began to trickle away. The hole was small and the quantity of poison was considerable but it leaked away slowly and, in time, it was all gone.

I didn't feel angry any more. I didn't endlessly and fruitlessly go on wishing he could have been different. It was pointless to expect otherwise. He could only be what he was. I had to accept that.

The psychological reconfiguration resulting from such thoughts was huge. The words lighter, emptier and cleaner spring to mind as descriptive terms of the way I felt, although they give little sense of the strength and the depth of the sensation.

And there I thought the matter would end; but there was one final stage.

Now I didn't have the anger clogging up my system any more, or impairing my judgement, I accepted how much there was of him in me that was good. His literary opinions, for example; as I read these in his diaries, I recognised them as if they were my own. I realised he decanted these into me. Suddenly, I felt grateful and that is the last emotion in the world that I ever thought I'd feel for him.

chapter seventy-four

Because of memory, nothing ends until you die. In my mind's eye, I see myself climbing Cannon Hill Lane – the image is a composite, constructed from the hundreds of times I made this journey.

The smog is both grey and also vaguely yellow; it reminds me of an old bruise. With each breath, I register the cold and the wet of the smog at the back of my throat. There is a tickle at the top of my lungs, a sure sign that the bore of my tubes must be narrowing.

I reach our house. I swing open our wet gate. It makes the grating noise it always made. I walk down the path; it is covered by a slimy patina, like the trail left by a snail.

The curtains are closed but I can see the lights are on in my father's study. I assumed that he must be at his desk. The woodbine that grows around and above the bay window is dripping.

I press the front door and find he has forgotten to put it on the latch. I press the bell, then take my finger away quickly;

a lengthy peal might annoy him and I don't want that. The shorter the peal, the better for me when he answers the door.

I hear his footfalls inside as he steps out of his study and comes along the hall. A second later, the door opens back and there he is.

I see his bald head, his dark eyes; I smell the lanolin that he has rubbed on his hands; it reminds me of the smell of lamb meat.

What is he going to say? Or will he say nothing? I try to judge by his face which it is to be. If I am lucky, he will say nothing; if I am unlucky, I could get a dressing-down . . .

What has changed, for me, is not that moments like this didn't happen; what has changed for me is that now I have something else to put alongside them. The things I was told, the things I found in the letters and diaries, together they went some way to explaining what made him into the man I knew.

Our relationship was a failure but my late discoveries humanised the old man. His death wasn't the best experience in the world but it wasn't the worst either. Because of these discoveries, I do not feel crushed by unresolved father-son business. I have a narrative that makes some sort of sense of what happened.

You can't change the past but, with understanding, you can sometimes draw the poison out of it.